Praise for *The Great Heist*

"In *The Great Heist*, David Shedd and Andrew Badger show us why every citizen should care deeply about the People's Republic of China's sustained campaign of industrial espionage against America. In this riveting and astounding story of duplicity and complacency, the authors have done their part to defend the United States from a hostile, ruthless rival. Read this book and demand that leaders in government, the private sector, and academia do their part to stop the Chinese Communist Party from stealing our future."
—H. R. McMaster, bestselling author of *Dereliction of Duty*, *Battlegrounds*, and *At War with Ourselves*

"*The Great Heist* is an alarming exposé of China's relentless campaign to steal America's intellectual property and data. However bad you think the problem is, the truth is far worse. David Shedd and Andrew Badger use their expertise as seasoned former intelligence officers to explain how China's systematic theft of our secrets puts every American at risk. This is a must-read for anyone concerned about our greatest national security threat."
—Senator Tom Cotton, bestselling author of *Seven Things You Can't Say About China*

"*The Great Heist* exposes the sweeping infiltration of Chinese espionage across America's technology and economy. Through gripping, well-documented cases of high-stakes industrial theft, this book lays bare the methods, motives, and scope of a covert campaign targeting the heart of US innovation. Meticulously researched, *The Great Heist* reveals the true scale of the hidden battle for economic supremacy."
—Michael Pillsbury, author of *The Hundred-Year Marathon: China's Secret Strategy to Replace America as the Global Superpower*

"This is the most comprehensive and gripping account yet of how the Chinese Communist Party has infiltrated, exploited, and hollowed out America's technological edge. *The Great Heist* reads like a thriller, but its facts are chillingly real. Every policymaker and CEO should read this book."

—Brigadier General Robert Spalding (USAF, Ret.), author of *Stealth War: How China Took Over While America's Elite Slept*

"America and China are locked in a technological arms race that may be determined by our ability to protect our own IP. *The Great Heist* is mandatory reading for anyone looking to understand how stolen American IP helped underwrite China's economic rise and why we must learn from these mistakes to ensure that American leadership in advanced technologies like AI and quantum doesn't power China's techno-totalitarian state."

—Mike Gallagher, head of defense at Palantir Technologies and former US Representative

"*The Great Heist* takes us on a tour of Beijing's successful criminal conspiracy to strip Americans of their most valuable intellectual property—a conspiracy that has yet to be seriously addressed by US universities, companies, and policymakers."

—Matt Pottinger, former US deputy national security advisor and CEO of Garnaut Global LLC

"A must-read for anyone concerned about national security and American competitiveness. Superbly written. Engagingly enjoyable and deeply sobering in equal measure, *The Great Heist* is a masterful telling of why—and how—for two decades, the PRC exploited the weaknesses inherent in our open society to perpetrate the most successful campaign of industrial espionage in history and emerge today as the greatest threat to that very way of life. Read the book, but buckle up. It's a frightening ride."

—Neil Wiley, former chair of the National Intelligence Council and former principal executive in the Office of the Director of National Intelligence

The Great Heist

The Great Heist

CHINA'S EPIC CAMPAIGN TO
STEAL AMERICA'S SECRETS

David R. Shedd & Andrew Badger

HARPER

An Imprint of HarperCollins*Publishers*

HarperCollins books may be purchased for educational, business, or sales promotional use. For information, please email the Special Markets Department at SPsales@harpercollins.com.

hc.com

FIRST EDITION

Library of Congress Cataloging-in-Publication Data has been applied for.

ISBN 978-0-06-345183-4

Printed in the United States of America

25 26 27 28 29 LBC 5 4 3 2 1

To the men and women on the front lines of America's defense—across intelligence, law enforcement, the military, and industry—who understand the scale and urgency of the threats we face, and who work with quiet resolve to safeguard our freedom, our innovation, and our future.

CONTENTS

A Note from the Authors

TEN YEARS ago, the United States saw firsthand the insidious threat posed by the People's Republic of China (PRC) and its Chinese Communist Party (CCP). It was 2015, and the Office of Personnel Management (OPM) data breach shocked the nation. The personal and sensitive information of more than 22 million government employees, the coauthors included, had been exposed to a foreign power with increasingly alarming capabilities.

The OPM data heist was just the opening salvo.

It wasn't a routine hack. It was an unprecedented theft of government records, including background investigations and personnel data of federal workers past and present. While the breach wasn't a direct theft of America's corporate intellectual property, it revealed a darker reality: that China had the power not only to steal vital data but to do so on a massive scale never seen before.

The OPM breach occurred during a pivotal year in China's ascent to global dominance. That same year, Xi Jinping, the general secretary of the Chinese Communist Party and premier of the People's Republic of China, launched Made in China 2025, an aggressive strategy designed to position China at the forefront of high-tech industries such as robotics, aerospace, and biopharmaceuticals.[1] Xi's motivation was to ensure that the CCP's grip on power would never be challenged, the "great rejuvenation of the Chinese nation" would be achieved, and the twenty-first century would be defined by Beijing domination over frontier technologies such as artificial intelligence (AI), quantum computing, semiconductors, space, and biotech. Never again would China suffer the shame of the "Century of Humiliation," when China was colonized and divided by foreign powers in the nineteenth century.

At the same time, as America was reeling from the implications of the OPM cyber-intrusion, China's military, bolstered by stolen US and Western technologies, embarked on an unparalleled modernization program. The People's Liberation Army (PLA) began transforming itself into a cutting-edge force infused with foreign innovations, including stolen weapons designs and classified knowledge, all aimed at preparing for a potential future confrontation with the United States, which had long been identified as its primary adversary. After a ten-year period, China has arguably achieved all of the ambitious goals it set out in Made in China 2025, in the process catapulting it to superpower status.

The events of 2015, underscored by the OPM breach and paralleling China's increasingly aggressive policies, marked the beginning of a distinct shift in the global balance of power. Through a combination of cyber-espionage and systemic theft, China has positioned itself as the United States' most formidable and long-term threat. The Great Heist—the theft of hundreds of billions of dollars' worth of critical data, intellectual property, and technology—has been a driving force behind China's rapid industrial and military expansion.

As former intelligence officers who had to face this threat firsthand, our motivation for writing this book is to issue an urgent wake-up call.

The CCP's unrelenting pursuit of stolen information has propelled China's economic and military might to heights previously unimaginable. Yet America and the West continue to underestimate the scale of this threat. It's time for the world to fully comprehend the depth and breadth of China's predatory behavior. Our national security depends on how we respond—and whether we finally wake up to the reality that China has already declared an economic war on the West using espionage at the forefront of its campaign. It already has a decades-long head start. The story of how we got here must be told, for it is not just about protecting sensitive information, it's about safe-guarding the future of our freedoms, our way of life, and our very existence on the global stage.

This book contends that China's rapid rise in geopolitical power is due, in no small measure, to its unprecedented campaign of state-sponsored industrial espionage—not just other factors such as its cheap labor force, command economy, or domination of any one in-dustry such as semiconductor chips. What this book seeks to make definitively clear is that China's supposed "economic miracle" is nothing less than a mirage—one that has been built not on ingenuity but rather grand larceny. Hopefully public discourse around China's rapid economic ascent can fully acknowledge this reality.

Our hope is to also show how the cumulative effect of indus-trial espionage (whether that be in the form of simple piracy, tal-ent recruitment programs, cyberattacks, forced IP transfer through lawfare, hijacked research at universities, nefarious acquisitions of emerging tech start-ups, or classic human intelligence spycraft) can transform the very foundations of the world's balance of power. Power, particularly power as defined by the twenty-first century, is *zero sum*. Sensitive IP or technological breakthroughs in things like AI, stealth fighter jets, or chemical formulas lost to an adversary do not happen in a vacuum. They lead, instead, to the very direct and very serious loss of the *relative* capabilities that define and underpin the balance of power within the international system.

To tell this story, this work is divided into three general sections. The first focuses on exploring the strategic impetus behind China's cam-paign of industrial espionage and the machinery behind it. The second looks at case studies of Chinese espionage in line with the industrial sectors outlined in the country's master intelligence collection guide, Made in China 2025, from electric vehicles to hypersonic weapons. Drawing upon numerous interviews with some of our country's top China, national security, and counterintelligence experts, the final section focuses on the recommendations, through two fictional sce-narios framed around nonfictional realities, that we believe will help the United States—and America's allies—successfully take on this threat.

This is a book for a broad audience, not just policymakers or intelligence professionals. Understanding China's espionage playbook and how to counter it will be of critical interest to a wide variety of readers. It's for every American who cares about the stability, security, and prosperity of our country: CEOs and blue-collar workers, accountants and high school students, software developers and academics, scientists and truckers, start-up founders and history buffs, service members and social workers, and everyone else in the tapestry of our nation. All have an interest in understanding this threat and how it has materially reshaped the global economy and balance of power in the twenty-first century.

Indeed, from Main Street to Wall Street, from the chemical industry to agriculture, American core interests have been irreparably impacted by this heist, eroding our economic and military competitiveness against an increasingly assertive geopolitical rival. Perhaps no sector has been more affected than the industries seeking to win the race to develop the emerging technologies that will define the commanding heights of both economic and military power in the twenty-first century. As the head of Great Britain's Security Service, MI5, warned the traditionally apolitical tech start-ups at Stanford University in October 2023, "If you're working today at the cutting edge of technology then geopolitics is interested in you, even if you're not interested in geopolitics."[2] Silicon Valley may have once harbored hopes about the power of the internet and technology to unite the world and usher in an era of peace, similar to those who hoped that liberalizing free trade would inevitably lead to further democratization. Such assumptions, however, have proven to be disastrously wrong.

The point of this story is not just job or quarterly earnings losses. As we move from a unipolar to a multipolar world, the prospect of a direct war between great powers is becoming ever more likely. The 2023 Annual Threat Assessment of the U.S. Intelligence Community concluded that President Xi has ordered the People's Liberation Army to develop the capabilities to invade Taiwan by 2027. In early June 2025, US Secretary of Defense Pete Hegseth went so far as to assert that the Chinese threat to Taiwan was "imminent." In the event such a conflict between the US and China were to in fact materialize, the side that develops—and controls—the ones and zeros that are at the root of power in the modern era will no doubt be victorious.

The stakes couldn't be higher. Our hope is that our leaders start to take this threat as seriously as it deserves and that this book—by capturing the full extent and severity of China's espionage against America—serves as the necessary wake-up call to make this happen.

David R. Shedd and Andrew Badger

The Great Heist

The Billion-Dollar Thumb Drive

ON A humid summer day in 2018, Tesla CEO Elon Musk stood in front of bright red curtains in Shanghai, clasping hands with a Chinese official, Ying Yong, the mayor of Shanghai. Ying's diplomatic smile, while broad, seemed disingenuous. Both men wore dark suits. Cameras clicked. Reporters buzzed. Musk, ever comfortable in any environment he finds himself in, had just pulled off what seemed like the boldest move of his career to date: Tesla would become the first foreign automaker in history to operate in China without a local partner. The standard business model for a foreign investor in China, which requires a joint venture, was waived as a requirement by the CCP. It was an economic coup.

At the time, no one—not the media, not the financial markets, not even Musk himself—knew exactly what that handshake would set into motion. While Tesla was breaking ground in Shanghai, China was preparing to dig into the IP that gave Tesla the competitive edge over its global rivals.

Within months of the photo op moment, one of Musk's top

engineers would quietly walk out the door of Tesla's sprawling white headquarters in the heart of Silicon Valley. In his proverbial digital back pocket? One of the vaunted "crown jewels" of Tesla's empire: the source code for Autopilot, the advanced driver assistance system that allows Tesla vehicles to drive automatically. Obtaining this jewel didn't require breaking into a bank or a vault. Rather it was simply uploaded to a cloud account and synced to personal devices. The billion-dollar technology, promoted as the future of electric vehicles, the end product of years of extensive research and development, sweat and toil, the brains of Tesla's self-driving software, would now be accessible with a simple cloud log-in. A critical technology for the future of electric vehicles and a closely guarded secret, stolen in seconds. Ones and zeroes representing material wealth and hard power, gone.

For Tesla, China presented the world's largest, most lucrative market-growth opportunities at the time. Achieving its ambitious quarterly earnings targets would be impossible without it. The pressure of the free market can be unrelenting. But the question that would soon haunt the Tesla offices and the desks of the FBI: Had Elon Musk just handed the keys of his company to the Chinese Communist Party?

Back in 2018, Musk was ranked fifty-fourth on *Forbes*' list of the world's wealthiest people.[1] In Shanghai, he was treated like virtual royalty. The announcement was explosive: Tesla would build a massive new "gigafactory" in China, a large-scale industrial factory to produce batteries for EVs, its most ambitious international expansion yet. Shanghai officials pledged that the factory would be operational in less than a year. Chinese state-run banks promised $521 million in loans to fund the project—a number that would eventually swell to $1.4 billion. The interest rates were so appealing that one of the Chinese ministers reportedly balked at the terms.[2]

It was no doubt a windfall and a highly strategic move on the industrial chessboard. Manufacturing in China domestically meant that Tesla could finally avoid the 25% import tariff that had long priced its vehicles out of reach for most Chinese buyers. Now, via local production, it could slash costs and pump its sleek, sophisticated electric machines into the world's largest car market. Owning a Tesla was more than just about saving gas money; it was a status symbol. And the Chinese market appeared primed to eat it up.

But beneath the fanfare was a startling precedent: Tesla would become the first wholly foreign-owned automaker in China. No joint venture. No mandatory tech-sharing clause that was typically associated with such deals. No local partner with open access to the blueprints. It appeared to be a jaw-dropping break from decades of Chinese Communist Party policy designed to be solely "China First."

In China, deals like that don't happen without approval from the top. The man who engineered it was Li Qiang, then Shanghai's powerful Communist Party secretary. Five years later, he would be named premier of China, the second most powerful position in the country.

Wall Street barely reacted to the news at the time. Tesla's stock price hovered between $20.80 and $21.85.[3] But in FBI field offices in Washington, DC, San Francisco, and Silicon Valley, the reaction was different. "We were having conversations regularly with the Bureau [FBI]," said one former Tesla insider. "They warned us: If you don't want your intellectual property stolen, don't open a factory in China."[4] Musk didn't seem to want to listen. "Obviously, I'm paraphrasing a bit," the insider added. "But Elon's attitude was essentially 'We're not skipping the biggest car market in the world because of espionage fears.'" Musk was not alone in this degree of hubris. Many Western corporate leaders had been guided by this approach toward the country for years.

Inside Tesla the warnings weren't ignored entirely. They were weighed between risk and the lure of future financial reward. Musk emphasized that Autopilot and Tesla's proprietary battery tech had to be protected at all costs. Engineers debated protocols: Who would have access to what information? Should anyone with source code clearance even set foot in the Shanghai facility?

Tom Zhu, the head of Tesla China, cut to the chase. "If we're putting stuff in China," he said, according to the insider, "we have to be essentially okay with the Chinese getting it."

Musk agreed but doubled down on the importance of speed. "We're more innovative," he said. "We'll move faster than them. By the time they catch up, we'll be ten steps ahead."

Beneath the swagger, one fear kept surfacing. "Elon always worried about the so-called billion-dollar thumb drive," said a former senior staffer. "A single USB stick with the Autopilot source code. That was the nightmare."[5]

Autopilot, the AI-powered driver assistance software that promised a fully autonomous driving experience, was Tesla's golden goose. It was the most sophisticated system of its kind on the consumer market at the time, and Musk knew that everyone wanted a piece of it. It was the exact type of technology that had allowed Tesla to revolutionize the auto industry.

Then it happened. The dreams became nightmares. On January 3, 2019, four days before construction of the Shanghai factory began, Dr. Guangzhi Cao, a Tesla engineer, resigned abruptly—effective the next day. Bespectacled, with frequently mussed hair, Cao wasn't just any engineer in the rank and file at Tesla. He was a seasoned expert in machine learning, computer vision, and electronic imaging, with a PhD from Purdue University[6]—and he had deep access to Tesla's Autopilot code.

Sometimes in the world of espionage, the most unassuming can in fact be the most dangerous. A post-exit review of Cao's computer activity after his sudden resignation triggered alarms within Tesla's in-house security team. According to court papers, they discovered that he had uploaded complete copies of Autopilot source code to his personal iCloud account. Tesla investigators alleged he then zipped the files—making them smaller, easier to move, and easier to extract—and later logged back in to his Tesla networks to clear his browser history,[7] an act that suggested clear efforts to cover his tracks.

Upon discovering the alleged breach, two senior Tesla executives immediately summoned Cao into their office. The confrontation didn't go according to plan. "His excuse was 'I uploaded it by accident,'" recalled the former staffer. "But this guy doesn't do anything by accident. He's too sharp."

Then came the real bombshell: Cao was going to work for XMotors, a Chinese electric vehicle start-up backed by powerful interests and flush with Chinese government money. Even worse? He had already flown to China a few months after receiving a verbal offer from the company.

This news sent a collective shudder through the Tesla security team, forcing members to grapple with an inescapable question. Had Elon Musk's billion-dollar thumb drive nightmare finally come true? Could it be that what started as a simple handshake in Shanghai would culminate in a security breach that would, in part, upend the global EV market?

They called the FBI.

CHAPTER I

Foreshadowings

IN THE middle of the sixth century, two hooded figures emerged from the clamor of Constantinople's busy streets and slowly climbed the steps of the awe-inspiring halls of the Sacrum Palatium—the Sacred Palace, the epicenter of the Eastern Roman Empire. The smell of frankincense, earthy and woody, wafted through the air. Christian Orthodox hymns resounded from nearby churches. Their robes were stained and threadbare, their sandals dusty from an arduous journey, but their eyes glimmered with the promise that only a secret of great worth could reveal.

The men were monks, disciples of Christ who had dedicated their lives to preaching his Gospel in faraway lands. Though of humble origin, they had requested an urgent audience with the most powerful man in the Christian world: Justinian I, emperor of the Romans. The "good news" they sought to share, however, was not one of the Kingdom of Heaven but rather earthly riches.

Determined to rival the majesty of Augustus, Justinian obsessed over the future of the Roman people. The ancient Roman Forum lay barren, surrounded by rubble, open marshes, and ghosts of past glory. Justinian believed in a New Rome that would rise from Constantinople, perfectly situated at the crossroads of Europe and Asia.

Justinian was a man of vision. A workaholic, he dreamed not only of constructing grandiose monuments and elaborate law codes but of establishing nothing less than *renovatio imperii*, the restoration of the Roman Empire to its rightful place as the world's superpower. Pax Romana, a Roman peace and golden age, would once again be reborn. Yet Justinian's dreams were constrained by harsh geopolitical realities: empty treasuries and barren coffers, seemingly never-ending wars, and, perhaps worst of all, trade dependence on the East. Military might has always depended on economic might; no empire can be rebuilt without the money to pay for it.

Silk, a luminous fabric with a soft texture and lustrous strength born of silkworm cocoons, had become the lifeblood of the ruling classes and a commodity of great worth. Senators demanded it. Courtiers flaunted it. Even bishops wore it beneath their vestments. Yet all silk flowed into Roman lands from the mysterious East through an ancient rival that had haunted the Romans for centuries: Persia. Leaders in Ctesiphon, the capital of the ancient Persians, were fully aware of the economic leverage the country held as a middleman between East and West through its control of key passages along the mighty Silk Road. Deliveries could be delayed. Fees were charged. Prices could become extortionate. And Justinian had had enough.

The monks came bearing a tale whispered in the borderlands beyond India. They spoke of a distant realm called Serinda, known to Rome as Serica, land of the Seres, the silk people. Its rulers, they said, referred to their domain as "The Middle Kingdom," for they believed it to be situated at the center of the divine cosmos. It was a holy land governed by men with a mandate from ancient deities to rule. There, in hidden groves and mulberry orchards, silk was not woven but grown, produced by creatures no larger than a fingernail: larvae fed on leaves, spinning threads finer than any loom could produce.

Obtaining these valuable creatures was easier said than done. Such larvae, delicate as dew, were unlikely to survive the arduous journey west. But their eggs—small, unassuming but budding with life—very well could. Packed in cool mud, hidden in dung, and most likely concealed within hollowed bamboo walking sticks, they could be carried across continents without arousing suspicion.[1] Such "tradecraft," hiding and protecting sensitive information through covert means and tools, was necessary. The punishment for being caught smuggling it was death.

Justinian, clad in imperial purple, no doubt recognized the opportunity for what it was: the theft of a trade secret that could become one of the empire's economic crown jewels. As the distant predecessor to Justinian's throne once put it: *Fortune favors the bold*. Nowhere is this wisdom perhaps more true than in the world of espionage.

Tasked by the emperor, the monks returned to China. Slipping past Persian patrols and hostile raiders, they threaded their way through treacherous mountain passes and barren deserts littered with the crumbling remains of Roman outposts from centuries of glory past. How exactly they were able to obtain the silkworms is lost to history. The great Byzantine historical chronicler Procopius, the ancient source of this story, did not share those details in his account.[2] What is known, however, is that they were successful. The monks returned home, their task complete. As they passed through the towering, legendary walls of Constantinople, the monks carried their great prize inside their hollowed-out bamboo walking sticks.

From that day forward, the Romans were able to eventually break the Chinese and Persian stranglehold of the silk trade. The elegant fabric, once a symbol of China's economic preeminence and Persian might, would now freely adorn the togas of Roman senators, the cloaks of bishops, and the curtains of Justinian's own court in the Sacred Palace.

In many ways the monks' single act of espionage bestowed upon the Byzantine Empire incalculable economic benefits, helping bankroll its *renovatio imperii*, no doubt helping fund Justinian's eventual reconquest of the city of Rome itself.

The identity of the two monks who undertook that incredible mission is now lost to history. The monks received no public honors for their bravery, as great Roman warriors of the past once did. There would be no triumphal processions through the forum. Their operation, like all great acts of espionage, was conducted in the shadows, and in the shadows their fate would remain. But their journey was perhaps one of history's most defining acts of industrial espionage, a heist that helped shift the global balance of economic power in the ancient world. It would not, however, be the world's last.

The Non-Assignment

In 1976, Ronald "Rudy" Guerin joined the FBI and was dispatched to the Oklahoma City Field Office. Traffic and activity were low, and for a while, the rookie found himself working in a one-man residence. "I was the FBI in three counties of Oklahoma," he recalled. "I looked about eighteen, and even though I was the only one there, I always went to work with a suit and tie on." He loved it. He met his future wife. The local sheriffs called him "Little Hoover."[3]

Three years later, he was transferred to the Washington Field Office. Excited at joining the FBI's largest division outside New York, he went to meet the special agent in charge to discuss his new assignment. "Go down to see Larry Torrence" were his orders. "You're on the China squad."

Guerin was stunned. "I felt like I got kicked in the groin," he recalled. "I was like 'China? What is that? Don't you have any real work? Fugitives, bank robberies, kidnapping?'"

His reaction was understandable. In 1979, China had no official presence in the United States. Its embassy on Connecticut Avenue in DC wasn't even an embassy. Insiders called it "LOPRC," short for the Liaison Office of the People's Republic of China. The only other PRC office in the country was its UN mission in New York. As assignments go, the China squad wasn't sexy. And it didn't seem that complicated, especially with only two primary targets to monitor.

Guerin stuck with the job for twenty-seven years. He watched as Beijing sent a massive influx of university students into the country. He worked with the CIA on developing intelligence sources. He was involved in many of the Bureau's biggest Chinese espionage cases, some decades in the making. He went on to a career advising businesses on managing risk in China. That boring assignment he once protested? It became exponentially more complicated.

"They [Chinese intelligence agents] grew real fast, and we didn't," he said. "When I left the Washington Field Office in 2001 for another assignment, we had seven Russia squads and one China squad." China was on the offense. America barely noticed. Soon enough the PRC would no longer be the backwater of American intelligence priorities. It would be the most formidable threat it ever faced.

Setting the Stage: Innovation by Acquisition

On June 30, 1984, Deng Xiaoping stood before a Japanese delegation in Beijing and delivered a speech that appeared benign and expected—at least on the surface. In reality the Communist leader was redefining the Chinese Empire's economic strategy for decades to come. Little did anyone realize at the time, but the world's tectonic plates of global capitalism would soon shift as a result. "Some people ask why we chose socialism," he said firmly, ". . . we had to, because capitalism would get China nowhere."

To the assembled guests from the Council of Sino-Japanese Non-Governmental Persons, Deng's words sounded both familiar and expected. China, still recovering from the chaos and violence of the Cultural Revolution, was signaling continuity: ideological stability in a time of social transformation. "If we had taken the capitalist road," he said, "we could not have put an end to the chaos in the country or done away with poverty and backwardness."[4]

But behind Deng's Communist cheerleading, the Party's apparatchiks were already beginning to execute a very different plan. By 1984, one government entity in particular, the Institute of Scientific and Technical Information of China (ISTIC), had been quietly pursuing a strategy steeped in capitalist principles: knowledge acquisition on a massive scale.

Founded in 1956 under the Ministry of Science and Technology, ISTIC had already amassed a staggering collection of Western intellectual capital. By the mid-1960s, its library held over eleven thousand foreign journals, 5 million foreign patents, and hundreds of thousands of technical reports, blueprints, and dissertations—a Cold War–era equivalent of Google Scholar, curated not for sharing with the wider world but for harvesting material to further the CCP's goals.[5]

While Deng spoke in political platitudes, ISTIC had been covertly mining the West's innovation ecosystem for decades. No mention of that made it into his speech. Instead, he offered a statement layered with typical obfuscation: "That is why we have repeatedly declared that we shall adhere to Marxism and keep to the socialist road. But by Marxism we mean Marxism that is integrated with Chinese conditions, and by socialism we mean a socialism that is tailored to Chinese conditions and has a specifically Chinese character."[6] It was the ideological equivalent of slight of hand: Marxism in appearance, capitalism in function.

There was no simple analysis for anyone trying to decode Deng's contradictory doublespeak. Was it economic pragmatism wrapped in revolutionary language? A rebranding effort? Or was it something else entirely, a doctrine of intentional ambiguity that would allow China to pivot strategically without having to concede a retreat from its founding principles? The answer became apparent two years later.

In March 1986, Deng's government unveiled the National High-Tech R&D Program, also known as the 863 Program, China's first formalized, state-sponsored initiative to compete with the West in emerging technologies. Framed as a national R&D push, the program identified its targeted priorities with surgical precision: space, biotech, lasers, automation, energy, information technology, and advanced materials. This was not ideological jargon; it was the foundation of an industrial policy with global ambition. It was the origins of a road map that would propel China to superpower status.

The 863 Program's stated mission was as bold as it was simple: to "enable China to approach or catch up with international pioneers by the year 2005." It was a declaration not just of intent but with a hard timeline.

Buried in the fine print of the 863 Program's "Relevant Measures" section, a particular paragraph would lay the strategic groundwork for decades of state-sponsored espionage to come: "Encourage innovation. In project award and evaluation, proprietary intellectual property right (IPR) acquisition is adopted as an indicator [of success]."[7] Proprietary IP? In a *Communist economy*? The seeds for economic innovation by illegal acquisition were laid.

Socialism with Chinese characteristics was no longer just an empty slogan. It was morphing into a highly orchestrated system designed to benefit from capitalism and free trade: seizing the by-products of its intellectual and economic progress through open competition without accepting its rules.

By declaring economic innovation a priority national objective and IP acquisition a critical metric of its success, China was effectively transforming espionage into industrial strategy. It would innovate where it could—and acquire, by any means necessary, where it couldn't. The end goal was clear; how the water flowed there didn't really matter. And with ISTIC, joint ventures, foreign academic exchanges, talent recruitment programs, and a rising tide of state-backed enterprises, it was building the infrastructure to do both.

Deng's genius was in his subtle, manipulative use of language to rally his people and shield his intentions from global competitors. He redefined the ideological underpinnings of the Party that had governed China for decades and in the process set in motion a grand strategy, purposeful and directed, of committing espionage on a scale never seen before.

Hedging between Party ideology and economic realities, China's foundational model for achieving power was born: state-directed capitalism, shielded by revolutionary language and powered by state-of-the-art technology—no matter where it came from or how it was obtained. And the West? It was still parsing Deng's speech, still playing by the rules he had never intended to follow.

Tea After Tanks: Business at Any Cost

On December 8, 1989, Brent Scowcroft, then the national security advisor, touched down in Beijing. Two days later, he was photographed sitting across from Deng Xiaoping, sipping tea beneath an elegant bouquet of flowers, both men smiling politely for the cameras. For the Chinese, it was a masterstroke of optics: projecting normalcy and diplomatic business as usual. For many Americans back home, it was a self-inflicted gut punch.

Just six months earlier, tanks had thundered into Tiananmen Square. Soldiers of the People's Liberation Army (PLA) had opened fire on unarmed civilian protesters. Hundreds—possibly thousands, the true figure is forever lost to Communist censors—of pro-democracy protesters had been killed. The world had watched in horror as the CCP had executed one of the most violent crackdowns on its own people in the history of China. And now the man advising the president of the United States on matters of global strategy was clinking teacups with one of the key architects of that repression.

The backlash was immediate. The writers of numerous editorial pages fumed. Human rights activists denounced the visit as a betrayal. Members of Congress called it appeasement wrapped in diplomacy. How could the United States, a bastion of human rights and the self-declared leader of the free world, cozy up to such evil?

But the photo op wasn't the real scandal. What came next was. Days after the picture was published, CNN reported that Scowcroft's visit hadn't been his first trip to Beijing that year; it was in fact his second. The first had taken place just *ten days* after the massacre. The mission had been kept secret: no press, no statement, no transcript.

According to later declassified documents, Scowcroft had flown into Beijing under orders from his boss, President George H. W. Bush, to deliver a personal message to Deng. The content of that message? A handwritten note from Bush himself—what one internal memo described as "warm personal regards."[8]

There would be no formal rebuke by the Americans. No condemnation. No sanctions for the vast violence and repression the world had just witnessed. The buds of democracy had been ruthlessly crushed by steel and lead in the heart of Beijing. But America's response was just quiet diplomacy and a handshake. Other incentives were at play.

The White House insisted that the first meeting had been to "convey America's deep outrage." But if that were true, critics asked, why do it in the shadows? Why offer warmth instead of warning? The answer, it turned out, was personal.

In the mid-1970s, Bush had served as the United States' de facto ambassador to China, the head of the Liaison Office before formal diplomatic ties were established. He admired Deng. He believed in the long game. He saw engagement with China not as an endorsement of its behavior but as a strategic imperative, given its robust demographic and economic prospects.

The massacre, in his view, was indeed horrific—but not reason enough to derail what he saw as a vital geopolitical relationship for the United States. But Deng had a more clear-eyed, long-term, and holistic understanding of the geopolitical chessboard. For all the moral outrage, all the fire and fury from various corners of Washington, Scowcroft's quiet visit was the signal Deng needed: The Americans would not hold the line when pressed. Trade would continue. Talks would resume. The sanctions would be superficial, and time would smooth over the rest.

The photograph of two statesmen smiling across a floral centerpiece wasn't a mistake; it was a message to the world. China had gunned down its own youth who were protesting for nothing more than greater transparency, fairness, and freedom. Six months later, a representative of the United States went back for tea with the same Party apparatchiks who delivered the execution order. And from that moment on, Beijing understood something fundamental about its most powerful rival: It could be managed, exploited, and even controlled.[9]

Stand Down: The Network That Never Was

In late 1995, something inside the CIA shifted. On the famous seventh floor of CIA headquarters in Langley, Virginia, the Agency's top leaders had come to a sobering conclusion: While America remained the economic and military superpower of the era—at least at the moment—it wasn't keeping pace with China in the realm of espionage.

For years, the Ministry of State Security (MSS), China's premier intelligence agency and CIA equivalent, had operated in near-total opacity. Chinese commercial strategy was expanding aggressively. Yet the US intelligence community knew remarkably little about what Beijing was actually targeting, why, or how.

So the Agency officers decided to try something new. The idea was simple, a blend of Cold War tradecraft and modern commerce. Instead of penetrating Chinese government agencies directly, which was becoming increasingly difficult, the Agency would go to where

China was looking outward: trade. As in an effective judo throw, China's strength, its unrelenting focus on industrial theft, would be turned against it.

The Agency assigned a senior CIA veteran to design the program. His remit: to embed deep-cover intelligence officers inside US companies doing business in China. Some were Fortune 500 companies; some were fast-moving start-ups. All of the agents had legitimate reasons to be on the ground—and plausible access to what the Chinese were trying to extract. "The goal wasn't to confront the MSS head-on," the architect of the program later recalled. "It was to understand the strategy behind their collection targets. If we could see what they were going after, we could see where they were headed."[10]

Cover identities were built. Assignments were drafted. American companies were quietly cooperative. After all, they had a stake in the outcome. America's economic interests were their interests and vice versa. Their IP was already being lifted, mirrored, and repackaged by Chinese competitors they'd never met halfway around the world. And that meant market loss and lower quarterly earnings. American jobs and 401(k) plans were on the line.

The officers went in. They joined companies, attended trade expos, took meetings in tech parks. Some were embedded in joint ventures. Others were placed in supply chain logistics or procurement positions, close enough to see how Chinese firms operated but far enough down to remain under the radar.

With their newfound commercial placements completed and covers for action in place, the CIA case officers would be set to execute their core mission: to recruit and handle human intelligence sources—or in other words, informants. Party members in Chinese firms, mid-level managers, factory floor liaisons—low- to midlevel officials and employees—could, with the right access to systems, meetings, or individuals, have just as much intelligence value as the most senior ones. Understanding their potential motivations, the life force that drives the willingness to commit espionage and in essence risk one's life, were key. Did they want money? Had their ego been damaged by their being passed over for promotion? Were they ideologically opposed to the crushing hand of Communist rule?

Then came the orders from Langley: "No recruitment pitches." "Just watch." The message was clear: The American agents could stay in place, but they couldn't engage with and try to recruit Chinese assets.

It wasn't a tactical call; it was political.

At the time, the director of central intelligence was John Deutch, a Bill Clinton appointee who had taken a cautious approach to doing anything that might endanger the White House's broader geopolitical strategy. The Clinton administration wanted to normalize relations with Beijing. Intelligence operations that might cause friction—even routine ones—were seen as too risky.

When George Tenet took over as director in 1997, the tone didn't change. If anything, it hardened. Inside the Oval Office, the mood was pragmatic, bordering on deferential. Trade with China was booming. Markets were opening. The logic of the moment (shared by economists and diplomats alike) was that engagement would tame Beijing. Why jeopardize it with risky spy games? So the commercially embedded case officers waited. And waited. Until the program was quietly shut down. No headlines. No scandal. Just silence. A network of skilled, embedded CIA officers who had never been activated. Could the potential clandestine access have provided a rare chance to see the MSS strategy from the inside and potentially preempt China's master plan to illegally acquire America's intellectual capital? We will never know.

All because the political interest—or will—to do so simply didn't exist.

The WTO Breakthrough:
A Virus Enters the System

On March 8, 2000, President Clinton walked onto the stage at the Johns Hopkins University School of Advanced International Studies to talk about what he called "one of the most important decisions America has made in years."[11] Behind him sat his cabinet members, senior advisers, diplomats, and policy elites. In the front row was Paul Wolfowitz, then the dean of the school, not yet the architect of America's next war in the deserts of the Middle East but already a true believer in the transformative power of US ideals exported abroad. The topic wasn't war, not yet at least, it was trade. More specifically, trade with China.

Clinton had come to sell to the American public what would become the single most consequential economic and strategic gamble of the twenty-first century: permanent normal trade relations with the People's Republic of China and support for its entry into the World Trade Organization (WTO), the body that governs trade relations and terms around the globe. It was framed as diplomacy, as engagement with a potential trading partner, possibly even a future ally. In hindsight, it was the moment the proverbial virus entered the global trade system and the launching pad for the CCP's Great Heist against America.

"I submitted the legislation to Congress," Clinton announced, "and I again publicly urge Congress to approve it as soon as possible." "It will advance our own economic interests." he went on. "Economically, this agreement is the equivalent of a one-way street. It requires China to open its markets—with a fifth of the world's population, potentially the biggest markets in the world—to both our products and services in unprecedented new ways. All we do is to agree to maintain the present access which China enjoys."

What followed was a 3,500-word tightrope walk, a balancing act between political constraints, economic optimism, and ideological hope. To his credit, Clinton didn't shy away from the obvious. "China is a one-party state that does not tolerate opposition," he said. "It does deny citizens fundamental rights of free speech and religious expression."

In Clinton's telling, China's admission to the WTO wasn't a reward for bad behavior; it was a tool to reform it, a mechanism through which liberal capitalism would eventually erode the country's illiberal authoritarianism. Over time, with trade and patience, China would naturally transform into a democracy—maybe one not exactly resembling the United States but perhaps its allies such as Japan and South Korea. After World War II, many observers had claimed that the establishment of Western-style democracy in those countries would be impossible, only to be proven wrong.

On paper, the deal seemed perfect: A new, large market would be opened to American titans of industry. Profit margins once inconceivable given the rising wage costs in the United States would soon be achievable. The stock market would boom. Americans' 401(k)s would grow, and America's economic dominance far into the twenty-first century would be ensured.

But in the world of power politics and grand strategy, not everything always goes according to plan. Clinton's logic was rooted in the post–Cold War orthodoxy that dominated Washington and the halls of Ivy League classrooms at the time: that economic integration would inevitably lead to political liberalization. Under this theory, exposure to markets, investment, and open information would be the "invisible hand" that over time, even if subtly at first, would nudge China toward democracy. That change would come not through outside pressure or at gunpoint but by China's participation in the American world order built from the ashes of World War II. To those at the time any other outcome seemed impossible. American self-confidence was brimming.

Despite warnings by some, with the tact of a true politician, Clinton gently dismissed the skeptics: "The choice between economic rights and human rights, between economic security and national security, is a false one." Then he took a more forceful and direct tone: "Membership in the W.T.O., of course, will not create a free society in China overnight. . . . But over time, I believe it will move China faster and further in the right direction, and certainly will do that more than rejection would."

In his speech, he seemed to dismiss the deep-rooted rot in the Chinese political and economic system regarding issues such as child labor, environmental abuse, political repression, and censorship. He even joked about what he believed would be China's futile efforts to suppress the internet: "Trying to crack down on the Internet," he quipped, ". . . That's sort of like trying to nail jello to the wall." Those in the room laughed. The very concept of a "Great Firewall" seemed, at the time at least, impossible.

Continuing with his grandiose vision, Clinton closed his speech with the full weight of presidential conviction and ideological certainty: "If you believe in a future of greater prosperity for the American people, you certainly should be for this agreement. If you believe in a future of peace and security for Asia and the world, you should be for this agreement. This is the right thing to do." It sounded like a rational strategy. But it was built on faith and sold behind the veneer of liberal moralism. What it became was something else entirely. China would indeed prosper, and many Americans would, too, in the process—but the real question would soon come into view: At what cost?

Soon the fruits of that great experiment in democratic idealism would be harvested. The results were objective and definitive. Within five years, China's economy began growing at double-digit speeds. Meanwhile, US employment in manufacturing entered a terminal decline. Jobs were lost. Families crumbled. Suicides increased. Empty cities across the Rust Belt were soon saturated with drugs such as oxycodone—and later the more potent fentanyl. Chinese firms flooded global markets with state-subsidized goods competing against those of competitors in the "free market." American exports diminished, and trade imbalances rose to never-before-seen levels. The American way of life didn't get better; it got worse.[12]

Beijing, now firmly implanted in the WTO, played by its own rules. Intellectual property theft accelerated. Joint ventures became Trojan horses, and state-sponsored espionage was scaled up with impunity. Washington had opened the gates to a foreign power with interests antithetical to its own, convinced that the future was going to lead to a China that would eventually change its predatory behavior and adopt the same liberal economic and democratic systems as its own.

But Beijing wasn't mirroring the West. It was mapping it, identifying its strengths and vulnerabilities, stealing the former and exploiting the latter. The Communist leaders in Beijing had closely studied the downfall of the Soviet Empire. They wouldn't follow the same path. They weren't so naive. They fully understood what Western leaders such as Clinton were trying to do, what their *true* end goals were by engaging in trade with China. And they weren't prepared to roll over and concede power. The CCP was about to go all in.

THESE ACCOUNTS and storylines each represent a key thread in the grand narrative that explains China's unprecedented economic and military rise in just under a quarter century. Many people have sought to explain this extraordinary ascension as being due to variables such as China's massive population, which has enabled it to achieve greater economies of scale and lower wages, its generous use of state subsidies, or its state-driven command-and-control economy, allowing it to commit to more long-term strategic plans without the vicissitudes inherent in democracies.

While these factors have no doubt been important, this book contends that a critical and largely underappreciated and underreported explanation for China's rise has been the scale, scope, and pace of its unprecedented campaign of state-sponsored industrial espionage, particularly over the past twenty-five years since entering the World Trade Organization in 2000. Quite simply, this is the story of the most consequential economic heist in human history. And it's one that has played, and will continue to play, a key role in redefining the global balance of power.

Over the past three decades, the CCP has orchestrated a global campaign to acquire—covertly and often illegally—trillions of dollars' worth of Western intellectual property, proprietary technology, know-how, and strategic data. The end goal was never subtle: to accelerate China's economic rise, modernize its military, and challenge the United States for technological and geopolitical supremacy. By all accounts and objective measures, from GDP growth to market capitalization in emerging industries such as EVs, the strategy is working.

The CCP's success of turning espionage into a tool of economic statecraft has redefined the nature of great power competition. Industrial sabotage has given way to strategic extraction. Beijing didn't just build factories; it built an entire ecosystem for harvesting knowledge on a large scale. What began with reverse engineering consumer electronics has evolved into the systematic theft of military designs, AI source code, next-generation energy solutions, and the architecture of advanced microelectronics. China, within our lifetimes an agrarian society, now dominates the filing of patent applications for some of the world's most cutting-edge technologies, filing more than twice the number of the United States in 2023.

US government estimates put the annual cost of intellectual property theft to the American economy at between $225 billion and $600 billion, almost all of it by China.[13] That sum almost matches the nearly $800 billion the United States spends on defense each year. These thefts include everything from counterfeit consumer goods to pirated software to the more insidious theft of trade secrets. And while the losses are staggering, they don't capture the full strategic cost: the erosion of Western competitive advantage in a zero-sum world and the strengthening of a rival whose ambitions are openly revisionist.

No doubt, cheap labor indeed played a role in China's economic surge. So did favorable trade terms and massive infrastructure investments guided by top-down, long-term state planning. But none of these variables explains the *speed* at which Beijing has closed the gap with America in sensitive sectors such as aerospace, electric vehicles, quantum computing, and telecommunications. That leap was powered in significant part by what can only be described as an epic level of state-sponsored espionage.

The numbers back up this claim. The Center for Strategic and International Studies (CSIS) conducted a survey of every Chinese espionage case in the United States since 2000. What they've found is a staggering 224 *reported* instances of PRC espionage against our country—meaning the "illicit acquisition of information by Chinese intelligence officers or their agents."[14] This does not include the numerous attempts of trying to smuggle export restricted or "controlled items" out of the country (such as munitions or other sensitive technologies) or the more than 1,200 cases of IP theft lawsuits undertaken by American companies against Chinese counterparts. China's espionage activities against the United States far outweigh that by any other nation, including Russia. This list, as large as it is, is not even fully complete. It only shows the number of cases *caught*. The true figure, including those where intelligence tradecraft prevented an agent's capture, is likely even higher.

Many Western firms have been complicit, both intentionally and unintentionally, in what has happened. In exchange for market access in China, they agreed to establishing joint ventures that left their critical intellectual property exposed. Years and millions of dollars spent on valuable R&D have been lost with the ease of plugging in a thumb drive. Other companies were infiltrated by employee insiders recruited by China's Ministry of State Security (MSS) or enticed by lucrative "talent recruitment programs" or targeted by cyberattacks launched from inside PLA command centers. In many cases, the thefts went undetected for years.

The consequences have been profound. American military technologies once considered strategic advantages—stealth aircraft, silent propulsion systems, hypersonic missile platforms—are now widely found in the inventories of China's armed forces. These thefts are not abstract; they represent very real threats to the American war fighters who one day may have to face down such advanced technology. The theft of these assets doesn't just threaten markets; it threatens lives. Indeed, their loss undermines the very military advantage that has underwritten decades of global stability and American primacy.

China's total R&D savings from this theft are impossible to truly quantify. Autonomous vehicle software, telecom hardware, chemical manufacturing processes, and semiconductor fabrication techniques developed in the West have reappeared inside Chinese state-owned enterprises. No model—economic or computational—can fully account for the acceleration enabled by this kind of acquisition. Research and technology can have exponential effects; opportunity costs are also impossible to quantify. What is clear, however, is that without this access to the global trading system and American firms, China's rise as a peer technological and military power would have taken significantly longer and been significantly more challenging.

None of China's economic ambitions were hidden. Since the early 2000s, China's leadership has issued formal policy directives outlining national goals in science, technology, and defense. Plans such as Made in China 2025 were not subtle; they named industries to be dominated and timetables to be met. Sectors ranged from advanced robotics and aerospace to biotechnology, semiconductors, and renewable energy. The plans were public. The means of reaching them, however, were not.

———————

THE MINISTRY of State Security (MSS) sits at the center of China's technology acquisition strategy. A civilian intelligence agency with a sprawling mandate, the MSS coordinates with other state organs, university systems, military institutions, and nominally private corporations to conduct clandestine operations around the world. Its mission is clear: to acquire critical technologies that serve national development goals, regardless of their origin and by any means necessary. Unlike in the United States, for Chinese agencies such as the MSS there is no distinction between civilian and military efforts. They are fused. China has truly pioneered a "whole-of-society" approach, marshaling every resource available to the state for the sole purpose of stealing intellectual property.

Targets for such theft have included nearly every major US tech and defense company: Lockheed Martin, DuPont, Cisco, T-Mobile, and many others. America's most prominent academic institutions, like Harvard University, have also been targeted. Sometimes the MSS uses students or researchers to access university labs. Sometimes it deploys front companies to buy distressed assets. Sometimes it recruits employees already inside a target organization. Sometimes it breaks in through the digital back door via custom malware or compromised third-party vendors. And sometimes it simply lifts a prototype off a desk and smuggles it out in a backpack.

From agricultural seeds to cutting-edge hypersonic technologies to paint formulas, the breadth, scale, and pace of China's Great Heist are truly astonishing. At one point in 2019, the FBI was opening a China industrial espionage case every twelve hours. Spies being run by China's notorious MSS have also been caught at the highest levels of the American government, from NASA to working on top secret military projects for our country's biggest defense contractors to even the CIA itself. American universities have been flooded with hundreds of thousands of Chinese students who, compelled by Chinese law and intelligence services that are unafraid to leverage their family and friends back home, have helped steal cutting-edge research, scientific innovations, and technical know-how.

Such theft is not simply a means of copying Western and American capabilities; it's a way of collapsing the entire R&D timeline. Each stolen design shaves years off development time. Each pilfered process reduces the need for learning by trial and error. Every copied algorithm can save billions of dollars in research costs. The compounding advantage isn't just economic, it's strategic. Every silent breach pushes China closer to technological parity—and possibly superiority.

Technology has always reshaped power. The Industrial Revolution upended empires. The Cold War was decided in part by computing, missiles, and satellites—material power first conceived and built by intellectual power.

Today, the technological frontiers that will define great power competition lie in artificial intelligence, quantum encryption, biotechnology, and microelectronics. In this new digital era, the weapons of war are no longer just bombs and bullets; they're lines of code, ones and zeros, networks of data. The country that controls them doesn't just win markets; it can shape economies, shape narratives, and shape the very nature of hard power and military might itself. And code stolen is just as valuable to a nation as code painstakingly developed from scratch.

China understands this. And unlike most of its competitors, including the United States, it has built an apparatus to act on it with a greater degree of urgency and commitment than fully appreciated by Washington. This book documents how that apparatus works—how espionage, state policy, corporate strategy, lawfare, and cyberwarfare have merged into a coordinated campaign of industrial acquisition on the largest scale in history. It examines how the CCP transformed its position in the global order not by competing fairly but by extracting the innovations of others, chiefly its greatest rival, the United States of America.

If Western governments and companies fail to recognize the true nature of this threat for what it is—a deliberate and highly successful

campaign—and act accordingly, they will continue to fall farther and
farther behind. The warning signs are no longer subtle. President Xi
has made his ambitions clear. The covert efforts to fulfill them have
already reshaped global markets and narrowed the West's margin of
error. China has already surpassed, and without serious countermeasures will continue to surpass, the United States on many of the met-
rics that define both economic and military power in the twenty-first
century.

The "great rejuvenation of the Chinese nation" is the end goal.
Made in China 2025 is the strategy and road map to get there. President Xi is the mastermind. The MSS are the lead henchmen. And a
whole-of-society call to arms, combining all aspects of both government and civilian capabilities, to acquire the information necessary
to achieve these ambitions (no matter how that information may be
attained, whether legally or illegally) is the means.

The question is no longer whether China is stealing the future;
it's whether anyone is willing to stop it. The great irony is that the
West helped build the arsenal that is now aimed at it. The outcome of
the next great power war won't necessarily be decided by what happens solely on the battlefield—rather by the scientific breakthroughs,
technological innovations, and strategic intelligence collection that
happens before the shooting ever starts. Stolen thumb drives, and
the powerful information they contain within, like silkworm larvae
hidden inside hollowed-out bamboo walking sticks, can define the
fate of nations.

CHAPTER 2

The Great Leap Everywhere

ON DECEMBER 11, 2001, exactly three months after the World Trade Center fell, China quietly stepped onto the global economic stage as the newest member of the World Trade Organization (WTO). Americans, for the most part, barely noticed. The US government was focused on other battles: deploying troops, hunting down terrorists, and refocusing intelligence priorities. President George W. Bush made no public remarks celebrating China's admission, but the US Trade Representative released a fact sheet about China's "accession" to the WTO.[1] At the time, America was immersed—and indeed distracted—by the Global War on Terrorism (GWOT) and its quest for justice in the wake of the terrorist attacks on September 11. Great power competition was seen as a relic of the Cold War, a bygone era. The White House mustered only a dry statement from the US Trade Representative. *The New York Times* relegated the news to three modest paragraphs—on page seven.[2]

But beneath that muted response, something profound was happening. China's entry into the WTO wasn't simply another trade deal. It was a strategic tipping point, one that would reshape global economics, politics, and security for decades to come. For President Bush, like Clinton before him, China's accession had been a priority.

"All of us who believe in a more open China—in advancing the rule of law and trade—must work together," he'd argued. ". . . We cannot let that work be undone."[3]

Sixteen days later, at his Texas ranch, he finalized the deal by signing a proclamation granting China permanent normal trade relations with the United States. In doing so, he erased the 1974 Jackson-Vanik Amendment, which had restricted trade with Communist countries that limited emigration rights.[4] The move was irreversible. Enforcement mechanisms were minimal. WTO rules, in essence, provided no way for removing a member state. It simply had never been done before. The so-called end of history, the ultimate conquest of economic liberalism, *it was assumed*, had been reached.

The deal thrilled both Wall Street and corporate America at the time. After decades of anxiety that European or Asian rivals would come to dominate the vast Chinese market, American firms finally saw their chance. Cheap labor, massive production capabilities, and hundreds of millions of new consumers were suddenly within reach. But no one celebrated more than Beijing. The CCP had pursued that goal for over fifteen years, ever since it had first applied for admittance to the WTO's predecessor, the General Agreement on Tariffs and Trade (GATT), in 1986.[5] Now the Party had it—and with it, something even more valuable: an open channel to the world's most advanced technologies and intellectual property.

By joining the WTO, China gained invaluable access to international markets with reduced tariffs and quotas, enabling it to boost its exports significantly. Members of the WTO benefit from what is called most-favored-nation (MFN) status, dictating that all members must treat one another equally in terms of trade. With benefits come obligations—at least on paper—including adherence to WTO rules. This includes requirements such as transparency on trade-related policies, a commitment to fair competition, and, perhaps most importantly, protecting intellectual property rights.

Amid the euphoria in Western capitals about the opening of a massive new market, China's strategic ambitions for joining the WTO weren't hidden. In 1979, Beijing's new joint venture law explicitly stated that foreign companies must provide "advanced" technology if they set up domestic operations in the country. One early partner was American Motors Corporation (AMC), whose joint venture launched the Beijing Jeep in 1985.[6] It was hailed as visionary at the time—until knockoffs started rolling off other Chinese production lines shortly thereafter. AMC's experience inadvertently became a template for CCP exploitation: The company entered optimistically, shared willingly, and hopelessly stood by as its technology was stolen and replicated. It was a playbook that would be repeated over and over in the years to come.

"I started going to China in 1986, when they couldn't manufacture a fork," recalled A. J. Khubani, the CEO of the TV marketing firm Telebrands. "They were an agrarian society. They couldn't manufacture anything. They didn't realize that a product had to be free of rust and that it had to be clean and had to be packaged properly. And you couldn't have defects. It took them a long time to get it right."[7]

In the mid-1990s, China's economic growth exploded. President Clinton's decision to grant China most-favored-nation status boosted American investment, despite lingering worries about adherence to fair trade terms. "If we could just sell one dollar of merchandise to every Chinese citizen, we'd make a billion dollars," hopeful entrepreneurs repeatedly told Duncan Jepson, then an enterprising young MBA at the small UK- and Shanghai-based venture capital firm Oscar Ventures in 1993. "You'd hear that all the time. That was the holy grail," said Jepson, who eventually traded a successful legal career to make films and work as a human rights activist based in California.[8] Yet Jepson, who is fluent in Mandarin and has been familiar with China since childhood, saw the truth behind the hype: The average Chinese citizen's purchasing power remained limited. The dream of gaining 1.4 billion consumers was always an illusion.

Unlike its American trading partners, the real value to China wasn't new markets for consumption; it was extraction. In return for foreign investors' pouring their money into joint ventures and manufacturing partnerships in China, they had to "willingly" transfer their know-how. "Every joint venture was explicit," Jepson noted. "They [China] wanted technology and IP, and everyone knew that was the price of admission."

Western optimism was first tested sharply in 1998 when the Guang-dong International Trust and Investment Corporation (GITIC), Chi-na's second largest financial institution, collapsed. Global banks and investors were left stunned. Jepson, part of the legal team handling the fallout, watched as furious Western bankers learned that Beijing would not make good their losses. When they were offered less than 30 cents on the dollar, shock waves ensued among the foreign invest-ment community. "We were in the Hyatt Grand ballroom, and the bankers were absolutely livid. I mean, they were just furious. I re-member a guy from Goldman standing up screaming," he recalled. "Everyone from Goldman's, Credit Suisse, First Boston, Dresdner, SocGen, Westdeutsche Landesbank, Citibank were all highly ex-posed. Western investors had assumed the Chinese government was going to stand behind it, and they didn't." China had been playing by its own rules, and foreign investors were left holding the bill.

Despite clear warnings, US policymakers clung to the belief that economic liberalization and growth would inevitably democratize China—a theory championed decades earlier by Seymour Martin Lipset, a Columbia University–educated political scientist, whose famous 1959 essay, "Some Social Requisites of Democracy: Economic Development and Political Legitimacy," argued that "the more well-to-do a nation, the greater the chances that it will sustain democ-racy."[9] The *faith* in the theory that capitalism would, in an almost magical sense, unlock democratic reform and progress would come to be a defining pillar of Washington's foreign policy establishment for many years to come. The end of the Cold War, and collapse of the mighty Soviet Empire, seemed to prove that conclusively.

Yet Jepson, working in China throughout the 1990s, saw no ev-idence of democratic stirrings on the ground. "To me, there were never any signs, going back to the eighties, that democracy was tak-ing root. There was no impression of that," he recalled. "In terms of large swathes of businesspeople, there was no interest at a civic level of pairing [democracy and human rights] together. It was about making money." Now that China was a member of the World Trade Organization, what did democratic reform matter? The WTO osten-sibly existed to settle disputes and protect intellectual property and patent laws. The world's biggest corporations could open for business and exchange in trade without fear of political interference. The free market, according to the assumptions of the day, would take care of the rest.

In Beijing, however, the plan was to do something different. Now that it was in the WTO, China's transformation accelerated dramatically. Its GDP soared from $1.3 trillion in 2001 to over $17 trillion by 2023.[10] China became the world's manufacturing engine, not just producing cheap consumer goods but dominating entire global supply chains. Piracy thrived openly as factories that once struggled with basic manufacturing processes now copied and replicated complex consumer product development with astonishing precision—often, according to Telebrands' CEO Khubani, from nothing more than photographs. With remarkable speed, many manufacturing facilities evolved from copycats into sophisticated innovation hubs capable of leapfrogging Western competition. Intellectual property was stolen without mercy. From Jepson's perspective, that theft was generally accepted. "The Chinese had long telegraphed that they wanted technology. They wanted IP. They wanted knowledge. And it was written bluntly in the 1979 joint venture laws." Western capitalists were focused on maximizing shareholder value for the next quarter; Communist Party strategists in Beijing were committed to the long game.

With its admission to the WTO, China had secured a strategic foothold in the global economic system, one that would help ensure that it would sustain continued economic growth. Doing so was a critical part of its mandate to rule and the social contract it had with the Chinese people. Mao Zedong's infamous Great Leap Forward from 1958 to 1962, a campaign of massive social and economic upheaval with the aim of transforming the Middle Kingdom from an agrarian society into a socialist industrial powerhouse, had failed disastrously. Millions upon millions of people had perished as a result, ending in one of the worst man-made disasters in history. But modern CCP high command was intent that the "Second Great Leap Forward" would learn from past failures. What Deng had started, his successor twice removed Xi Jinping would see to fruition: China's economy would be revolutionized, and in turn the country would become an economic superpower.

The ambitions were truly grandiose. And the master plan to achieve them all started with a simple PDF document uploaded onto a government website in 2015.

IN THE marble-lined halls of Zhongnanhai, the secretive compound in Beijing where China's elite leadership crafts the strategies that govern some 1.4 billion people, the outlines of a revolutionary economic manifesto began to emerge in late 2014. Behind its high walls and guarded gates, in effect China's White House, President Xi Jinping had summoned his closest advisers, economic strategists, intelligence chiefs, and influential industrialists for a series of highly confidential meetings. What emerged from those secretive gatherings would soon be unveiled to the world as Made in China 2025, an audacious plan to catapult China from the factory floor of the world economy to its commanding heights.

Stressing the critical importance of manufacturing, the opening paragraphs of Made in China 2025 declared that establishing its production capabilities was "the only way China can enhance its comprehensive national strength, ensure national security, and build itself into a world power."[11]

The plan was more than a mere economic proposal; it was a comprehensive geopolitical strategy. The CCP leadership, still haunted by memories of humiliation in the 1990s—particularly the image of US aircraft carriers forcing China's hand during the Third Taiwan Strait Crisis of 1996—understood that technological supremacy was no longer just desirable but essential to military power. Economic independence and technological dominance would become the twin pillars of China's future security and strategic autonomy.

A dedicated group of officials from Beijing's Ministry of Industry and Information Technology (MIIT), in close coordination with intelligence and national security organs, was tasked with drafting the plan. They pored over data from Chinese industries, studied classified analyses of Western and Japanese innovation strategies, and ultimately zeroed in on ten sectors: information technology, robotics, aviation, maritime engineering, advanced railways, new-energy vehicles, electrical equipment, agriculture machinery, new materials, and biomedicine. The priority was clear: to ensure that China would achieve 70 percent domestic production in those sectors by 2025 and global leadership in them shortly thereafter. It was a catch-up by any means necessary strategy, one the CCP did not publicly acknowledge. In essence it bore many of the hallmarks of the Manhattan Project, a zealous commitment and dedication of resources toward achieving a state policy deemed existential.

Of course, the CCP has yet to release an inside-look documentary into the making of Made in China 2025. But given Party protocol and culture, one can readily devise what likely happened. Senior leaders were explicit in their instructions: the road map must guarantee strategic autonomy. The MIIT teams and their advisers in academia and industry systematically mapped out their objectives. They undoubtedly discussed the ways in which foreign technology could accelerate the country's industrial ambitions, albeit masked by carefully chosen euphemisms to placate the concerns of the outside world. As China's premier intelligence gathering apparatus, particularly after Xi's commitment to significantly expand its relative role and capabilities, it's a safe assumption to make that the MSS from the earliest planning phases was consulted on how to achieve the desired outcomes of Made in China 2025.

The strategists dissected previous national strategies—the failures and successes of China's past technological pushes. They closely examined Germany's Industry 4.0 initiative and America's industrial internet strategies, absorbing relevant lessons but determined to surpass their foreign counterparts. Their directives were simple but ambitious: Build indigenously, innovate independently, dominate globally.

Over the course of a few months, the plan was fine-tuned under scrutiny by the Party's Politburo Standing Committee. No doubt Xi himself demanded that the document hammer home a single uncompromising reality: that China would not tolerate technological

dependence on foreign powers any longer. The world's leader in manufacturing would now dominate the frontiers of global technology
development, going from an agrarian country, to an industrial manufacturing powerhouse, to ultimately the leader of developing and
controlling emerging technologies. Doing so was critical if other political goals were to be achieved. To one day capture Taiwan, China
would need to be free from any fear of sanctions or dependence on
Western resources.

The plan was formally unveiled in May 2015, presented with carefully choreographed speeches, glossy brochures, and meticulously
prepared talking points. Publicly, Chinese officials marketed Made in
China 2025 as a necessary economic transition to the modern world,
promoting domestic innovation and high-quality manufacturing. But
internally, as Western intelligence would soon learn, this was in fact a
strategic blueprint that would drive China's global espionage activities.

The MSS shouldered a vast new responsibility. Its senior officers
ensured that Made in China 2025 wouldn't be just theoretical, but
operationalized. The MSS delivered vital inputs on global technological trends, foreign R&D vulnerabilities, and acquisition targets. They
briefed top-level officials on Western academic research networks
and hot new start-ups that could be quietly tapped for knowledge extraction. What emerged was a dual-track strategy: above board, the
Chinese would pursue innovation via public investments, research
park development, venture capital, and international partnerships.
Below the surface, however, they would pursue a secondary track
of cyber-intrusions, recruiting insider moles, and pilfering sensitive
information from joint ventures and academic exchanges, aimed
at achieving the goals of Made in China 2025 and manifesting Xi's
dream of the "great rejuvenation of the Chinese nation."[12]

Based on their subsequent actions, the MSS and PLA were clearly
assigned priority targeting directives based on the plan. They
mapped out where breakthroughs were happening in each of the ten
sectors and issued collection requirements to operatives around the
world and provincial bureaus. Effective strategy is the prioritization
of limited resources: Made in China 2025 set out where Chinese spies
should focus their efforts.

Within months of the plan's unveiling in May 2015, Western cyber-security firms and intelligence agencies began detecting unusual patterns. Semiconductor labs in California experienced simultaneous phishing campaigns and cyber-intrusions. Aviation firms in Toulouse, France, and Wichita, Kansas, were approached by "visiting scholars" who had deep but inexplicable knowledge of proprietary engine technology. Start-ups working on quantum encryption in Canada found themselves under cyberattacks from previously unknown advanced persistent threat (APT) groups later attributed to MSS affiliates. These were not random hits or smash-and-grab assaults; they were coordinated, sequenced, and sector specific. The MSS had started targeting new sectors and technologies with a zealous pace and commitment not seen before.

Declaring Made in China 2025 to be sacrosanct CCP policy meant that it was more than just a plan. It was a fuse, an explosive directive that mobilized every lever of Chinese state power. Provincial governments, state-owned enterprises, the military, and other state subsidiaries were now all launched toward a single unifying goal: achieving technological self-sufficiency for China.

The plan would eventually become the center of focus for alarmed China watchers in the Western world. Intelligence assessments in Washington, London, Brussels, and Tokyo pieced together a mosaic of espionage campaigns and technology theft—all of which directly answered the call of Made in China 2025. In the years that followed, the FBI would open thousands of counterintelligence investigations connected to Chinese espionage, as would the domestic security services of Western governments everywhere.

What made Made in China 2025 so alarming was its scope and its ruthless execution through a multipronged fusion of government and civilian levers of power. Chinese universities and research institutions were funded lavishly to repatriate top scientists from Western labs, who brought with them critical know-how. PLA cyberteams were deployed to breach Western technology firms and vacuum up intellectual property on a large scale. MSS agents accelerated their recruitment of insider threats in key foreign corporations, exploiting financial inducements, ideological appeals, coercion, and carefully engineered "academic exchanges." Each successful espionage operation fed directly into China's domestic innovation pipeline, cutting R&D costs and speeding up breakthroughs in aviation, robotics, artificial intelligence, and quantum computing—the future of power in the twenty-first century. While in Western nations billions are spent on conducting espionage through a handful of agencies, the remit for conducting such operations is relatively limited. China would face no such constraints. Truly *all of society* would be wielded and directed toward helping the state acquire, by whatever means necessary, the information it needed, whether done so legally or *illegally*.

As 2025 approached, the dedicated measures of China's intelligence apparatus had helped the CCP reach many of the goals it had laid out in its plan in 2015. The Australian Strategic Policy Institute (ASPI), which analyzes scientific and research innovation publications in critical technologies such as advanced explosives and energetic materials, magnets and superconductors, AI algorithms, hardware accelerators, and electric batteries, concluded that China now leads in thirty-seven of the forty-four fields of emerging critical technologies it tracks (almost all of which were sectors or technologies targeted by Made in China 2025). That is above an 80 percent success rate for achieving global leadership in many of the defining technologies of the twenty-first century.

The ASPI's reporting and analysis track well with other economic indicators of rapid development in China. With technological prosperity (whether achieved licitly or illicitly) comes economic prosperity. The United States and China have been moving in opposite directions for three decades in terms of income growth, job loss and creation, standard of living, and even life expectancy. These societal benchmarks provide strong evidence that the MSS's vast array of active measures targeting every sector of the American economy hasn't just crippled corporations and venture capitalists, but has also helped fray the very fabric of our nation and sparked a realignment of global power.

Indeed, IP theft can lead not only to job losses but potentially to battlefield losses. One notable segment ASPI tracks is advanced aircraft engines, including hypersonic technology. The institute reported that "China generated 48.49% of the world's high-impact research papers into advanced aircraft engines, including hypersonics, and it hosts seven of the world's top 10 research institutions in this topic area."[13] As demonstrated by battlefields in both Ukraine and the Middle East, such hypersonic technology will no doubt prove critical to shaping military supremacy in the future.

China's domination of this key technology may come as a surprise to casual observers, given that, for decades, NASA first led the world in hypersonic research and currently administers the Hypersonic Technology Project in conjunction with the Department of Defense. In August 2021, however, the PLA conducted a test that left US military and aerospace experts in shock: it launched a hypersonic missile with nuclear capability on a glide vehicle. Traveling at a low altitude at five times the speed of sound, the missile traveled around the globe and landed about twenty-five miles from its intended target. The velocity, low trajectory, and ability to alter course midflight pose serious challenges to the US military in both detecting such weapons and defending against them.

The baffled sentiment of outside observers at the time was best captured in a now-infamous comment by a Pentagon official in the *Financial Times*: "We have no idea how they did this."

To those who truly grasped the stakes of Made in China 2025, Beijing's audacious plan to achieve strategic autonomy and catapult China to superpower status, and the extent of the CCP's ambition to achieving it by any means necessary, the outcome was less surprising. What few outside the intelligence world grasped was that behind this epic campaign stood a shadowy organization few had ever heard of, quietly pulling the levers of China's rise.

CHAPTER 3

Inside China's Intelligence Labyrinth

THE EPICENTER of China's espionage machine lies hidden in the shadow of imperial glory of a bygone era. Just beyond the picture postcard serenity of Beijing's Summer Palace—its placid lakes and sculpted pavilions echoing the legacies of the past emperors who once resided there—sits a compound with no hordes of tourists, no signage, and no official public history. This is the Ministry of State Security (MSS), China's vast, sprawling intelligence apparatus, an agency that combines the capabilities and mandate of America's CIA and FBI.

The MSS has rapidly evolved into one of the premier intelligence services in the world, and one that has revolutionized the very concept of espionage in the twenty-first century. Under President Xi Jinping, it has become a hypercharged nerve center of economic theft. Its primary target is proprietary information: America's most sensitive military blueprints, its crown jewel commercial technologies, and its cutting-edge laboratory research.

Since rising to power, Xi has redefined espionage as a strategic instrument of national transformation unbridled by any other constraints. Term limits that once reined in unchecked authority were discarded. Political rivals were neutralized under the guise of anticorruption measures. And the MSS, elevated above any other apparatus in the Chinse security establishment, was supercharged. "We had some corporate espionage activity previously," recalled William Evanina, the director of the National Counterintelligence and Security Center (NCSC) from 2014 to 2021 and one of America's top China watchers. "When Xi Jinping comes to power. Everything changes. I mean, overnight, everything changes."[1]

Evanina is literally a straight shooter—he obtained sniper certification during his twenty years at the FBI, where he rose to lead the Counterintelligence and Counterterrorism Divisions of the Bureau's Washington Field Office. A baseball-loving jock turned G-man, the Pennsylvania native also has a master's degree in educational leadership, which likely accounts for his astute manner in analyzing China's assault on America. The changes he described weren't metaphorical; Xi decided to go all in on developing a new, state-of-the-art playbook that would promote China's intelligence apparatus to the proverbial Premier League. "Xi and his inner CCP circle more than doubled the size of the MSS from 2013 to 2015 because they knew that they were going to [increase their IP theft]," said Evanina, who now monitors China's machinations while heading the Evanina Group. "They needed resources and capabilities. I'm going to say they went from a hundred twenty thousand to almost three hundred thousand bodies in twenty-four months, which is incredible." Other intelligence apparatuses within the PRC, such as those in the People's Liberation Army, were soon relegated. The MSS became the primary vehicle to operationalize and execute the Great Heist, and its reach wouldn't be constrained.

The model that inspired Xi was audacious: the Kaspersky concept. Russian intelligence had covertly embedded surveillance capabilities in antivirus software. It turned personal computers in effect into intelligence collection devices. Xi saw not just the brilliance of the method—weaponizing the openness of the capitalist system—but the potential exponential impact if it were to be applied across every sector of Chinese power. Corporate espionage could be scaled up.

It could be systematized and made more effective than ever thought possible.

The result was a perfect storm of cyber-intrusions, human recruitment, legal manipulation, and investment front operations. MSS operatives no longer needed to sneak into government buildings or break into defense labs. The internet—and the social platforms that connected the global workforce—was the new playground of spies.

From its headquarters in Beijing, the MSS launched what would become the most sustained campaign of intellectual property theft in modern history. LinkedIn became one of its primary recruitment pipelines. Universities were seeded with students under deep-cover directives. Joint ventures were structured as Trojan horses. Start-ups were acquired—not for their future growth and potential investment returns, but rather because they had the missing know-how that could fill a CCP technology gap. And American firms, slow to react and lulled by the promise of lucrative market access in China, willingly let the fox into the henhouse.

Xi's vision wasn't just about regime survival; it was about national supremacy. Made in China 2025 called for self-reliance and eventual market domination in critical technologies, from semiconductors and AI to aerospace and biotech. But Xi knew the truth: China was lagging behind. The only way to leap ahead on the timeline he envisioned was to steal things that the West had already built.

So the MSS adapted to the mission requirements laid out by its commander in chief. No longer simply shadowy spies lurking in alleyways, MSS operatives became in effect economic agents, research collaborators, venture capitalists, and graduate students. In this new model, everyone—every Chinese citizen, at home or abroad—could be a sensor, a conduit, or a tool. Intelligence was now in effect crowdsourced. Under China's 2017 National Intelligence Law, citizens were legally compelled to aid the MSS when asked to do so.[2] If the MSS wanted a database, a prototype, a human genome, it would be obtained. There were no rules—just results. No other spy agency in history had such a mandate and the resources at its disposal than the one built by Xi.

Enter the MSS

The MSS is no longer a shadowy backwater relic of Cold War bureaucracy. Once dismissively seen as the "junior varsity" of intelligence organizations, it's now a sprawling, multitiered intelligence leviathan with specialized bureaus capable of conducting sophisticated espionage operations both within China and around the world.

Western analysts estimate that at least eighteen bureaus operate out of the MSS headquarters in Beijing, alongside three other major offices in the capital. Each bureau has a distinct, often overlapping mandate, revealing the breadth, depth, and precision of China's modern intelligence machine. Like any other government entity, the MSS is subject to frequent reorganization, and its exact structuring will never be fully known, at least by the outside world.

That said, what we do know is that the First Bureau focuses on domestic counterintelligence and foreign target operations *inside* China. Its officers operate under deep cover as employees within various Chinese government ministries and agencies. Their mission: to identify, monitor, and recruit foreign diplomats, businesspeople, researchers, and travelers while they are on Chinese soil. These officers are trained not just to surveil but to seduce and manipulate, cultivating relationships that can be harvested long after the visitor returns home.

But the First Bureau doesn't stop at China's borders; it also recruits Chinese citizens headed abroad: students, scientists, engineers. This outbound recruitment effort is vital to MSS's technology acquisition strategies. Placing the right graduate student in the right PhD program, particularly in American research labs or elite universities, is often the first step in a long-tail operation that may bear the fruit of IP theft only years, if not decades, down the line.

The Second Bureau operates what Western intelligence professionals would recognize as classic foreign espionage. Its employees are officers deployed overseas under diplomatic or nonofficial cover, posing as journalists, attachés, cultural liaisons, and technology specialists. In US intelligence parlance, they are case officers, the individuals responsible for spotting, assessing, developing, and running human sources. These sources are in effect "moles" within an organization that collect and share sensitive, proprietary, or nonpublic information.

In addition to the eighteen bureaus, the MSS has many provincial and municipal offices. Prior to 2017, these units were involved in targeting foreign nationals, according to Nicholas Eftimiades, a former Defense Intelligence Agency (DIA) analyst on Chinese intelligence. A digital worker in Shanghai with ties to Taiwan, for example, might be targeted by the local division, as opposed to the Fourth Bureau, which focuses on Taiwan, Macau, and Hong Kong. In his book *Chinese Espionage Operations and Tactics*, Eftimiades reported that after a recent MSS reorganization, targeting assignments seem to be driven by functional divisions, rather than by geographical centers.[3]

The United States remains the MSS's top intelligence priority. And for that reason, the Eighteenth Bureau exists. The Eighteenth Bureau, also known as the US Operations Bureau, is the MSS's dedicated operational wing for conducting espionage against US targets. It's tasked with the identification, acquisition, and exploitation of American technology, IP, and state and corporate secrets. It functions as both a command post and a clearinghouse, distributing assignments to other bureaus and coordinating across various collection platforms both controlled by the government and indirectly controlled or influenced by it.

The Eighteenth Bureau works in concert with other bureaus to develop Chinese sources within the United States and handle inbound intelligence leads, direct operations against US personnel abroad, and analyze and translate acquired intelligence into final analytical products for China's high command. Two of its most critical partners for driving Great Heist targets are the Thirteenth Bureau, the Bureau of Network Security and Exploitation, responsible for cyberintrusions and information system penetration; and the Fourteenth Bureau, the technical reconnaissance division, which is tasked with intercepting telecommunications, monitoring signals, and overseeing technical surveillance.[4]

Together, these bureaus form an interlocking, mission-driven system designed to target America's most sensitive assets. No collection target is off the table; scientific research, defense innovations, infrastructure blueprints, and commercial breakthroughs are all fair game. Targeted by this vast apparatus, the United States should have no illusions about being enemy number one of the MSS. And unlike its American counterparts, the MSS operates under a completely different set of rules.

Legalized Espionage

In 2017, China passed a law that would quietly reshape the global landscape of intelligence, innovation, and international business. It didn't come with headlines or dramatic announcements—just a terse statement from the National People's Congress (NPC) and a handful of clauses that seemed, at first glance, like bureaucratic filler.

But hidden in that legalese was something extraordinary: a framework not merely for spying but for citizens' compulsory participation in the Chinese state's intelligence operations. The law, called the National Intelligence Law of the People's Republic of China, made clear that spying on behalf of the CCP was a legal requirement enforced by the full power of the state.

The law's cornerstone is Article 7, which states with chilling simplicity, "All organizations and citizens shall support, assist, and cooperate with national intelligence efforts in accordance with law."[5] If there were any ambiguity left, Article 14 erased it by reiterating that "National intelligence work institutions lawfully carrying out intelligence efforts may request that relevant organs, organizations, and citizens provide necessary support, assistance, and cooperation."

In effect, those lines transformed every Chinese citizen, anywhere in the world, into a potential extension of the MSS. PRC citizens or ethnic Chinese such as a PhD candidate working at a US university, an engineer at a German automotive firm, an entrepreneur at a Canadian biotech start-up—all were now legally on call by the Chinese intelligence apparatus. They could be asked to hand over files, access internal systems, or relay conversations, and they would be required by law to do so. Failure to do so can have very real consequences, including being whisked away to a secret prison. What made the framework particularly unnerving wasn't just the mandate itself but the total lack of any oversight or limitations on its reach. There was no provision in the law for appeals, no carve-outs for ethics or privacy, no exceptions for dual citizens or foreign nationals. If you were within Beijing's sphere of influence, you were within the MSS's command structure.

American spy agencies operate under a very different set of constraints. Notably, Section 702 of the US Foreign Intelligence Surveillance Act of 1978 as amended in 2018—which allows the US government to collect foreign intelligence information from non–US citizens located outside the United States—bears a stark fundamental difference to China's 2017 National Intelligence Law. Section 702 does authorize significant surveillance capabilities and has generated criticism, particularly for so-called backdoor searches involving Americans. However, it does not forcibly conscript ordinary citizens into collecting intelligence on the government's behalf. In other words, there is no equivalent in US law that *requires* that ordinary people turn over sensitive data for intelligence collection purposes or assist in clandestine activities under penalty of prosecution. China's law is both broader in scope and deeper in its implications. It erases the line between civilians and government intelligence operatives, with significant implications for counterintelligence officials in other countries tasked with combating the threat. It marks a distinct fusion of civil and legal powers underpinning China's whole-of-society approach to espionage.

To incentivize compliance and cloak its coercive character, the Chinese law does offer some carrots in addition to sticks. Article 9 states, "The State gives commendations and awards to individuals and organizations that make major contributions to national intelligence efforts," adding a patina of honor to what is essentially mandatory support for government surveillance efforts. To provide further diplomatic cover for these authoritarian provisions, Article 8 attempts to reassure the world by promising that all intelligence efforts will be "conducted in accordance with law" and will "respect and protect human rights." The contradiction is stunning: a legal obligation to spy by everyday citizens, paired with a promise to uphold the very rights that the law itself nullifies. This is not a contradiction to rule by the CCP; it is a feature of it. In the logic of one-party rule, the law is what the Party says it is.[6] Such doublespeak would have likely impressed Orwell himself.

China's National Intelligence Law of 2017 is only one piece of a larger legal infrastructure that enables and amplifies the MSS's global reach. The Cybersecurity Law of the People's Republic of China of 2016 adds another layer by providing legal cover for targeting foreign firms. It mandates that any operator of "critical information infrastructure" must store all personal information and important data collected or generated in China within its borders.[7] In other words, if companies want to transfer its data in China abroad—say to a headquarters in California, a server in Frankfurt, or a cloud provider in Singapore—they need prior approval from Chinese authorities. The definition of what qualifies as "critical" is intentionally vague, but sectors explicitly covered in the law include telecommunications, finance, energy, transportation, public services, and defense technologies. That means that nearly every foreign enterprise operating in China, from car manufacturers to health-tracking apps, in effect fall under the mandate of this law.

The result of this legal infrastructure is a form of protectionist digital mercantilism. Whereas Western democracies try to regulate data for privacy and security, China regulates it for control. Its cybersecurity framework operates not to protect consumers but to harvest data and transfer it within state boundaries, where it can be monitored, exploited, and reverse engineered. This isn't just a firewall; it's a funnel. While Beijing tries to keep so-called dangerous information from its citizens—stories critical of China or promoting democracy and civil rights—it also harvests every nugget it can find and keeps it under tight Party surveillance. That said, the CCP doesn't need to hack every company or infiltrate every research center; it simply requires the ability to demand access and it now has that ability, empowered by law. These legal tools give the MSS something that Western intelligence agencies could never dream of having: official, comprehensive, and legally enforceable access to an entire nation's

data network and to the global diaspora beyond the country's borders. The impact of this advantage for the rest of China's intelligence
capabilities is exponential.

China's modern legal regime reframes the very idea of espionage.
Whereas the CIA and Britain's MI6 still depend on trained officers
and cultivated informants, China has built an architecture that renders espionage ambient—ever present, always available, triggered by
a legal clause and a phone call. There is no longer a need for limiting
the spy business to cloak-and-dagger meetings in parking garages;
a WeChat message to a Chinese graduate student might suffice. A
quiet request at a consulate for a well-positioned national in a foreign
country can yield terabytes of information. And the risks are relatively minimal because the CCP legal framework is, of course, on
Beijing's side. For Chinese operatives, the law is their cover and the
state is their accomplice. MSS operatives would wield this national
advantage to great effect, supercharging their talent recruitment
drives.

The Thousand Talents Mirage

Perhaps one of the most effective MSS recruitment operations was the
now-infamous Thousand Talents Program (TTP), launched in 2008
under the public mirage of fostering academic and scientific exchange
with the outside world. The hidden objective, like the vast majority of
CCP international initiatives, was never just about idealistic notions
of peaceful innovation. It was about cold, hard acquisition—of data,
of designs, and of secrets through the people who know them.

Participants in the TTP, most often Chinese nationals or ethnic
Chinese working in US academia or industry, were lured with money,
prestige, and promises of permanent appointments at elite Chinese
institutions. Building up their ego, stoking their academic accolades,
or facilitating a meeting with a high-ranking official, potentially
offering them the inside track to building and growing a business,
are indeed powerful motivators. Alongside the manipulation of
these motivations to recruit talent from abroad, TTP contracts often carried with them the explicit or implied obligation to transfer

foreign-developed intellectual property, conceal participation from employers, and replicate research labs in China. Such clauses make clear that the TTP wasn't merely a "talent recruitment program"; it was rather a new, more insidious form of espionage. Billions of dollars worth of research and IP, from universities across America and the world, were stolen and used to advance Chinese interests.

When US intelligence and academic watchdogs finally caught on to the true mission of the TTP, Beijing responded not by shuttering the program but by obfuscating it. The TTP was rebranded, fragmented, and repackaged into an ever-changing mosaic of new initiatives under new names, such as the High-End Foreign Expert Recruitment Plan, Changjiang Scholars Program, and Young Thousand Talents Program. While the public titles were changed, each had the same fundamental mission at its core: to bring knowledge to China while masking its true intent from the rest of the world.

MSS operatives worked hand in glove with provincial state security departments to identify and approach high-value individuals for the program, particularly those in the critical industries laid out in Made in China 2025: science, biotechnology, aerospace, and semiconductors. Offers to potential recruits often came from official-looking university-affiliated front groups or talent liaison offices connected to regional governments. The goal of the TTP was nothing less than to create a parallel research ecosystem in China by poaching the best minds—and, most importantly, the best ideas—from around the world.

The role of the MSS in executing the TTP highlights the federated nature of its operations. While the Beijing headquarters sets strategic priorities, provincial state security bureaus act as field offices for the execution of such priorities, recruiting, surveilling, and tasking a wide range of operatives locally and abroad. All that matters is obtaining the information, not how or from whom. From Jiangsu to Sichuan, from Guangdong to Shanghai, each provincial office acts as a collection node, exploiting both local industries inside China and their international ties in order to feed the central apparatus.

Often, these provincial bureaus work with universities and innovation zones to embed operatives into seemingly legitimate academic collaborations. Chinese state security officers can impersonate—use as "cover"—talent recruiters, embassy cultural attachés, or even start-up entrepreneurs. Behind these often friendly public masks, however, are Communist apparatchiks working with a singular mission: to funnel foreign technical expertise directly to the CCP. Other organs of the CCP around the world hold similar missions.

The United Front: Espionage in Plain Sight

Another critical, albeit less publicized, pillar of the CCP's intelligence infrastructure is the United Front Work Department (UFWD), an entity that operates at the crossroads of soft power, political influence, and covert intelligence.

Though on the surface the UFWD is a Party liaison group responsible for building support among non-Communist organizations and diaspora communities abroad, its hidden mission is to ensure the MSS goals and objectives are aligned to the CCP's plans to co-opt, coerce, and control overseas Chinese populations. While its mandate also includes supporting espionage activities, the primary focus of the UFWD is shaping global opinion in favor of the CCP.

The UFWD secretly coordinates with Chinese embassies, consulates, and overseas student associations to monitor political dissent, track critics of the CCP, and even mobilize local community leaders to carry out CCP-friendly puff initiatives. In recent years, UFWD affiliates have been publicly linked to such operations disguised as cultural exchanges, diaspora charity events, and trade delegations. In the fall of 2024, for instance, a former aide in the governor's office for the state of New York, Christine Lee, was charged with using her role to secretly advance Chinese government interests. Per Chinese state media reports, Lee had met a top UFWD official in 2017 who told her to "be an ambassador of Sino-American friendship."[8] The UFWD's murky public mandate and broad overlap with other Party organs help provide it with a valuable degree of plausible deniability.

In addition to trying to shape the global narrative in the CCP's favor, the UFWD also works in concert with provincial MSS bureaus to "spot" (i.e., identify, in nonspy parlance) talent and potential assets in foreign countries. UFWD-linked associations have invited foreign professors and tech executives to "friendship forums," while behind the scenes, MSS officers aggressively probe the participants for potentially exploitable connections, vulnerabilities, or IP access. The forward and direct questions by these officials are often reported by those subject to them to be unrelenting and deeply uncomfortable.

The UFWD has historical, deep roots within the CCP ecosystem. As far back as 1939, Mao called the United Front one of China's "three magic weapons," along with armed struggle and the CCP.[9] Communist Party leaders have always understood that power is just as much immaterial as it is material. Xi Jinping echoed its importance in 2015, declaring "United front work is party-wide work."[10] In practice, that magic weapon is a mirage, like the TTP providing the polite face of a covert intelligence-gathering and malign influence infrastructure. The world would eventually find out that modern-day China conducts espionage unlike any other state power before it.

China's Human Intelligence (HUMINT) Machine: A Different Kind of Spycraft

Case officers, from Langley to Moscow's Lubyanka to Beijing, are fundamentally hunters. At the core of their craft lies the relentless pursuit of finding, developing, recruiting, and handling foreign assets, human sources capable of providing valuable, secret information (human intelligence, or HUMINT). Case officers must be a finely tuned blend of psychologist, strategist, actor, and diplomat. Handling human sources is both an art and a meticulous professional discipline. Screening programs to find these select few often require years to carry out and lead to some of the most intense and demanding training any government offers.

Spies, the actual human sources of intelligence handled by case officers, navigate a perilous world; exposure is almost always catastrophic. To be caught often means a sudden arrest, imprisonment in a frigid cell, or sometimes even a bullet to the back of the head.

With such stakes, both the source (agent) and the handler (case officer) must possess nerves of steel. Espionage is not an activity for the faint of heart.

To effectively recruit new sources case officers must wield an expansive tool kit, adeptly interpreting emotional cues to uncover deeper motivations and exploitable vulnerabilities. They require cultural fluency as well as an understanding of local customs, social hierarchies, and power dynamics. Under extreme pressure, when carefully laid plans collapse in the face of real-world "friction," case officers must remain composed, resourceful, adaptable, and decisive. To such officers "Murphy's Law" is an ever-present reality in the world of HUMINT operations: What can go wrong will go wrong. They must think ahead, anticipate how people may react or an operational meeting may fail, and plan the appropriate responses accordingly. They operate comfortably in ethical ambiguity—the so-called gray zone—setting aside moral judgments about those they recruit, understanding that the world is not simple, not black and white, and that sometimes the greater mission requires a moral compromise in working with unsavory characters.

The relationship between handling officer and agent can be intense and deeply personal. Case officers must earn and maintain absolute trust; agents must see them as a patient on the operating table sees a neurosurgeon or a passenger on an airplane sees a pilot. Operational security, strict attention to detail, and impeccable tradecraft—avoiding surveillance, securing communications, conducting clandestine meetings—are nonnegotiable, and an officer's proficiency in them is what ultimately builds the required trust and confidence for a recruited agent to sustain an effective, long-term clandestine intelligence relationship.

At the core of any case officer's craft is the ability to effectively assess three key variables about a potential agent: their access, suitability, and motivations. These form the cornerstone of any successful HUMINT recruitment. Traditionally encapsulated by the broad acronym MICE—money, ideology, coercion, ego—motivations often overlap and evolve. They can also be multifaceted. A primary motivator, such as the lure of a prospective business opportunity, may be further supported by secondary ones, such as ideologically driven concerns about the political nature of a regime. The motivations that drive one to commit espionage are hardly ever as simple as they appear on the surface. An ideological drive may fade, giving way to financial or ego-driven incentives that ultimately sustain the relationship. Human nature can prove fickle; passion and commitment will flare up only to dissipate months later. As such, motivations can fluctuate unpredictably. A case officer must dig beneath the surface to find what makes a potential agent truly "tick"—a task much easier said than done. The best case officers are able to find the proverbial missing piece of an asset's psychological mosaic, aligning fundamental desires to shifts in their behavior—namely, risking their life to commit espionage. While ideology can no doubt be a primary motivator for agents, financial motivations often ultimately enable greater control by the handling officer. Cash frequently incentivizes actions once the more emotion-based drivers fade during the twists and turns of a clandestine intelligence relationship. When an agent's relationship is in fact driven primarily or exclusively by financial incentives, an effective case officer must understand the deeper reason behind why such money is a driving factor for an agent (for example, using the funds to pay for a child's education or medical bills).

The best spy recruiters are those who are externally, not internally, focused. They know themselves just as well as they know those they are trying to approach. Truly deciphering the human nature of others invariably first requires understanding one's own. They are able to enter the minds of their potential recruits, seeing the world as they see it, *feeling* the world as those foreign spies feel it. Most importantly, recruiters speak in terms of their agents' interests, identifying what matters most to them and equating requested actions (e.g., stealing information) to material benefits aligned with an agent's deepest motivations.

The nature of an agent's access is critical to any successful HUMINT operation. Most importantly, a potential source or agent often must have "natural" access to information through their placement in an organization or through their relationships. Going outside the normal parameters of their roles within an organization could

attract unwanted attention or lead to a counterintelligence flag spark-
ing an investigation. Asking too many direct questions, seemingly
out of the blue and not related to an agent's logical area of responsibilities or need to know, can also potentially trigger such suspicions.

In this recruitment formula, the suitability of a potential HUMINT
source is also important. A recruited asset must have the temper-
ament and fundamental skills required to follow a case officer's
taskings, receive training, and understand how to safely elicit information. In fulfilling a "tasking" requirement, they must be able to
separate what information is most important from what is not, while
also remembering seemingly trivial details that may in fact be of
great intelligence value to analysts back home. The agents must also
be capable of deciphering and explaining the chain of acquisition—
how the information was obtained—so that its credibility can be
accurately judged by these analysts. They must also have the technical know-how to effectively use covert communication equipment
to relay information if necessary. Perhaps most significantly, an effective intelligence source must have solid operational judgment: the
ability to make good decisions in complex, sometimes highly ambig-
uous, situations and under extreme duress.

While the fundamental equation of intelligence recruitment—
access plus motivations and exploitable vulnerabilities plus suitability
equals recruitment—is universally relevant, its application across different intelligence services varies drastically. The CIA, for example,
emphasizes targeting carefully vetted, high-value sources for recruitment within strict legal and operational frameworks. Its case officers
are meticulously trained to identify and recruit sources with strategic
insights into things such as political leadership, weapons programs,
terrorism, and geopolitical threats. Recruitment most often involves
a formal, explicit decision, marked by a definitive pitch and clear
commitments by both sides. Officers, often under diplomatic or nonofficial cover, often meticulously manage only a handful of high-value
agents cultivated over years, employing sophisticated and cautious
tradecraft to avoid exposure or diplomatic fallout. Internal oversight
and legal constraints strictly limit their scope of action, especially
regarding any relationship that may involve private sector entities.

China's MSS, on the other hand, operates under a completely different doctrine with a strategic philosophy rooted in its history, shaped by its unique culture, and engineered to capitalize on the new tools of the modern world. China is not new to espionage; it's been perfecting the art for over 2,500 years through countless battles and wars among competing kingdoms and fiefdoms and with foreign "barbarians." As early as around 500 BC, Sun Tzu, the great military philosopher, underscored its importance in *The Art of War*. His counsel was as wise as it was simple: "If you know the enemy and know yourself, you need not fear the result of a hundred battles." The influence of this classic book continues to significantly shape the psyche of China's approach not only to warfare, but also to intelligence.

In *The Art of War*, Sun Tzu dedicated an entire chapter to "On the Use of Spies."[11] The great military philosopher emphasized that effective governments and militaries always place a premium on and investment of resources in conducting espionage to obtain what he called "foreknowledge" of the enemy. Wars inflict a terrible cost on any people through expended blood and treasure, sometimes over many years. Wise rulers, he advised, are those who understand that espionage—knowing the "conditions of opponents"—is critical to achieving the quickest victory possible and therefore best serving the interests of any ruler's people. In fact, not aggressively prioritizing espionage, and thereby minimizing the costs of war, in his eyes, is nothing less than immoral.

In his manifesto, Sun Tzu noted that the foreknowledge essential to defeating enemies (i.e., intelligence) cannot be found out by wishful thinking, divination, reverting to historical analogy, or "calculation" while sitting at some desk. It must be obtained by people on the ground, "people who know the condition of the enemy." The best intelligence has always come from humans with the right access. Only humans can truly read other humans, capturing the nuances and insights critical to understanding the intentions driving an adversary's strategic planning and decision making. The intelligence value of understanding such *intentions* far outweighs simply counting up the number of war chariots on a battlefield. The wisdom that any ruler can gain from well-placed human intelligence sources is not outdated: in an era like our own, which is becoming ever more reliant on technology, it's in fact as important as ever. Even the most sophisticated satellite or cyberattack cannot get inside the head of an adversary as a close friend, family member, or colleague can.

Notably, Sun Tzu outlined five types of spies, which, he stated, are essential for a leader to understand and deploy. Centuries later, China's emphasis on a fluid, multipronged approach to intelligence gathering echoes this philosophy. The categories of agents Sun Tzu identified include local spies (recruited from a ruler's own people), inside spies (recruited from enemy officials), reverse spies (recruited from the enemy's spies; in other words, double agents), dead spies (those who transmit false intelligence to enemy spies), and living spies (recruited agents who have the ability to go back and forth between enemy territory).[12] The last category, while somewhat vague, appears to be later reincarnated in China's twenty-first-century Thousand Talents Program: members of the Chinese diaspora and those sympathetic to the Middle Kingdom who live abroad recruited to return from abroad to report on enemy developments.

Indeed, signs of China's future espionage apparatus can be found in the types of intelligence requirements that Sun Tzu recommended be targeted centuries ago, everything from knowing the identities of enemy generals to those of their aides, their visitors, their gatekeepers, and even their chamberlains. Every piece of information, no matter how seemingly small or insignificant, can be crucial to effectively building a larger, strategic picture of an adversary's strengths, weaknesses, and intentions. This tactical understanding and strategic appreciation of the inherent value of espionage, even its smallest strands, could readily be pulled from a MSS training manual from today.

Fascinatingly, buried within one single rather long sentence, are astute analysis of and recommendations on how to approach recruiting potential human sources. While Sun Tzu clearly understood that recruiting spies could be achieved through simply bribing them, he also recognized the value of the often harder (but more effective) method of *inducing* them into committing espionage. According to the ancient Chinese philosopher, this latter approach requires great sagacity—in other words, the ability to notice and understand even the smallest psychological cues, especially those that are subtle and not immediately obvious. He also noted that it requires understanding who the targeted source is, what motivates them, and what their access to sensitive information may be—in other words motivations, access, and suitability. Ultimately, the brilliant Chinese strategist recognized, as any good case officer today would, that the effective recruitment and employment of spies requires the ability to understand human nature on a very fundamental level: what motivates people at their deepest core, what truly makes them "tick," what their most profound interests and dreams are, what, in other words, might drive them to spy on your behalf. Sun Tzu closed his chapter on espionage by identifying and emphasizing what he believed is its most critical factor: subtlety. The best spies avoid the obvious; infiltrate through obfuscation; pursue the indirect, not the direct.

The principles of espionage recorded by Sun Tzu centuries ago have undoubtedly played a fundamental and significant role in shaping the way China has long approached the use of intelligence. Those principles would shape Mao Zedong's rise during the Chinese Civil War and World War II, aided by the spymaster Kang Sheng, who institutionalized the "thousand grains of sand" doctrine: gathering intelligence through a vast web of informal, often unwitting sources so broadly dispersed that counterintelligence services must struggle to detect it. Under such an approach, quantity (even tidbits of seemingly small bits of intelligence) can have a quality of its own.

The legacy of Sun Tzu persists within the modern-day Chinese intelligence apparatus as well, from the PLA to the MSS. While long associated with the seemingly less sophisticated "thousand grains of sand" strategy, the competence, professionalism, and effectiveness of Chinese intelligence officers has progressed rapidly in recent years. Two decades ago, they were often viewed as relatively amateurish. They could even be reckless and sloppy, using elementary and predictable covers for action. Military officers, pretending to be civilians in order to collect on unwitting targets, often failed to hide their army grunt–like demeanor. Everything from their clothes to style of speaking betrayed their cover. Recently, however, China's intelligence collectors have become much more advanced, grasping and mastering the traits and skill sets of effective case officers described above. Their emotional IQ is higher, their manners more natural, and their language abilities (notably in English) much stronger. They are more suave and more charismatic. As one former official who closely tracked their development stated, "Now this is the norm. They really have learned quite a bit and grown up."[13]

China's approach to HUMINT, like its approach to intelligence gathering at large, is, in simple terms, to do whatever it takes to accomplish the mission. This mindset is reflected in the way it appeals to the motivations of potential human sources. By and large, ethnonationalism is the predominant factor behind why individuals spy for China and the preferred appeal of MSS officers, who have historically shied away from working with vulnerable or unstable personality types. "They want good people to do bad things," explained Paul Moore, a former top China expert at the FBI. "They convince them it would be good to help China modernize."[14] Stealing information, in other words, is not "betrayal"; rather, it's simply helping China achieve its rightful place in the world alongside other great powers.

In framing their recruitment pitches in such terms, Chinese intelligence officers, like all good case officers, seek to provide the proverbial fig leaf to intelligence sources. In other words, recruiters offer reassuring words in trying to assuage any potential moral quandaries an agent might have. They also seek to reframe the activity itself, crafting narratives, for instance, about helping a poor country like China develop and rise peacefully. According to Moore, MSS officers typically seek to avoid more direct recruitment approaches in which agents formally and psychologically cross a clear line; rather, they try to have agents "give [secrets] away by manipulating them into certain situations."[15] Based on his career at the Bureau, Moore noted that Chinese pitches are often framed with such statements as "Scientific information should recognize no political boundaries," an appeal that no doubt resonates in particular with more left-brain-driven researchers and academics who believe in the universality of human development, intellectual exchange, and open dialogue. Such recruitments are most often incremental and often largely unspoken in the early stages. Targets rarely realize when they have crossed from friendly information sharing (legal) to stealing sensitive or confidential information on behalf of a foreign government (illegal)—the indirect approach of leveraging influence over the direct pitch. Subtlety, as Sun Tzu noted centuries ago, is the key to effective espionage.

In making appeals framed in terms of ethnonationalism, China has traditionally targeted ethnic Chinese sources almost exclusively. A joint CIA/FBI report to Congress in December 1999, in the wake of a high-profile Chinese penetration of America's nuclear secrets, highlighted this issue: "Because most Chinese share a common cultural and historical background, Chinese leaders refer to all individuals of Chinese ancestry as 'overseas' Chinese. When approaching an individual of Chinese origin, the Chinese intelligence services attempt to secure his or her cooperation by playing on this shared ancestry."[16]

That said, in recent years, as China's intelligence apparatus has become more sophisticated, it has broadened its target set to prioritize recruiting from a more diverse range of human sources, not just those of Chinese ethnic descent. Appeals to foreigners are still often framed in terms of a sentimental "obligation" to help China modernize and develop; it's only fair, the pitch might go, given the Western colonialism that "exploited" the Middle Kingdom. Officers frequently target foreigners who have spent a significant amount of time living and/or studying in China and who often speak the language and admire Chinese culture and history. For instance, shock waves rocked Great Britain's Parliament in 2024 when it was discovered that a parliamentary researcher named Christopher Cash was allegedly spying on behalf of China. Cash, the director of Tory MPs' China Research Group, who has insisted he is "completely innocent," previously spent almost two years in China, before he was accused on espionage charges of sharing information with Beijing based upon his access to the corridors of power in London.[17]

While China's approach to HUMINT recruitments is predominately centered on patriotic appeals, MSS officers do not shy away from using financial motivators as well. While historically, Chinese case officers tended not to prioritize recruits who were fundamentally motivated by monetary compensation, according to former FBI agent Paul Moore, under the new "whatever it takes" collection philosophy and supercharged by the imperative of achieving the goals set out in Made in China 2025, Chinese operatives are ready and willing to pay high prices for high-value intel. Monthly retainers for sources can sometimes reach the tens of thousands of dollars. In relative terms, such payments can be worth their weight in gold. Moving an advanced spy satellite orbiting thousands of miles above the earth to obtain information can cost millions of dollars; getting the same information from a simple chat with a human informant over coffee can cost far less.

Unlike more risk-averse Western agencies, which are constrained by moral norms and laws, China is not afraid to employ "honeypots," romantic partners who get close to someone with access to sensitive information—a tactic that has been historically used to great effect from French diplomats such as Bernard Boursicot to FBI agents and American politicians. CCP officers can also make coercive threats to potential sources against their family and friends in mainland China, and use the more subtle tactic of entrapment. As the former FBI senior counterintelligence agent William Evanina warned, Chinese operatives try to get targets to pass over sensitive information by degrees. An initial request is generally benign but later requests evolve into something much more significant. A snare is then set. "When they get that [first] envelope, it's being photographed. And then they can blackmail you. And then you're being sucked in," he told *The Atlantic*. "One document becomes 10 documents becomes 15 documents. And then you have to rationalize that in your mind: 'I am not a spy, because they're forcing me to do this.'"[18]

Another unique trait of Chinese case officers is their commitment to playing the long game. They can invest decades cultivating a single source, staying close, developing the relationship, and never breaking cover. The source then eventually joins an organization in a low-level position, with less access to sensitive information and therefore less scrutiny. Eventually, however, they rise to the top, where they can gain access to more valuable and hard-to-access secrets. MSS officers, for instance, might identify a bright young lieutenant in a foreign military service not for what he knows today but for what he might know in the future, when he one day becomes a general. In contrast to the US intelligence community, in which postings typically rotate every twenty-four months, Chinese case officers may remain in assignments for a decade or more. They become part of the source's life—"Like family," as one China analyst put it, not having to worry about a potentially awkward or rough turnover to an unknown handling officer.

Chinese operatives also tend to place much greater emphasis on developing personal rapport than Western officers typically do. Years are spent cultivating the relationship with a source before any official request is made. When one finally does come, it's often built around emotional leverage: shared dinners, photographs, favors, or perhaps even family connections. By such a stage the target may find it nearly impossible to refuse—not out of fear of the consequences of espionage but out of the sincere belief their "friend" would never betray them. The intelligence relationship is more person to person, not person to institution. China's greater commitment to playing the long game and its strategic patience can pay massive dividends that more short-term focused approaches do not.

The best HUMINT assets, no matter where their motivations may fall on the MICE spectrum, almost always have a deep level of personal rapport with their recruiting officer. While largely universal to espionage, the critical role such personal rapport plays in China's human intelligence operations is unique and cannot be overstated. In fact, the acronym MICE should, for China-related cases, be rather categorized as MICE + G, with the *G* standing for *guanxi*, a concept that is hard to pin down in Western thinking. In essence, it's a system of networking that includes unstated obligations built into relationships that are based on mutual dependence. In highly simplistic terms: "You scratch my back and I'll scratch yours." This concept has been deeply rooted in Chinese culture for thousands of years, shaped by Confucian thought. Chinese often keep a mental tally kept of favors done and debts owed. Social debts are tracked. This system of reciprocity is deeply ingrained in relationships and remembered over a lifetime. Within this mental framework, not repaying a favor is seen as a moral wrongdoing, in effect a grave sin.

Under the principles of Confucianism, interpersonal duties are the foundation of relationships. Chinese colleagues will expect a partner to honor their commitments, not because of any signed contract but because *guanxi* holds them accountable to their part of the agreement. The critical role personal rapport and relationships play in Chinese human source recruitments is no surprise when one understands these deep cultural nuances. They are also the reason why Chinese case officers place such a premium on extending favors to potential targets and sources, especially early in the recruitment wooing process: such debts must one day be repaid.

The concept of "face" is also intricately tied into the idea of *guanxi*. Ensuring that face is protected through the sharing of utmost respect in how a relationship is handled is critical to building it. Demonstrating genuine personal concern and care for others, beyond just business interests, is also critical for successfully building *guanxi*. The traditional exchange of favors is ultimately rooted in informal emotional ties, not formal economic interests. This means the relationship between agent and handler is often viewed as personal, not institutional. In contrast, American intelligence officers are trained to ensure that recruited agents understand their relationship is with the US government, not the handlers themselves, so that when the officer inevitably rotates out, the intelligence can continue to flow without disruption.

In addition to concepts such as *guanxi*, another unique aspect of China's intelligence apparatus is the sheer scale of the number of potential intelligence targets it's willing to pursue or is capable of pursuing. "In 2020, we had great visibility into the MSS and PLA folks that were facilitating their LinkedIn recruitment," William Evanina told us. "They were sending out thirty thousand emails per hour."

This astounding number—never before reported—showcases Beijing's commitment to mass recruitment that can best be described as a "flood the zone" strategy. The MSS doesn't need all its targets to respond. Just a handful can be enough; a single successful recruit can make the entire endeavor worthwhile. The Chinese intelligence system, unlike the United States' or even Russia's, doesn't focus on select, high-value targets alone. It traditionally works on volume, breadth, and the law of large numbers, as previously noted. Combined with advances in artificial intelligence and social media scraping, the MSS has developed an approach that vastly multiplies its outreach to potential intelligence targets around the world. "Bumping" targets to initiate contact in places like a coffee shop, a gym, or an airport by a single case officer focused on a single potential source has been injected with steroids.

Greg Levesque is a cofounder of the preeminent security advisory firm Strider Technologies, an award-winning company that designs applications and software to identify bad actors within its clients' organizations to protect IP and prevent its theft. In assessing the impact of the tools installed by Strider with clients in over ten countries, he called the past and current scale of MSS onslaught "humbling."

"The scope and scale of China's activities are beyond what I even imagined," he underscored in an interview. "I think we have a good idea of how the model plays out and replicates itself, which has been very helpful for us to kind of peel back the onion. But I have yet to see a Fortune 1000 company anywhere in the world that is telling us at Strider they haven't had an incident. *All of them have had incidents.* And all of them are currently conducting investigations into anomalous activity, not cyber. So that's a phenomenon that has metastasized in the past five years."[19]

In addition to the huge and unrivaled scale of its operations, the MSS excels in the use of proxies and unwitting intermediaries in executing espionage operations—what can be described as "access agents." A Chinese scientist might meet a foreign academic at a Starbucks, ask harmless questions, and report back to their handler in Beijing—without ever realizing that they've become part of an intelligence collection chain. That scientist may later receive five "follow-up questions" for the same academic contact, still unaware that they're collecting sensitive information for government agencies. The primary source in this scenario, the foreign academic, will also likely never know the identity of the ultimate end user of the information they share. They may think only that they are simply helping a fellow researcher, one with an established background and public credentials in their area of expertise. This opaque system of collection and the use of such cutouts, in which even the collector may not know what they're collecting, provides the MSS with layers of insulation and deniability, as well as a unique competitive advantage in skirting foreign counterintelligence agencies such as the FBI.

In executing these clandestine intelligence operations, the MSS and other Chinese intelligence agencies employ a wide range of tradecraft—the tactics, equipment, and methods intelligence officers use to protect and mask their activities. These can include everything from the more primitive methods of hand carrying SD cards across borders to stuffing confidential information inside a bag during a visit to an office or laboratory, to employing classic spycraft such as dead drops, in which items or information are left at prearranged (often concealed) locations for another person to pick up to ensure that the asset and handler are never seen or caught together.

China's use of such tradecraft has become more sophisticated in recent years, due in no small part to the effectiveness of the FBI in locating its sources. Such counterintelligence victories can no doubt be important windfalls in breaking up networks and disrupting adversary activity, but they can also enable foreign agencies to adapt and improve upon their past mistakes. Evolutions in China's tradecraft include the use of end-to-end encrypted commercial messaging applications such as WeChat. As another measure of operational security, MSS officers invariably instruct their assets to create a new account on a different phone for every contact with their handler. A classic tradecraft practice deployed by the MSS involves meeting clandestine sources in third countries in order to raise less suspicion with the source's own domestic security services. Meeting in a third country can also put intelligence assets more at ease, providing them the psychological comfort to more freely divulge secrets or let their guard down. It can also enable the handling officer and agent to engage in more informal activities, allowing the latter to "let their hair down" and a greater rapport to follow suit.

While its shadowy and less known background tends to accentuate its ominous profile, it's important to recognize that MSS officers are by no means infallible and have made what can only be described as rookie mistakes in the execution of their tradecraft—most commonly in their failure to detect surveillance by adversarial services such as the FBI. The apparent number of high-profile blowups of Chinese intelligence cases, however, should be taken with a grain of salt. They are undoubtedly part of what is called "selection bias" in statistics. In other words, the public learns only about the intelligence cases that *failed*, not those in which clandestine tradecraft worked effectively and remained secret. High-stakes espionage failures in the West generally and the United States specifically are broadcast to the world, resulting in things like congressional hearings and investigations. Success remains hidden in the shadows. Like any other service, China's intelligence apparatus, including the MSS, has gone through growing pains and evolution. While starting with more primitive methods embodied in the "thousand grains of sand" collection strategy and "smash and grab"-type heists, it has evolved rapidly through cold, hard experience and dedication. Its officers should not be underestimated but rather respected as formidable masters of their craft capable of executing highly sophisticated penetration operations of even the hardest targets. Perhaps only decades from now, when Communist archives are finally opened or sources pass away from old age, will we ever learn just how successful China's intelligence services have truly been at penetrating the halls of power in the United States from Wall Street to Washington, DC.

The comparison between the CIA and MSS in particular reveals two different philosophies of HUMINT. The CIA is more selective about whom it recruits and is limited by legal constraints. It targets the collection of state secrets based on intelligence requirements that are shared only within the government under a strict classification system. In contrast, the MSS is systemic, patient, and almost entirely unconstrained by moral or traditional legal norms. It casts a far broader net in the sources it targets and the information it collects and is much more dedicated to playing the long game. Whereas the CIA focuses on recruiting official sources who are vetted and subjected to a formal recruitment pitch, China builds ecosystems of informants under both direct and indirect control.

In the global contest for technological and political dominance, the CIA and MSS don't just differ in method; they represent competing models of how intelligence can be used as an instrument of national power. One is selective and focused; the other is systemic, sprawling, and unapologetically opportunistic.

Perhaps the most significant difference between the two agencies is simply one of will: Who wants the information more? Who's playing for higher stakes? And, perhaps most significantly, who's willing to pay the higher price? Dennis Wilder, a former deputy assistant director for East Asia at the CIA, emphasized that China's leaders don't just see America as another competitor on the global stage; it's viewed as an existential threat: "This is a constant theme in Chinese intelligence—that we're not just out to steal secrets, we're not just out to protect ourselves, that the real American goal is the end of Chinese Communism, just as that was the goal with the Soviet Union."[20]

For decades, from the highest levers of power on down, China has been dedicated to waging a ruthless shadow war against America, framing the stakes as nothing less than existential. For decades, Americans hardly knew that such a war was occurring.

Sun Tzu's maxim "Know your enemy and know yourself, and you need not fear the result of a hundred battles"[21] is buried deep within the psyche of Xi's and the CCP's grand strategy. It's nothing less than the philosophical principle at the heart of China's foreign and domestic intelligence apparatus. The principles of espionage first outlined by Sun Tzu, the deeply embedded role of his teachings in broader Chinese strategic thought, and the influence of other particular cultural and political factors such as the concept of *guanxi* and Marxist-Leninist Party principles have molded China's unique approach to espionage and intelligence collection, rendering it one of the world's most formidable services. It is undoubtedly the world's largest.

One operation, however, can break any illusion of infallibility—one MSS officer, one LinkedIn message, one American engineer. A single misstep would pull back the curtain, show the world the machinery underneath, and reveal Beijing's hidden playbook.

CHAPTER 4

The Playbook Exposed

BRUSSELS, EASTER Sunday, April 1, 2018. The spring air in the Royal Galleries of Saint Hubert was thick with tourists, chatter, and the scent of fresh pastries from a nearby café. But hidden among the crowd were Belgian federal officers and American FBI agents, tense and focused. At precisely 3:00 p.m., a man—square-faced, compact, and flanked by a nervous-looking colleague—entered the ornate shopping arcade. He didn't know it, but he was walking straight into history.

Within moments, Xu Yanjun, a senior officer of China's Ministry of State Security, was surrounded and arrested. In his pockets: thousands of euros in cash. In his backpack: an encrypted hard drive and memory cards. On his iPhone: secrets that would help peel back China's modern-day industrial heist. The arrest would be the beginning of the path for the first Chinese intelligence officer to ever be extradited to the United States to face trial.

The man who orchestrated the sting, from beginning to end, wasn't your average G-man. At first blush, Bradley Hull might not seem like central casting's idea of an FBI special agent. His pre-agent days suggest a nerdy genius, with more in common with characters on *The Big Bang Theory* comedy series than lethal agents in Bourne thrillers.

The Ohio-bred, Oxford-educated Hull received his PhD equivalent, a DPhil, in the United Kingdom, in archaeological science. He spent his leisure time as a member of Oxford University Lightweight Rowing Club, a group devoted to dueling their Cambridge University rivals on the Thames River in an annual 6.8-kilometer race.

When not sculling with his mates, who were victorious in three of the years Hull raced, the scholar worked on a dissertation with a title that exhibited a natural curiosity and nose for investigation: *Social Differentiation and Diet in Early Anglo-Saxon England: Stable Isotope Analysis of Archaeological Human and Animal Remains.*[1]

Newly graduated, Hull decided to put his knowledge of isotope geochemistry to use joining the FBI's lab in Quantico, Virginia, in 2008. He studied isotopes—the smallest, purest fragments of matter—taken from the teeth of corpses and tried to determine their place of origin. Then he had an epiphany. "I realized I was a very educated ditch digger," he said.[2] He decided to change disciplines, became an FBI special agent, and was assigned to counterintelligence work in the Boston and Cincinnati field offices.

In 2017, China's espionage-driven efforts to obtain US intellectual property, trade secrets, and data had shifted into overdrive. One staggering assault involved hacking into Equifax, one of the three largest consumer credit–tracking companies in the United States, in May of that year. Bill Evanina called it "one of the CCP's greatest intelligence collection successes." Elaborating further, the former FBI China watcher explained, "More than 145 million Americans had all their financial data, nicely aggregated, [and provided] to the CCP. That is more than half of the American adult population. Stolen along with all the personal data was Equifax's business process and trade secrets on how they acquire and share such data from financial institutions, data brokers, and credit bureaus."[3] Such bulk data can be critical for finding new intelligence sources and understanding exploitable vulnerabilities such as massive levels of debt.

While Equifax's entire network and databases were penetrated by PLA hackers who gained entry to the company's dispute resolution website, an MSS agent was busy targeting one of America's leading technology companies, General Electric Aviation. He planned to use a different collection tactic than a simple hack: developing a clandestine human source inside the corporation. Now called GE Aerospace, the company at the time was a global leader in manufacturing jet and turboprop engines and integrated systems for military vehicles. It was a lucrative target for the MSS, and it was headquartered in Cincinnati, meaning that it was on Hull's turf.

The MSS agent orchestrating the penetration of GE Aviation was a fourteen-year MSS clandestine case officer named Xu Yanjun. At the time he was deputy division director of the MSS's Sixth Bureau in Jiangsu Province. An outsider might conclude that Xu was on the upper rungs of middle management. Xu's writings, however, later made public in FBI documents, tell a different story. His personal emails and diary entries, revealed by using sloppy tradecraft and a shared iCloud account, paint a portrait of a professional spy who was a resentful midlevel bureaucrat coping with heavy expectations and bosses he disliked. Separated from his wife and with one son, he wrestled with midlife agonies, was saddled with debt, and frequently moaned about women rejecting his advances. He was a far cry from a Chinese version of James Bond.

Those mundane realities aside, Xu was nonetheless a professionally trained case officer. He had several aliases he used as covers for his operational work, including one elaborate facade as the deputy director of the Jiangsu Association for International Science and Technology Cooperation. It was an ideal cover. When officials at other government agencies or his superiors in the MSS requested specific information, he could adapt his official-sounding persona to the target and approach and recruit experts with access to the desired American and Western technology trade secrets. That was always the first step. Ideally, he'd arrange for recruits to "bring"—a polite term for "steal"—specific plans to China.

Xu also built his own outreach team. One person he reportedly worked with was a vice dean at the Nanjing University of Aeronautics and Astronautics (NUAA) Office of International Cooperation and Exchange, who apparently invited technology-savvy foreigners to speak at the school. According to a comprehensive *Bloomberg Businessweek* report, Cheng Feng stumbled across the LinkedIn profile of

David Zheng, an engineer at GE Aviation's office near Cincinnati. He cut and pasted Zheng's name into the top of his form letter offering a speaking engagement, made a quick edit to reference GE, and hit send. The fawning letter cooed over Zheng's "wealth of engineering experience in well-known companies such as GE Aviation."[4] The missive was aimed at stoking Zheng's ego. "I felt honored to be invited to give a talk," he recalled later. The open-ended invitation was convenient, too. The talk was scheduled to coincide with a trip he was already planning to take to see friends and attend a family wedding in China.[5]

Zheng responded, saying that he was interested. He was an expert in the construction of fan blades, which are used in sophisticated airplane engines, as well as in the light but robust fibers used to make them. When Chen proposed a topic for his speech, "Application, Design, and Manufacturing Technologies of Composite Materials in Aircraft Engines," Zheng readily agreed.[6] Zheng knew that he couldn't divulge GE Aviation trade secrets in his presentation, something he told Chen. But under the pressure of delivering a public address that would be up to par with the hype his host had connivingly already built up, he downloaded several GE Aviation–related documents to his personal laptop, planning to use the images and information in them to augment his PowerPoint presentation.[7] It would end up being one of Zheng's biggest mistakes of his life.

Entrapment

Exactly how Zheng first triggered suspicion as an insider threat at GE remains unclear. The FBI does not want to reveal the surveillance methods that uncovered the MSS operation. Early reports out of Cincinnati credited GE Aviation's own internal vigilance. Subsequently, FBI Special Agent Hull tried to pass the recognition to the company's cybersecurity team, testifying that "GE looks for employees within its companies with red flags."[8] But Eric Ridder, GE Aviation's vice president of cybersecurity, would later divulge in court that Bureau agents had alerted the company to a possible breach by a company engineer.[9]

After being tipped off, Hull had several engagements with GE security managers about Zheng. Any successful counterintelligence investigation in the private sector often relies on law enforcement working closely with the security managers at the impacted companies. On November 1, 2017, after the firm's cybersecurity team conducted extensive forensics on Zheng's communication devices, Zheng was called to a meeting with GE Aviation security officers, according to news accounts. There was no beating around the bush; he was asked directly about his trip to China. Clearly nervous and stumbling through his alibi, Zheng recited a tale about attending a college reunion and spending time with friends and family. His travelogue had holes in it. He made no mention of downloading GE files, going to Nanjing, giving a talk, or receiving $3,500 in cash for expenses and an honorarium from his overly generous hosts.

Hull and another agent then entered the room and flashed their FBI badges. The tension in the room shot up a notch. The agents quizzed Zheng about his China trip and got the same abbreviated version about the school reunion and visits with family. But Zheng's body language betrayed his story; he was visibly shaking.[10]

Hull took his time, rephrasing his questions, saturating them with doubt, prodding Zheng to think again and come clean with his travelogue. But the engineer remained evasive. Hull seemed to have Zheng dead to rights with the easiest of all convictions: lying to an FBI agent, a charge that can land someone in prison for up to five years and as much as a $250,000 fine.[11]

But catching Zheng in a lie wasn't Hull's goal; he had bigger plans. He told Zheng that he thought the engineer was lying. And he had proof; he brandished several documents revealing that Zheng had visited the Nanjing University of Aeronautics and Astronautics and consorted with several individuals who were definitely not family members. They were spies.[12]

Hull pointed out to Zheng that he was in serious trouble. Some of the files he had taken to China were under federal export controls. He was suspected of stealing GE Aviation secrets and transmitting them to China. At that very moment, the FBI was searching his home and his car. But Hull had a proposition: If Zheng would cooperate with the FBI and work to string MSS officers in Jiangsu along, Hull would return the favor. Zheng was about to become one of Sun Tzu's reverse spies, what today we would call a double agent, one of the riskiest gambits in the great game of espionage. Zheng, who had a wife and child in the United States, not to mention a $130,000-a-year job he was about to lose, agreed and was not charged. He was not about to sacrifice in effect his life for the greater good of the CCP.

One of the people Chen introduced Zheng to in Nanjing was Qu Hui, the deputy director of the Jiangsu Association for International Science and Technology Cooperation. The association, at least according to its public website, is a "provincial, professional, non-profit social organization" whose goal is to "serve for the construction of an 'industrial technological innovation center with global influence' in Jiangsu."[13] For anyone versed in CCP technology acquisition operations, the organization might sound like a front. But for Zheng, it raised no alarm bells and appeared credible.

Qu Hui was one of Xu's MSS aliases. At Hull's direction, the FBI took over communications with Xu, instructing Zheng on what to say and when to say it. Meanwhile, the Bureau ran down two email addresses Xu used to communicate with Zheng and learned that the accounts had been backed up via an iPhone to an iCloud account. They obtained warrants to access the iCloud account and found a mother lode of documents detailing MSS operations: years of Xu's communications, personal diary entries, audio recordings, and personal documents, many revealing additional operations that Xu had spearheaded. Xu had committed a rookie error and costly mistake in his tradecraft: tying his operational phone to his personal account.[14] Looking through Xu's files provided a moment of vindication and irony. The FBI had legally obtained sensitive data the easy way, the very thing that Xu was obsessed with stealing through an onerous HUMINT recruitment process. Now the Bureau could analyze thousands of files and reverse engineer a version of the MSS espionage playbook.

It became clear that Zheng was not Xu's first rodeo. Access to the spy's iCloud account provided investigators with details of several other operations. One case they were able to piece together from it involved targeting Frédéric Hascoet, a project manager at Safran

Aircraft Engines, a French aerospace leader working with GE Aviation on advanced engine design. Safran built parts of its engines in Jiangsu. Xu had two employees at Safran's Chinese facility on his payroll. One, a Chinese engineer, had helped Xu install malware on Hascoet's laptop to enable remote access to it. When Hascoet returned to France, however, his laptop had connectivity problems, and the malware was detected.[15] To this date, Hascoet has not been legally charged with any wrongdoing. The case would highlight the MSS's tactic of using HUMINT to enable cyberoperations—a potentially lethal combination.

The MSS agent also ran a young Chicago-based spy named Ji Chaoqun. A registered alien, Ji had served in the US Army Reserves under the Military Accessions Vital to the National Interest program. He had been busted after telling an American undercover agent that he used his military identification to gain access to *Nimitz*-class aircraft carriers to take photos of them. Xu, FBI investigators discovered, had also instructed Ji to obtain biographical information to help recruit engineers and scientists in the United States. Due to Xu's carelessness, the Army reservist Ji would ultimately be sentenced to eight years in prison for betraying his oath at enlistment and spying for a foreign power.[16]

As revealed by the iCloud account, Xu also coordinated a hack of an engineer from the British firm Stork Fokker (now part of GKN Aerospace), which had sensitive information about US military airplane designs. During the engineer's visit to Jiangsu, Xu arranged for an associate to distract the engineer by accompanying him to a banquet while he himself broke into the engineer's hotel room and copied the contents of his laptop.[17] He also targeted Arthur Gau, an engineer at Honeywell Aerospace, who reportedly accepted $5,000 from Xu in exchange for an Aviation-related presentation and later pled guilty to exporting items without a license in 2021.[18]

Xu hadn't come up with these operations by himself. He was in frequent communication with engineers at Chinese government-owned aerospace and turbine companies, trying to clarify the precise IP the companies were after. In other words, he was developing taskings for his agents in response to high-level intelligence requirements (targeting the same sectors and technologies, in effect, as those outlined in Made in China 2025). In that way, the MSS operated in essence like a consulting firm that didn't charge its customers: It conducted research, met with potential clients, developed recruitment strategies to obtain HUMINT employees, and analyzed the potential return on its investments. And unlike at traditional intelligence services, its end-user customers were not always government or military entities but private sector companies.

To support those "clients," the MSS frequently targeted tech and aerospace companies such as GE Aerospace. Xu used open-source intelligence (OSINT), everything from social media to sites like LinkedIn, to find new human sources to approach who could answer his questions. Such tools offered a simple but effective means of "targeting" that the Chinese would continue to utilize for years.

The Backstory

Xu's espionage activities directed against GE Aviation reveals the extent to which MSS operations are committed to the long game. As various CCP-issued five-year plans made clear, aviation and aerospace are viewed as critical technology sectors, both militarily and commercially. That strategic framework empowered the MSS and officers such as Xu to steal vital technological secrets in sync with the priorities of the Chinese aviation industry and have the bandwidth and resources to dedicate years to executing such collection operations.

Xu's targeting of GE Aviation and Safran was no accident. In 2007, the State Council of China approved plans to develop a domestic passenger jet, and one year later the newly formed Commercial Aircraft Corporation of China (COMAC), a state-owned enterprise (SOE), announced plans to produce C919 passenger planes. In 2009, COMAC hired CFM International, a joint venture between GE Aviation and Safran that made state-of-the-art LEAP-X engines. The new Chinese entity would shortly thereafter build a less sophisticated engine, the LEAP-1C, for its new plane.

Meanwhile, COMAC and a second SOE were also engaged in

building their own versions of CFM's turbofan engine, the LEAP-8, according to a report from the cybersecurity firm Crowdstrike. In 2016, COMAC and China's giant SOE aerospace company Aviation Industry Corporation of China (AVIC) became the joint owners of a company producing the CJ-1000AX engine, a suspected knockoff of the LEAP-X. Without precise specs, Crowdstrike analysts noted, it's difficult to assess whether CJ-1000AX is a virtual clone of LEAP-X. But, they suggested, "it is highly likely that its makers benefited significantly from the cyber espionage efforts of the MSS . . . knocking several years (and potentially billions of dollars) off of its development time."[19]

Curiously, in 2017, the year Xu targeted Zheng, China's leading news service, Xinhua, produced an article about the overdue maiden flight of the C919 titled "China-Made C919 No Challenge to Boeing, Airbus Dominance." Was it a forthright appraisal? Or was it another page from the MSS playbook, a journalistic misdirection to lull Western aviation leaders into a false sense of security that their sensitive IP wasn't being stolen and replicated back in China?

If that was the case, such misdirection can work both ways.

The Bust

Through Zheng, Hull was behind the scenes, pulling the strings of MSS officer Xu. It was an incredible opportunity to examine an MSS operation in action. Xu, unaware that the Bureau was monitoring his accounts, believed that he was engaged in a picture-perfect HUMINT operation. In reality, he was the unwitting victim of Hull, who was choreographing a beautiful counterintelligence ballet. The goals of the dance were clear: to arrange a secret handoff of vital GE Aviation technology—and lure Xu out of China for the exchange while continuing to gather as much MSS intel as possible and, ultimately, making the FBI's first arrest of a known MSS officer. It was a high-wire act with no room for error.

Acting on Hull's instructions, Zheng continued to communicate with Xu, who invited Zheng to return to China again. Eventually, Zheng provided GE Aviation plans—vetted, of course, by GE Aviation engineers and supported by the FBI—relating to the GE9X engine, the holy grail of its jet engine design. He also asked for Zheng to provide a copy of the file directory for his company-issued computer, which Zheng also provided after GE security scrubbed the document.[20] That "chicken feed" was the perfect dangle—just interesting enough to keep Zheng on the hook while not providing anything of true intelligence value.

When Zheng himself floated the idea of a second trip, Xu was thrilled. But Hull had no intention of allowing Zheng back into China. Rather, it was part of a bait and switch, with Zheng announcing that his boss had suddenly ordered him to attend meetings in Europe. Xu, eager to make his higher-ups at the MSS happy and acquire GE's sensitive blueprints, replied that he would do his best to meet his recruit there.

The two men hatched the operational details on WeChat. Xu pushed for a meeting in Amsterdam. From the FBI's point of view, that would have blown up the mission; the Netherlands was not always receptive to US extradition cases. Belgium, however, usually was, meaning that Hull and Zheng had to figure out a way to steer Xu to Brussels, not to Amsterdam, without raising Xu's suspicions.

Hull came up with the cover. Two days before the scheduled Amsterdam meeting, Zheng announced his boss had scheduled him to work in Brussels. With his work demands, logistically it would be impossible for him to go to Amsterdam. Unless Xu met him in Brussels, a meetup was not going to happen.

By that time, Xu had already flown to the Netherlands. He was all in—an aggressive case officer on the hunt, about to snatch his next scalp. On April 1, 2018, he arrived in Belgium with another MSS officer, Xu Heng, and immediately scouted out the assigned meeting place with Zheng, a Le Pain Quotidien coffee shop at a popular Brussels tourist spot. Evidently, nothing he saw raised any red flags during his pre-meeting reconnaissance.

Around 3:00 p.m., the planned time of their meeting, Hull, along with Belgian federal police officers acting on a warrant that Hull had coordinated with the US Department of Justice, swooped in and arrested Xu Yanjun and Xu Heng. Xu Yanjun had about €7,000 in cash on him; Xu Heng, who was not named in the arrest warrant and not accused of any wrongdoing, and who was quickly released, had a similar amount in US dollars. They had brought a hard drive and some memory cards. Xu Yanjun had two phones, a Huawei model and the iPhone with which he had so diligently documented his personal and professional life on. Twenty-four hours after his arrest, an unknown person accessed the iPhone remotely and wiped it clean.[21] Xu was arrested, out of all days, on April Fool's Day.

Xu Yanjun was extradited to the United States and indicted on multiple charges, including conspiracy to commit economic espionage and conspiracy to commit trade secret theft. The actual prosecution of espionage cases can prove more challenging than the broader public may suspect; Hull's meticulous crafting of the case to show clear intentions by the actors involved and material damages suffered by the company was therefore critical to making the case stick. Naturally, PRC Foreign Ministry spokesman Lu Kang denied all charges, saying "The U.S. accusation is something made out of thin air."[22]

At the trial, Bradley Hull took the stand and shared a bizarre detail about Xu's pursuit of Zheng: FBI agents had found a trove of photographs of Zheng, the GE Aviation engineer, and members of his family on Xu's phone. The material, more suited to an ominous stalker than a professional intelligence officer, suggested one thing to investigators. "The presence of over 200 images brought to a meeting in a foreign country could be used as a manner of coercion . . . he still has family in China," Hull testified.[23] On November 5, 2021, Xu was convicted on all counts.[24]

Xu and Hull were involved in a shadow war—albeit one in which only one side was witting. It was the game of espionage at its finest. This time, the American was victorious.

Before sentencing Xu, US District Court Judge Timothy Black sought to assess what the monetary damage to GE Aviation would have been had Xu succeeded in obtaining the corporate secrets that would inevitably have been used by a PRC rival developing its own composite fan blade engine. The conclusion, based on GE Aviation's 55 percent market share of the $73 billion aircraft engine market in 2019 and a series of assumptions to calculate the projected loss if Xu's heist had succeeded, was $50,094,000.[25] Despite the shock value of that figure, experts watching the case viewed it as relatively small, considering that it did not factor in GE Aviation's R&D costs or account for the inevitable erosion of future sales to a foreign rival. They estimated that the losses to GE could have been billions of dollars.

Xu, forty-two years old at the time of his conviction, was sentenced to serve twenty years in prison.[26] In November 2024, however, he was released from US custody as part of a prisoner exchange. Three Americans detained in China were returned as part of the swap. The current whereabouts of Xu are unknown.

The Playbook

Xu's arrest and trial gave the world a front-row seat to the CCP's espionage doctrine in action—its playbook. Defined below are some of the core tenets of Beijing's modus operandi in executing its Great Heist:

Academic and professional exploitation: Xu's sophisticated cover as a scientific official exemplifies China's use of academic institutions to recruit unsuspecting professionals, exploiting their desire for recognition, career advancement, or simple financial incentives. It also underscores the breadth of resources at China's disposal in crafting sophisticated cover stories that can enable access to targeted sources with access to sensitive information around the world.

Whole-of-society approach: Chinese espionage involves an ecosystem of all sectors of society—academic institutions, private companies, and SOEs—working in tandem toward one common objective: stealing secrets and helping the CCP achieve its economic and technological goals. Underpinned by the 2017 National Intelligence Law, Chinese citizens, such as Chen Feng, the vice dean of NUAA who helped lure the GE Aviation engineer Zheng to China, are legally required to support this espionage mission.

Incremental entrapment: MSS operatives gradually escalate demands from innocuous academic interactions, such as Zheng's presentation at the conference, to explicit requests for sensitive technologies, making the collaboration seem harmless until it is too late. The taskings set by such officers often escalate over the course of a relationship, from acquiring relatively benign information such as a corporate directory at GE Aviation to stealing more damning articles such as sensitive engine blueprints. This "boil the frog slowly" approach is a lethal psychological ploy calculated to entrap unwitting victims.

Covert technology acquisition: MSS operations often align directly with the state-backed Made in China 2025 initiative and other national development plans, targeting critical technologies such as jet engines, artificial intelligence, and advanced manufacturing through both cyber- and human intelligence methods. These strategic doctrines serve as the intelligence "requirements" that drive the Chinese collection cycle, from targeting new OSINT sources to recruiting agents, to conducting debriefings.

Recruitment via social media: Platforms such as LinkedIn and other OSINT tools have become prime hunting grounds for Chinese intelligence operatives, enabling them to rapidly identify, approach, and cultivate targets with unprecedented precision and on an unprecedented scale. "Flooding the zone" by creating a large quantity of such approaches practically ensures that some of those contacted will respond and, playing the numbers game, eventually be recruited. Quantity can have a quality all of its own.

Financial and familial leverage: Cash payments, family pressures, and subtle coercion (such as Xu collecting personal information on Zheng's family) are systematically employed to ensure the compliance and ongoing cooperation of recruited sources. In the CCP's approach to espionage there are no rules.

Cyberenabled HUMINT: China's espionage campaign can integrate both cyber-intrusions with traditional HUMINT operations, maximizing their intelligence-gathering effectiveness. A human agent can be recruited or compelled not only to provide information about what they know but also to physically plug a thumb drive into a sensitive IT system filled with malware (demonstrated by the way one of Xu's recruited assets tried to install malware on the laptop of an employee of the French aircraft firm Safran Aircraft Engines). Even the best cybersecurity measures will find it difficult to prevent a hack enabled by an employee with legitimate access to its systems.

Smash and grab: Xu's case also demonstrated that China is willing to employ the more primitive methods of its past, including luring a potential intelligence target away from their hotel room and then breaking into the room and rummaging through their personal property to hunt for valuable secrets. At the end of the day, getting the information is all that matters, not necessarily how "sexy" the means are for doing it. Sometimes the simplest methods work best.

Xu Yanjun's conviction wasn't just a victory for the FBI; it shone a spotlight on the hydralike architecture of China's intelligence collection apparatus. Xu was Exhibit A in how the CCP is stealing its way to global economic dominance—one LinkedIn message, one insider, one conference at a time. This is not the Cold War espionage of diplomats at cocktail parties; this is asymmetric economic warfare using every available means of acquisition. And sophisticated HUMINT operations weren't China's only means in conducting it. In fact, acts such as simple piracy of goods could prove just as effective.

CHAPTER 5

The Attack of the Clones

ON A bitter January morning in 2025, buried deep within the gray prose of a government report, a single word shattered decades of diplomatic illusion. It didn't come from a leaked memo, a viral video, or a fiery congressional hearing. It was included—dryly, deliberately—in the annual report of the Office of the United States Trade Representative (USTR). The one-word verdict on the People's Republic of China's compliance with World Trade Organization rules: "Poor."

There were no footnotes, no diplomatic caveats, just the blunt truth. After twenty-three years of legal theater and economic shadowboxing, Washington had officially called a spade a spade: China was not just bending the rules it had agreed to when it signed up to the WTO nearly two decades before; it was ignoring them as though they were written in invisible ink.

The clearest evidence of noncompliance comes from US Customs and Border Protection (CBP). CBP isn't all that focused on technology transfer per se as its core mission, but it amasses evidence of billions of dollars' worth of PRC property rights violations, unsanctioned manufacturing, and intellectual property (IP) transfer every year. In other words, it aims to thwart China's knockoffs by focusing on stopping the fruits of previous transfers, copyright and patent violations, and the manufacture and importation of pirated goods.

"Seizures from China and Hong Kong accounted for approximately 90% of the total quantity seized," the agency reported in 2024. Over $5 billion worth of pirated goods was captured at US ports, airports, post offices, and monitoring express consignments. Over $5 billion in lost market share for American companies. By the CBP's accounting, jewelry was the top smuggled product, with $1,654,738,737 of valuables seized (the agency uses the manufacturers' suggested retail price when calculating values), followed by $1,442,665,050 worth of watches, $1,086,024,208 worth of handbags/wallets, and $414,106,770 worth of sunglasses.[1] None of these numbers, it should be noted, includes smuggled goods that went unconfiscated, which would surely make them even higher.

The Piracy Jungle

One person who isn't surprised by the number of counterfeit items pouring out of the PRC is A. J. Khubani, the entrepreneur behind Telebrands and its multimillion-dollar-selling infomercial-fueled products, such as the PedEgg callus remover and the Reusable Sticky Buddy Picker Upper. Khubani, who has been fighting against Chinese pirates of his products for decades, says that an incalculable amount of piracy takes place online in America every day—and that Amazon, Walmart, eBay, and dozens of other online vendors are the conduits for sales of pirated goods sent from China. After years of vociferous complaints by American manufacturers, including Khubani himself, Amazon would finally implement a "Transparency program" and Amazon Patent Evaluation Express (APEX), giving manufacturers a process to stop illegal sales. While these enhancements were welcomed, the scale of Chinese piracy meant that US patent owners could end up being caught in an unending Kafkaesque retail nightmare. Khubani lived this nightmare out firsthand.

"We have a product called the Pocket Hose, an expandable garden hose that we have 126 patents on. Before the APEX program, there were thousands of infringers on Amazon. We went to the APEX program last year, right after it started. And Amazon accepted the Expandable Hoses infringer path. We started taking down all the infringers. To date, we've taken down over eight thousand infringers off of Amazon. The problem is, if you go to Amazon now, it's still filled with infringers. And you wonder, 'Well, A.J., you've taken down eight thousand infringers. So why, when I go to Amazon, is it filled with infringers?' Because one hundred new infringers, without exaggeration, pop up every single week. Then we file the takedowns of all those infringers, and Amazon takes several days to several weeks to take each infringer down. And the moment you take them down, the people selling simply put the listing back up under a different name with the same exact photographs, the same copy, same everything under a new company name. We call it Whac-a-Mole. It's a game you can't win."

For Khubani, who often manufactures his products in China, the onslaught of piracy is facilitated by a perfect storm of factory capacity, engineering skill, online shopping, and complete lack of any moral scruples. The nation that once, in his words, "couldn't make a fork," can now produce anything at any time and in any quantity. Pirates monitor the bestseller lists of Amazon, Alibaba, and other commerce sites looking for products to copy, he said. "All they need is a picture of a product online, and they are in business. They can order it online and have it the next day. In a matter of days, they can sell it, claiming it's the real thing, at half the price of the original or less."

Ironically, although Amazon's Transparency program may protect manufacturers with deep enough pockets to join the initiative (companies must pay for a QR code sticker to be placed on every individual manufactured item), the app can actually end up *helping* counterfeiters, according to Khubani. That's because counterfeiters can see what products are listed as Transparency products, and the system automatically blocks counterfeiters from attaching their pirated products to the real listing. "That's telling the counterfeiters, 'Okay, don't bother with this one,'" Khubani added. "The app right here is telling counterfeiters what they can counterfeit and telling them what the best sellers counterfeit. Amazon does this because Amazon wants the cheapest price. They know they're creating competition even if it's illegal."

Seven years after the initial 2016 Transparency launch, Amazon was proudly bullish on its program. Dharmesh Mehta, vice president of Amazon's Worldwide Selling Partner Services, said Amazon Transparency had verified "more than 900 million product units across the supply chain" for over thirty thousand brands, "effectively eliminating the threat of counterfeiting and giving customers peace of mind when shopping for these products in Amazon's store."[2]

But listening to Khubani and other struggling retailers impacted, it's hard not to conclude Amazon, eBay, and many other sites that allow unregulated listings of pirated products that violate IP and patent laws in effect enable de facto legal black markets. The low prices have forced other traditional retailers such as Walmart, the Home Depot, Macy's, and Best Buy to offer marketplace-like retail experiences and partner portals to compete, thus expanding the market for counterfeit goods even further. Khubani advocates holding online retailers to the same liability standards facing brick-and-mortar stores. "Amazon's position is 'I'm only the intermediary. You can't hold me accountable for anything sold on Amazon, You can't hold me accountable for intellectual property infringement. You can't hold me accountable for nonpayment of tariffs.'"

Noting Amazon's political power and its advertising might—in 2022, the company was the number one Big Tech spender on lobbying[3] and the biggest ad buyer in the United States[4]—Khubani doesn't see any meaningful legislative changes on the horizon. But he has a dream that President Trump will fix things with a few well-placed sentences. "The Consumer Product Safety Commission says you can't go after Amazon for selling dangerous products," he said. "We need an executive order that changes that."

The Backstory

China's piracy problem isn't new. It has simply evolved and metastasized. In the 1980s and 1990s, visitors on the backstreets of every major Chinese city and Hong Kong were witnesses to a constant, albeit fairly innocuous wave of criminal commerce. You could find videocassettes of recent Hollywood movies and audiotapes of hit

Billboard albums being sold for pennies on the dollar. Looking for cheap designer blue jeans? Familiar-looking denim pants bearing brand-name labels were stacked high at suspiciously low prices on Shanghai street corners.

Part of the equation for the pricing was rooted in China's economy. The average Chinese worker, whom Beijing was offering as a low-wage alternative to Western labor costs, couldn't afford the prices of Western goods. That said, the CCP was bullish on the nation's manufacturing future as part of its long-term strategic economic plans to surpass the West. Those two realities created a perfect storm for piracy: profit-seeking foreign manufacturers, cheap labor, a growing factory base, and a huge domestic market for low-cost counterfeit merchandise.

"This prevalence of copycat goods, pirated CDs, gray market goods disappearing out the factory door, or through some warehouse into the local market—that was an annoyance, but it wasn't necessarily a major threat," said Lee G. Branstetter, an economics professor at Carnegie Mellon University who has written widely on technology transfer and intellectual property issues. "Things got more serious as the capability of indigenous Chinese manufacturing firms rapidly increased, and it became increasingly possible for these enterprises to take something close to frontier technology and produce it about as well as Western firms. Now Western companies not only have a significant competitor in this gigantic Chinese market that you're trying to claim for yourself, but you're also seeing these goods show up elsewhere in the world."

A long history of piracy and copyright violation festers beneath the 2025 USTR report, lurking like a sneaky, recurring, and predatory virus that initially feigns a symbiotic relationship with a foreign business. Once entangled in it, the proverbial virus demands access to critical technology, replicates inventions, and destroys its host.

The USTR's first WTO report in 2002 was at least aware of the threat. Written soon after China's admission to the WTO, it avoided adjectives such as "poor," no doubt in an effort to continue the West's nascent courtship of Beijing to engage within the terms of its economic order. Still, the report warned of ominous signs ahead: "The lack of effective IPR [intellectual property rights] enforcement remained a major challenge. If significant improvements are to be achieved on this front, China will have to devote considerable resources and political will to this problem.["] Not surprisingly, the WTO report would end up falling on deaf ears to Communist leaders in Beijing.

Efforts by US politicians, diplomats, and trade groups to combat Chinese IPR violations would ultimately prove toothless. At the same time, the CCP mastered the art of positioning itself as a willing partner in upholding the rules that drive the WTO, while simultaneously ignoring them. Indeed, China went through the motions of upgrading its IP laws in 1979, in 1990, and then again in 2001, upon its accession to the WTO. And it has continually made promises during negotiations to fix the widespread predatory practices of its state-owned and privately owned companies demanding technology transfers. Promises that were made but not kept.

The preponderance of evidence clearly suggests that the PRC never intended its actual approach toward things like WTO trade requirements to be anything more than lip service. "China's misappropriation of foreign technology violates World Trade Organization (WTO) principles and China's obligations under its accession agreement to the WTO," wrote Branstetter, the professor at Carnegie Mellon. The economist pointed out that China had originally committed to ensuring its state-owned enterprises would operate based on market principles rather than national industrial policy—highlighting that it had signed the WTO Agreement on Trade-Related Aspects of Intellectual Property Rights (TRIPS), pledging to safeguard the patents, trademarks, copyrights, and trade secrets of foreign companies operating within its borders.

Despite these pledges, however, the reality is much different, as Branstetter reported: "China's requirements for technology transfer . . . are imposed instead through extralegal means; hence, few firms are willing to make their complaints public."[6] Like a bully or mafioso, Beijing has pressured corporate victims of piracy to stay silent or suffer the consequences of either legal or economic retaliation, WTO commitments be damned.

The Strategy Encoded

In 2006, the PRC published a document that was as telling as its title was long-winded: The National Medium- and Long-Term Program for Science and Technology Development (2006–2020).[7] This document outlined China's national attitude toward technology acquisition and, by extension, piracy. In 2018, the Office of the United States Trade Representative called it "the seminal document articulating China's long-term technology development strategy." The USTR's 215-page report on the issue was written to determine, at President Trump's request, if an investigation into whether "China's law, policies, practices, or actions" might "be unreasonable or discriminatory and . . . may be harming American intellectual property rights, innovation, or technology development."[8]

The question was answered with an avalanche of official documentation. The report zeroes in on the core of Beijing's strategy: the NML Program's directive to "Introduce, Digest, Absorb, and Re-Innovate" foreign intellectual property and technology—a process known as IDAR. This approach, the report makes clear, is no accident. It's the product of deliberate, close coordination between the Chinese government and domestic industry to systematically extract and repurpose the innovations of others. The USTR further cites follow-on CCP blueprints—such as the 2012 12th Five-Year National Strategic Emerging Industries Development Plan and the Made in China 2025 road map—which place the accumulation of scientific and technical expertise at the heart of the PRC's ambition to dominate global technology.

The bulk of the report lays out instances of relentless pressure campaigns and private threats by CCP private and public sector officials to force technology transfer—almost all done covertly—as well as discriminatory policies that allow the use of unlicensed patented technology and other acquisition scams.[9] It also documents cybertheft cases, including a case involving Guangzhou Bo Yu Information Technology Company Limited's targeting and stealing of geospatial positioning technology from three firms, including an American technology powerhouse, Trimble. Perhaps most importantly, the report does not mince words about the long-term threat of these practices, stating that the investigators found that "China's technology transfer regime continues, notwithstanding repeated bilateral commitments and government statements."[10]

Once again, the Office of the United States Trade Representative chose its words tactfully, wary of upsetting America's largest trading partner. But the conclusions are impossible to escape: When it comes to fair trade, the CCP is a government of liars and thieves, and China is a nation pretending to operate according to free market principles while cynically violating them to fight an undeclared economic war. The purported "miracle" of China's economic growth wasn't due to enlightened CCP state policy planners. Rather it was the fruit of cold hard theft on a scale never seen before in the global economy.

Absorption as a Strategy

When Tai Ming Cheung, a journalist who spent six years covering Hong Kong and China for the *Far Eastern Economic Review*, *Institutional Investor*, and other publications, traded in his reporter's notebook for a consultant's briefcase in the mid-1990s, he decided to put his geopolitical knowledge of East Asia to work as an analyst and risk adviser. The new gigs weren't that different from the old one, although PriceWaterhouse and Kroll Associates definitely paid better than journalism did. Outside of his desk jockey job reading and writing reports, he attended conferences, banquets, and dinners, engaging diplomats and government officials when he could, asking questions in his clipped British accent, and building relationships— the kinds of pursuits that might suggest the fine arts of business, journalism, and intelligence gathering are not always very different.

But in the early 1990s, when Cheung served as defense correspondent for various outlets, the PLA purchased the SU-27, Russia's leading twin-engine fighter jet, developed in the late 1970s. It would end up buying dozens of the fighters for around $35 million apiece.[11] The CCP backed a 1995 deal with Shenyang Aircraft Corporation, a subsidiary of the massive state-owned Aviation Industry Corporation of China, to license the production of the supersonic fighter from Russia and produce it domestically. Cheung heard about the deal over vodkas with Russia's military attaches in Beijing. "They didn't like what was going on," he said. "They were critical of the Russian defense industry giving away technology. One of them said, 'It's like we're selling off the silverware.'" On a trip to Moscow, he met more men with military ties who expressed concern about the SU-27 deal. Russian jets, they told him, should be made in Russia.

As it turned out, the Russians were right to worry. "The Chinese were licensing, producing, and assembling the SU-27 in Shenyang," he said. "But they also built another factory they didn't tell the Russians about. And that's where the J-11B gets produced, almost side by side."[12] Design-wise, the Chinese version was a dead ringer for the Russian plane, cloning its signature aerodynamic look. There were plenty of other overlaps as well: each version of the plane had two turbofan engines and matching radar and weapons systems. Whatever nuances the Shenyang engineers might have added were only slight or would be implemented in future iterations.[13]

Cheung eventually left the consulting business for academic pursuits. He is currently the director of the University of California Institute on Global Conflict and Cooperation and a professor at the School of Global Policy and Strategy at UC San Diego, where he writes extensively about Chinese national security, technology, and political structure and their ties to China's economic development.

From his academic vantage point, he now sees the creation of the J-11B as both a pivotal event in the PLA's modernization efforts and, in a larger context, a grand operational achievement that embodied a template for China's future technology growth and modernization copying foreign innovation where possible. That model, he noted, is Introduce, Digest, Assimilate, and Re-Innovate (IDAR) in action. It was the embodiment of the same phrase that had caught the eye of the Office of the United States Trade Representative when describing the CCP's National Medium- and Long-Term Program, which called for "promoting digestion, absorption, and re-innovation of imported technologies."

For Cheung, obtaining technology plans had not been the central problem for China's developing economy—or that of other Communist nations with fledgling market economies. He pointed to the intelligence gleaned from the famous French-run Farewell Operation, in which a KGB mole had obtained and then shared mountains of technical intelligence obtained by the Soviet Union. For years, both China and Russia had the means to steal IP but, for a variety of reasons, neither was particularly adept at analyzing the specs and taking the more difficult step of actually building on them. Manufacturing the J-11B changed that dynamic, Cheung said. "The reason why the SU-27 is really important for understanding the PLAs technological absorption capability was that it was about two generations ahead of anything that the Chinese military aircraft industry was building at that time."

The aircraft was, quite simply, a game changer.

Cheung has written extensively and compellingly about IDAR, most recently in his book *Innovate to Dominate: The Rise of the Chinese Techno-Security State*. Although he ties the concept back to 2006's National Medium- and Long-Term Program, which declared its guiding principles to be "indigenous innovation, leapfrogging in priority fields, enabling development, and leading the future,"[14] and other documents, Cheung credits Xi with turbocharging the initiative. He noted that the CCP leader "attributes China's inability to leverage its massive size into global strength to a chronic lack of innovation" while also prioritizing "national state security as a means to defend the country's expanding external interests and safeguard internal stability."[15]

The framework identified by Cheung as IDAR is in principle related to a slightly more crass framing of Chinese predatory practices called "capture, raise, and kill," a term favored by some China intel experts. In simple terms, under this framework for dissecting a clear pattern, China first lures in foreign companies into its ecosystem; it raises and then grows a domestic consumer market for the related goods while also learning the mechanics of how to replicate them; and then it kills off the foreign competitor through lawfare and other tactics while propping up its newly established Chinese clone. The SU-27 licensing deal has all the hallmarks of the strategy. A CCP-backed defense-focused company, Shenyang Aircraft Corporation, lured advanced technology into the country, built a factory to use and master it, and then, having built its own aircraft, had no need to continue the deal. Russia was kicked to the curb. As underscored by the development of the J-11B, acts of piracy by China were no longer relegated to the scale of handbags or watches, but advanced fighter combat jets. The technical and industrial know-how to not only copy but in fact replicate and produce, at scale and with their own modifications, advanced technology had been unlocked. The significance of this breakthrough would have profound implications for years to come.

Walking the Piracy Plank

Given the by now well documented practice of IDAR—or catch, raise, and kill—it's hard to fathom why any American CEOs would agree to do business in China, aside from the obvious lures of the proverbial billion-person consumer market, supply chain efficiency, and large supply of low-cost labor.

For Michael Brown, a former director of the Department of Defense's Defense Innovation Unit (DIU), that motivation is eerily familiar. Early in his career, as the CEO of Quantum, he sought to sell his company's disk and tape drives in China. Over time, he witnessed many of China's coercive business tactics, and by the time he became the CEO of Symantec Corporation, a cybersecurity firm and the world's tenth largest software company with more than ten thousand employees worldwide, he had learned enough to avoid doing any business with Beijing whatsoever, if at all possible.

"We should be highlighting these stories so more executives understand what has happened," Brown noted when asked about why so many Western CEOs continue to do business there. "While more business executives are aware today than a decade ago, we can increase the awareness even further as there have been more examples that make the pattern clear."

Brown distilled the experience of Western executives doing business in China as having three distinct phases. Drawing on several reports from the Mercator Institute for China Studies (MERICS), a nonprofit German think tank founded in 2013 by Stiftung Mercator that focuses on China, those phases are described in the following manner: "First, you're excited about the prospect of being in China and you agree to a joint venture. In the second phase, there's disillusionment with the joint venture the Chinese government forced you to set up because there's been IP theft. The third phase is: *you're screwed*. China now has your IP and they've set up a competitor that's being subsidized by the government. It's only a matter of time before your business stops growing and becomes unprofitable, forcing you to withdraw from China. It's only a matter of time: you're in one of those three phases depending on the evolution of your technology. Every American businessman should understand that pattern before doing business with China."

Branstetter, the Carnegie Mellon economist, sees the answer as an understandable deal with the Devil and even evokes the kind of doomed bargain offered by Marlon Brando's Vito Corleone character in *The Godfather* as a relevant analogy. "US firms are basically feeling that the Chinese government and their Chinese standard enterprises are making them an offer that they can't refuse, right? And so they actually enter into an agreement to transfer technology to indigenous, top Chinese entities. But it's an agreement that they enter under certain duress." Branstetter cited the pressure that companies such as General Electric and Siemens might encounter if the head of a Chinese utility company offered to buy their turbines only if they agreed to transfer valuable technology to Chinese manufacturers. "As the Chinese market is too big to ignore, GE and its multinational competitors all realize that the short-term costs of refusing to play by Chinese rules are quite high—since, if one firm refuses to play, another is likely to acquiesce."[16] While the costs for not entering the China market can indeed be high for multinational companies, doing so most often comes with far greater dangers.

From Name Brands to High Tech

Online sales of pirated American goods are obviously not limited to Telebrands products. Nor are they limited to the United States. Some of the most heavily trafficked websites in the world, many in China, sell bootlegged products. In 2023, the USTR continued its aggressive stance against China's IP theft, naming WeChat, AliExpress, Baidu Wangpan, DHgate, Pinduoduo, and Taobao as leading sites for the sale of counterfeit goods.[17]

As for precisely what goods are pirated, counterfeiting victims often choose to suffer in silence with regard to the cloning of their products. Similar to the companies that remain silent about IP hacks out of concern that they will reflect poorly on them, manufacturers are hesitant to publicize piracy, which might be seen as negatively impacting their profits or corporate stability and therefore their valuations. While the 2018 Office of the United States Trade Representative Report named a few victims specifically, such as SolarWorld and U.S. Steel, which have sought remedies for IP theft, it also cites several manufacturers and trade groups that said they had not pursued even low-level legal action to protect their IP against the suspect Chinese companies because they feared crippling retaliatory action.

These activities cost American and Western companies billions of dollars in annual sales. But there is other damage as well. China's counterfeiting ultimately pilfers revenue and jobs from American manufacturers. The knock-on effect denies government further tax revenue to spend on things like defense. In some instances other harms are more direct. Pirates often exploit child laborers to make their goods as cheaply as possible. There is no upside to these cheaper, illegal, and inferior goods beyond expanding the PRC's workforce, earning the country underserved foreign capital, and ultimately helping tip the scales of the global economic balance of power in their favor.

The theft or reverse engineering of the specifications of high-priced sneakers by Nike or Telebrand's water hose may not have the geopolitical importance of, say, blueprints for a stealth jet, advanced AI programs, or a quantum computer. But they are undeniable IP thefts nonetheless, and another important prong of the CCP's master campaign to leapfrog the West through hijacking its trade secrets. Given the CCP's obsession with state security and its constant monitoring of all digital data—on social media sites, on email, and on the movement of people and goods—the idea that Beijing lacks the means to control rampant piracy within its borders is absurd. It's clearly the result of a lack of will.

During the covid pandemic from 2020 to 2023, Beijing's leadership shut down entire cities and rigorously enforced quarantines affecting tens of millions of people. It has astounding, frightening internal security and monitoring abilities. Given this fact, it can no doubt be safe to assume that piracy has been and remains an unspoken national strategy. "Introduce, Digest, Assimilate, Re-Innovate"—IDAR—may be a catchy acronym. But it helpfully and clearly defines piracy as a systematic Chinese state policy. When a product is introduced, reverse engineered, and then "reinnovated" via mass production, it's not reinvention. It's simply government-backed theft.

Bill Evanina developed a formula to articulate this CCP policy at FBI briefings. "I called it 'eighty-five times thirty.' Basically, we said any kind of technology the US was going to make, China would steal it. They would only provide eighty-five percent of the capability for thirty cents on the dollar. That was their strategic plan. Say we built a widget. The Chinese would steal the technology and build that same widget, but with only eighty-five percent of the capability because it's cheaper, and then it would sell it globally for thirty cents instead of a dollar. That was the whole construct, a strategic plan for China, which worked very, very well and allowed them to dominate the global market."

And that is ultimately the root of the Great Heist: state-sanctioned larceny to catapult China to the commanding heights of the world's economy. Eventually handbags and sneakers wouldn't be the only products stolen by Beijing at scale. Some of the world's leading frontier technologies and industries would be targeted as well—including a company led by one of the world's most famous and wealthy men.

CHAPTER 6

Crossed Circuits

The Electric Vehicle Wars

IN 2018, two months before Tesla's panicked security team contacted the FBI over fears that Guangzhi Cao had smuggled out Autopilot, the Trump administration's Department of Justice (DOJ) announced the start of its China Initiative. Devised as its strategy to counter Chinese national security threats, the initiative was a long-overdue, aggressive solution to counter and prosecute Chinese espionage. Everything from theft of trade secrets to cybercrimes. After nearly two decades of a relentless campaign targeting American industrial secrets, academic research, and private sector data, as well as rampant Chinese piracy, American law enforcement was finally offering, in theory at least, a response in kind.

But for Tesla, there was a hitch when it later came to prosecuting Cao. "We used to have the *anti*-handbook handbook," explained a former senior staffer, noting there was never an official document. "Elon was against written policies because he viewed it very much as bureaucracy." When it came to pressing charges against Cao, the company's lack of rigorous checks and balances proved to be problematic, the insider said. For example, while Tesla stated that it had some policies prohibiting employees from storing confidential company information on personal devices, those policies often weren't enforced. In Tesla's high-speed development culture, copying a snippet of code to work on at home was common and forgivable, said the former staffer. Missing a deadline, in contrast, was not. That kind of fast-and-loose work culture posed a serious legal obstacle to anyone trying to prosecute trade secrets violations in a court of law, said the former staffer.

Musk himself has been quoted in favor of breaking rules and questioning managerial authority, offering up five commandments that made up what the CEO called "The Algorithm." Number one: "Question Every Requirement. You should never accept that a requirement came from a department, such as the 'legal department' or the 'safety department.' You need to know the name of the real person who made that requirement. Then you should question it, no matter how smart that person is. Requirements from smart people are the most dangerous, because people are less likely to question them. Always do so, even if the requirement came from me."[1]

Anyone familiar with corporate legal protections might wonder what role, if any, Tesla's general counsel had in implementing security policies. But Musk was quixotic in that regard. In July 2018, a search to replace Tesla's general counsel, Todd Maron, who had gotten the job after serving as Musk's personal divorce lawyer, began, and an eye-raising series of rotating general counsels ensued. Over a four-year period, five general counsels were hired and put onto the legal hot seat. One reportedly lasted only about a month. Some of the lawyers were pushed out by Musk, while others "quit over security and policy battles," recalled the Tesla insider. "They said, 'I'm not going to be personally liable for this.'"

Discussing the Cao data theft allegations with the FBI, the specter of another insider breach hovered over the Tesla team. About six months earlier, a trade secrets case had surfaced involving XMotor, a leading Chinese EV manufacturer, recruit stealing an American company's EV-related plans. The American company impacted this time was Apple, and the employee, Xiaolang Zhang, had worked on Project Titan, Apple's secret self-driving car initiative and one of the company's most high-profile expansions into new product lines in decades. Zhang's role was designing and testing circuit boards for EV sensors. On April 30, 2018, after returning from a paternity leave trip to China, he told his supervisor that he was quitting to take care of his mother in China. During that meeting, he indicated that he was in reality taking a job at XMotor.

Tipped off, Apple immediately investigated Zhang's computer usage. They identified a dramatic increase in download activity only days before his departure. Apple security uncovered two more ominous facts in its investigation: Zhang had copied a confidential twenty-five-page document containing schematic drawings of a critical circuit board used in Apple's autonomous vehicle to his wife's laptop, and he had been caught on camera taking circuit boards and a Linux server from Apple's labs.[2] Ten days after he was interviewed by the FBI and admitted to his actions, he bought a one-way ticket to China. Before he was able to board his plane he was busted by federal agents.[3] He subsequently entered a guilty plea to theft of trade secrets in exchange for a mere 120-day prison sentence and three-year supervised release. As Apple's CEO would later recount, the punishment didn't appear to truly match the crime.

Indeed, such a sentence might suggest that Zhang's actions had inflicted relatively limited damage on Apple. While Apple didn't officially pull the plug on its autonomous vehicle program until 2024, a conversation the former senior FBI counterintelligence agent Bill Evanina had with Apple CEO Tim Cook in 2018 suggests that it was in fact a cataclysmic cause for the product line's failure. "It [Zhang's theft] basically neutralized and eliminated Apple getting in the autonomous vehicle race. Nobody drives an Apple car now, right?" Evanina said. "I asked Cook, 'Hey, could you tell me what the net dollar value loss is for you, losing this autonomous vehicle from ideation to manufacturing?'"

"Bill," Cook said, "you're missing the whole point here. The actual substantial threat isn't that we're out of this business. It's the fact that, (A), yes, we're out of this business. But (B), the ten factories I was going to build in the US and the hundred thousand employees working there are now gone—that's the long-term threat here."

The Cao case at Tesla shared many of the hallmarks of the Zhang case at Apple. Despite the obvious similarities in tactics, it quickly became evident that the FBI thought there was no clear route to prosecuting Cao like they had Zhang, the former Tesla staffer said. Musk's unofficial *anti*-handbook attitude made that virtually impossible from a legal point of view.

For all the hype about Autopilot, the software hadn't been adequately secured and protected as a trade secret.

The Tesla source familiar with security standards was unsurprised that the DOJ passed on targeting Cao, despite the new China Initiative started under the Trump DOJ. To prosecute cases in court, companies need to mark and designate all sensitive documents as confidential and sufficiently demonstrate they have robust security protocols in place to protect assets. Plus, "economic espionage is an almost ridiculously high barrier to prove," the former staffer noted. "Not only do you have to prove the theft, but you've got to prove the transfer to a foreign government along with evidence of the compensation in return." Catching or stopping industrial theft can sometimes prove relatively simple; prosecuting it in the court of law is another ball game entirely.

Frustrated by the high legal bar to prosecuting Cao on criminal grounds, Tesla's legal team wound up launching a civil suit against Cao in March 2019, alleging misappropriation of trade secrets, breach of contract, and breach of employee's duty of loyalty. The case was eventually settled, with Cao later admitting he had copied and retained Autopilot source code. He apologized to Tesla while also paying an undisclosed fine.[4]

While Cao confessed to uploading Autopilot code, he denied transferring the technology to his new employer in China. A later investigation was not able to surface such evidence that XMotor had indeed ever received the code—a determination, however, that can ultimately neither be proved nor disproved given the inherently opaque barriers to outside scrutiny and transparency constructed by the CCP to protect Chinese firms. If the code was smuggled into the Chinese ecosystem, it seems unfathomable, at least to any reasonable outside observer familiar with CCP tactics and other historical cases, that it was not repurposed and used for illicit purposes.

In the wake of the breach, and as the opening of its flagship Chinese factory in Shanghai approached, Tesla set about tightening its security protocols, according to insiders. Or at least, it tried to. Between balancing the material risks and financial promises of the vast Chinese market, the company continued to learn the hard way. A third-party AI-powered security program identified several Tesla employees who had ties to China's Thousand Talents Program, its global recruitment campaign to bring the world's best and brightest back to China. One such employee was found with files about thermal management control—a vital and highly sensitive technical capability for battery-powered cars that allows them to extend their charge length—on his laptop, which had accompanied the employee on annual trips to China and a visit to Vienna, Austria—an infamous hot spot for Cold War document drops.

When the employee was flagged as a potential security concern by the company's in-house security team, the Tesla legal department asked what specific policy violation had occurred. The answer, according to the former staffer, was none. At the time, Tesla still hadn't required applicants and employees to disclose their outside work with other organizations, codified the parameters around the use of personal and private equipment, or required the disclosure of travel plans.[5] "It's much better now," said the source. That being the case, much of the damage was already done.

While these internal security gaps were later identified and patched, Tesla's Gigafactory Shanghai manufacturing hub, dedicated to the mass production of EV batteries, was completed in a record 357 days.[6] Its first Model 3 rolled off the assembly line on December 30, 2019. Despite a three-week shutdown in Shanghai during covid, business hummed. Tesla even paid off its huge loan from China's generous state-owned banks. Yet instead of the American company's continuing to dominate sales, the global EV market would be turned upside down. Even the great business oracle Elon Musk wouldn't see that coming. Nor would many others.

Assaults and Batteries

One segment of the EV technology market rivals—and arguably surpasses—self-driving operating systems in importance: EV battery production. Without a power source to propel an engine—and activate self-driving software—electric vehicles go nowhere. Given that sophisticated, powerful, lighter-weight batteries that hold their charge are critical to their success, battery manufacture is essential to every EV manufacturer's future. If the cars do not have sufficient range, comparable at least to that of automobiles with combustion engines, potential markets will undoubtedly dry up.

To help propel its battery technology forward, in 2019, Tesla purchased Hibar Systems,[7] a leader in automated precision dispensing pumps and battery assembly lines based in Canada.

Within the next year, two Hibar employees, a Canadian named Klaus Pflugbeil and Yilong Shao, a Chinese national, left the company to set up their own firm, Ningbo Psycho Machine Company, in Ningbo, China.[8] Like their former employer, the duo sold technology for the manufacture of batteries, including batteries used in EVs.

While Pflugbeil and Shao confidently expanded their start-up to operations within China, as well as in Canada, Germany, and Brazil, their actions also raised red flags to American counterintelligence officials in the process.

In September 2023, US undercover agents met Shao at a Las Vegas trade show. Using a business cover, the agents expressed an interest in purchasing a battery assembly line to manufacture batteries at a Long Island, New York, facility. On November 17, 2023, Pflugbeil emailed his interested "customers" a sixty-six-page technical documentation proposal that contained several schematics, including trade secrets of Tesla's battery assembly processes and techniques. Soon after, Pflugbeil was busted on Long Island on a charge of conspiring to send trade secrets belonging to Tesla.[9] He pled guilty in June 2024, while his coconspirator Shao evidently remains untried back in China. Prior to his sentencing, Pflugbeil had yet to remove a particularly telling quote on his personal LinkedIn profile by the nineteenth-century University of Oxford classicist Benjamin Jowett:

"The way to get things done is not to mind who gets the credit for doing them." Pflugbeil apparently had no moral qualms about taking credit for the years of Telsa research and investment.

Compared to its global rivals, the extent and scale of China's commitment to EV development has been unparalleled. A study by the Center for Strategic and International Studies (CSIS) determined that the Chinese government provided $230.9 billion in EV industry subsidies from 2009 to 2023, with annual support tripling from 2018 onward. The Washington think tank also reported EV R&D spending alone has averaged nearly $4 billion in recent years.[10]

While the extent and scale of such state subsidies has assuredly helped propel China's EV industry, the high-profile corporate espionage cases related to companies like Apple and Tesla undoubtedly also played a key role. American firms weren't the only targets in China's relentless campaign to achieve the aspirations of Made in China 2025. In January 2024, Svolt Energy Technology Korea, a subsidiary of the fourth largest player in the Chinese EV battery market, faced allegations that it had stolen battery technologies from two Korean firms, Samsung SDI and SK On. According to initial reports, five former and current employees of the two Korean battery makers were referred to prosecutors for allegedly having provided designs of the Korean companies' proprietary battery cells to the Chinese subsidiary.[11]

Svolt, owned by China's SUV powerhouse Great Wall Motor, and which denied all such allegations, was said to have targeted Korean workers by offering above-market salaries and big bonuses. It raised alarms when, after relocating to Seoul in 2021, it subsequently produced a cobalt-free battery within months—a truly shocking speed and one that would only presumably be possible with a collapsed R&D timeline.

Clone Cars

The theft of trade secrets within the automotive industry has a long and rather illustrious history in China. Long before the red-hot EV and battery markets erupted, and even before Beijing joined the World Trade Organization in 2001, piracy was rife within the

Chinese car industry. The first documented IP theft involved the earliest US-China automobile joint venture. In 1985, American Motors Corporation (AMC) and Beijing Automotive Industry Corporation (BAIC) celebrated their collaboration, producing the Jeep Cherokee XJ and the BJ212L, an updated version of the Chinese armed forces' similarly named jeep, which was manufactured by Beijing Auto Works.

As the Dutch automotive expert Tycho de Feijter has reported, when Cherokee XJ sales surged in the mid-1990s—by which time Chrysler had acquired AMC—"A dozen or so smaller Chinese outfits created their own Cherokee clones." Those gray market automakers improvised extensively, even developing entirely new Cherokee-inspired variants such as four-door pickups and wagon-like vans. While the Cherokee knockoffs dominated China's burgeoning clone market, de Feijter noted the country's roads were also crowded with other unauthorized adaptations, including imitations of the Nissan Patrol and the Toyota Land Cruiser.[12]

By 2004, car cloning had become a major issue for American firms setting up shop in China that could no longer be ignored. General Motors was the first to take legal action. In 2002, the American behemoth had acquired a Korean subsidiary, Daewoo Motors, and the plans for its minicar, the Matiz, which in America was called the Spark. When China's state-owned Chery Automobile unveiled its QQ in 2003, it was immediately reported to be the Spark/Matiz's identical twin. "A Matiz door can fit on a QQ and a QQ bonnet fits on the Matiz," asserted a GM spokesman.[13] The company filed suit in a Chinese court charging that Chery Automobile had stolen the designs of the Matiz. The suit against a government-owned firm, heard in a government-run court in China, predictably went nowhere.

In September 2005, the China National Intellectual Property Administration held that the Spark design had never been patented in China and therefore had no legal protection in that country. Two months later, the companies reportedly reached a settlement, without a public admission of wrongdoing, revealing only that no more further legal action would be taken by either party. "All parties highly appreciate the efforts that have been made by relevant governmental authorities for the purpose of further clarifying the intellectual property rights issue and relevant legal frameworks," GM said.[14] Decoding that kowtowing statement in hindsight, it's clear that GM knew it had lost the battle and was likely afraid of losing future access to one of the world's largest car markets. It seemed as though the automaker was clinging to the hope—as many American companies before it had done—of achieving future wins in China.

Despite the lucrative nature of such prospects, revenue was continuing to evaporate from other sectors of the American automotive industry in China as domestic competitors ate away at its market share. Its global market share also suffered as a result of broadscale piracy. In 2006, Michigan Senator Carl Levin reported annual losses of $12 billion in the US auto parts industry to counterfeiting. According to Levin, an estimated 75 percent of those fake auto parts—$9 billion worth—were made in China.[15] As distressing as the losses were, the idea that untested and unregulated products such as brake pads, hydraulic hoses, engine and chassis parts, suspension and steering components, and airbags were making their way into the American market created significant safety concerns. Still, the vast cheap labor pool and the lure of market access continued to attract more investment from foreign and American firms in China largely unabated.

Electric Dreams and Interferences

Like many other Western business executives who displayed a degree of hubris toward their Chinese rivals, Elon Musk discounted the threat posed by Beijing's plans to corner the EV market. His rationale for ignoring China's technology theft—"By the time they get caught up, we will be ten steps ahead"—appears to have gone unchallenged within the company. Musk has a remarkable record of building out his dreams, disrupting markets, and crushing historical monopolies. But his visions of leaving the competition behind, at least in the Chinese EV market, would not go all according to plan.

While he is now the face of Tesla, Musk did not in fact start the company. He joined Tesla Motors in 2004, after it was founded in 2003. One year earlier, on the other side of the world, BYD, a leading

Chinese rechargeable battery company, bought Xi'an Tsinchuan Auto Company, a small state-owned automaker. In 2008, both companies launched their first vehicles. The Tesla Roadster, modeled in part on the luxury Lotus sports car, outfitted with revolutionary lithium-ion battery cells, was the first EV to achieve a range greater than two hundred miles per charge.[16] In parallel, BYD's debut effort, the F3DM, was the world's first mass-produced plug-in hybrid compact sedan. It didn't need a dedicated charging station; owners could simply charge the "dual mode" car by plugging it into a wall outlet. Like Tesla's Roadster, the F3DM used a lithium-ion battery, but it was far less powerful. A single charge powered a car for a paltry sixty miles. BYD was significantly behind its American rival.

Despite being founded in a "Communist" country, BYD's F3DM debut was soon boosted by a major injection of Western capital. Warren Buffett, the "Oracle of Omaha," and his right-hand man at Berkshire Hathaway, Charlie Munger, plunked down $230 million to buy a 10 percent stake in the Chinese company. Buffett and his team were doing what they'd always done: placing bets on the future to grow Berkshire Hathaway's coffers.[17] The cold hard interests of shareholders, not geopolitical considerations or patriotic sentiments, were at the forefront of their investment calculus and decision making.

In purely financial terms, it's clear now that Berkshire made a savvy investment. "I have never helped do anything at Berkshire that was as good as BYD," said Munger fifteen years after the initial investment.[18] In 2011, though, Musk was not, naturally, as pleased. That year, Bloomberg TV anchor Betty Liu mentioned BYD during an interview with Musk. His response was to laugh long and hard derisively. "Have you seen their car?" he scoffed.

"You don't see them at all as a competitor?" Liu asked after a second round of laughs.

"I don't think they have a great product," he said, adding that its car wasn't "particularly attractive" and that he thought that BYD might not even survive China's own cutthroat auto market.[19]

While the ensuing decade brought existential challenges for both companies, from battery and charging infrastructure challenges to scaling up production to meet customer demand to shaping consumer preferences, none of them would prove financially fatal to either company. Tesla assumed the mantle of global market leader of luxury EVs first, establishing a network of charging stations in the United States. Its valuation climbed to staggering heights—a credit to both the product and the CEO's business acumen. In the United States the Model Y and Model 3 dominated sales by a wide margin, even as other American competitors began making market inroads with models such as the Chevrolet EV Bolt and Ford Mustang Mach-E.

Meanwhile, in China, BYD grew with a variety of low-cost, efficient "new-energy vehicles," including the e6, an all-electric compact crossover SUV with a range of around 186 miles, and other hybrid sedans, compacts, and buses. Additional Chinese firms, such as NIO, XPeng, and DiDi, entered the market with their own electric vehicles. Fast-forward twelve years from Musk's laughing dismissal of BYD during his Bloomberg TV interview, and the picture for Tesla quickly turned not so rosy.

In the fourth quarter of 2023, BYD's lower-priced EVs outsold Tesla globally for the first time, marking a key turning point in the global EV wars. In a January 2024 earnings call, Musk confronted some hard competitive truths, noting, "Frankly, I think if there are not trade barriers established, they will pretty much demolish most other car companies in the world."[20] By April 2024, Tesla's China sales plummeted by 18 percent from the previous year.[21] In response, the company issued a limited-time offer of 0% interest rate loans to attract new buyers.[22]

Musk's confidence in the ability of Tesla to out-innovate its rivals in China proved to be overstated. In China, by 2025, a new car model is released on average every two days, including ever-increasing breakthroughs in cutting-edge technologies. Perhaps most notably, since 2020, Tesla has launched a total of only four new models or refreshes in China. In contrast, BYD has released 129 such updates in the same time frame, according to Automobility, a Shanghai consultancy.[23]

Despite those setbacks, Telsa remained one of the most highly valued companies in the world in 2024. (In the wake of Donald Trump's reelection, it would end the year with a market cap around $1.4 trillion). With capital to spare, Musk pivoted in several new and unexpected directions. Less than two weeks after President Joe Biden announced that the tariff rate on EVs from China would increase from 25% to 100%,[24] Musk backtracked from his previous comment that trade barriers would be necessary to protect non-Chinese car companies. "Neither Tesla nor I asked for these tariffs, in fact, I was surprised when they were announced," he said, criticizing Biden's move at a Paris tech conference. "Things that inhibit freedom of exchange or distort the market are not good."[25]

Anyone who is curious about why Musk had such a dramatic change in perspective on trade protections might wonder about a "surprise" visit to China that he had made a month before making that comment. Flying in on his private jet, Musk met with Chinese Premier Li Qiang. He was on a mission, seeking Beijing's permission to deploy full self-driving (FSD) software on its vehicles in China and to transfer the data the cars collected overseas.[26] On the day of his meeting with Li, the China Association of Automobile Manufacturers (CAAM) released a statement that Tesla's Model 3 and Y vehicles had passed China's data security requirements for FSD.[27] The timing of the announcement seems unlikely to have been a coincidence.

A few weeks earlier, *The New York Times* hypothesized about a potential CCP long-game strategy toward Musk. "Musk's reliance on the Shanghai factory may give Beijing leverage over him," the paper noted amid Tesla's struggling sales. "That's a concern because a second company of Mr. Musk's, SpaceX, has sensitive Pentagon contracts and controls much of the world's satellite internet through its Starlink network."[28]

In addition to Tesla, three other Musk companies are undoubtedly of interest to the CCP: Neuralink, SpaceX, and X, the company formerly known as Twitter. These assets make Elon Musk "a nation-state to himself," according to the former Tesla senior staff member quoted earlier, and one that China naturally has an interest in remaining close to.

While ranked among the top three wealthiest men in the world, Musk's status with the CCP is likely less rooted in his lobbying power than in the titanic value of the companies he runs. SpaceX is the world's dominant satellite company. Neuralink develops revolutionary chips to implant in brains and connect the human body to computers, a technology with an understandable appeal to a totalitarian government that believes in thought control and denies freedom of expression for its citizens. X is among the loudest, most influential social networks in the Western world, with the power to shape and amplify worldviews.

Perhaps Musk's meeting with Li was just Musk being Musk: trying out new ideas, failing, launching new products, tackling new markets, forging new alliances, adjusting old ones. But the former Tesla staff member pointed out a possibly fatal flaw of his old boss: "Elon's public persona is very much 'We're going to iterate faster than anybody who's going to try to copy our products.' That may be true. But if it costs you a billion dollars to make your first pill and the next guy spends five cents to make the next pill because he stole the formula—at a certain point that doesn't scale." Such sentiments echo Bill Evanina's "eighty-five times thirty" theory described earlier: Stealing technology formulas drastically reduces the cost of product launches, cutting R&D costs and allowing thieves to undercut the competition.

That strategy eventually took down Jeep's joint venture in China, whose chain of ownership eventually landed with Stellantis. Jeep's China play would come to an unglamorous end in 2022, when Stellantis CEO Carlos Tavares ended the company's agreement with the Chinese state-owned Guangzhou Automobile Group (GAG), citing losses and "broken trust" with GAG as well as frustration with CCP policies that provide unfair advantages to domestic automakers— perhaps an ominous foreshadowing of Tesla's possible future fate.[29] Even for an automotive titan like Jeep, or Telsa, Beijing's ruthless pursuit of China First in its economic policies can prove nearly impossible to compete with.

Stalling

With his very public stature and larger-than-life persona, Musk is the ultimate example of the many American and Western CEOs who have sought to justify their commitment to large-scale investments in China. In exchange for access to the country's vast cheap labor pool and a vast consumer market, they must also agree to forced technology transfers that may ultimately, and perhaps even unintentionally, put the future of their companies at risk.

In March 2025, there was no major stock in the world as volatile as Tesla's. Shortly before Musk joined the Trump administration in January 2025, Tesla's stock price soared for three months, peaking at $479.86 in December 2024 before losing around 50 percent by the middle of the month.[30] But all that activity occurred *after* it became apparent that critical aspects of its IP had been exposed to competitors. In its rush to expand into the world's biggest auto market, it appears Tesla has now in effect hand-delivered its factory plans to CCP government agencies twice—once for the Gigafactory Shanghai and once to manufacture energy storage batteries called Megapacks, also in Shanghai.

More disturbing are the implications of Musk's meeting with Premier Li and the security of Autopilot, the FSD data-generating software used in Teslas. As noted earlier, after Musk's meeting with Li, the China Association of Automobile Manufacturers (CAAM), in effect the industry's regulator in the country, announced that Tesla had met its data security requirements. The company's EVs' operating systems must anonymize data collected from outside the vehicle. That includes blurring facial images, having a default setting that prevents the collection of cockpit data, in-vehicle processing of certain data, and a prominent notice regarding how personal information is handled. In the case of Tesla's self-driving vehicles, the operating system that needed to be assessed by Chinese regulators was its proprietary Autopilot technology.[31] "Absolutely. No doubt," said national transportation news correspondent Mike Caudill when asked if he thought the AACM must have examined Autopilot to make such a determination.[32] Such an examination surely also included an under-the-hood look at how it worked—a peek that no doubt shed valuable insights on how it was made to help dissect how it could be replicated.

Indeed, the auto industry expert is convinced that there are no real EV secrets in China. "Tesla was the number one vehicle sold in China," Caudill continued. "They've [the Chinese] got those cars broken down every which way to Sunday. They know every nook, cranny, bolt. The way BYD has built its business—if you go and look at some of their models, they're very Tesla-esque. Some of their original models are very reminiscent of models 3, X and Y. So I can make the argument 'Yeah, there's a facility there, and yes, they're going to have easy access to proprietary information.' But the truth is, they already have it." Making the strategic decision to manufacture in China came with great financial upsides to Tesla; it also came with great costs.

A month after its regulatory approval for Tesla's self-driving technology, the Shanghai state government issued a list of data types that can be transferred overseas without having to undergo security assessments. They included sales, used-car sales, parts and procurement, and auto design research. There was no mention of performance data, safety data, sensor data, or anything related to the actual self-driving operations.

Outside observers are rightfully not reassured by the steps taken by the Shanghai government. As noted earlier, under Chinese cyberlaws, Beijing claims ownership of *all* data created, used, or contained within its borders. To service its vehicles, Tesla has a data collection center in China to monitor its vehicles sold and operating there. And presumably, CCP agencies know all about that center since Tesla had to provide the plans before building its factory. There is also nothing stopping CCP agencies from demanding access to Autopilot from Tesla—the brain that processes the data—given its use within China and legal frameworks like the 2017 National Intelligence Law. What CCP apparatchiks did with such data can only reasonably be presumed.

Not surprisingly, in February 2025 BYD released a free advanced self-driving system dubbed "God's Eye," which was also the same technology that underpinned its newfound entrance into other product lines, such as using drones for logistical work in the so-called low-altitude economy. BYD made the decision to roll out twenty-one new models of EVs with the God's Eye self-driving system without charging fees to purchasers of the vehicle. As a result, the move raised serious questions about the viability of Tesla's hope of unlocking future revenue streams by selling expensive subscription services for its own advanced driving system, Autopilot.[33] BYD had achieved the same type of self-driving source code that took Tesla years to develop and test with an exponentially quicker R&D timeline, directly under-cutting the ability of Tesla to one day reclaim its primacy in the EV market.

It remains to be seen if Musk has the power and clout to influ-ence or shape CCP business rules to address issues such as piracy for forced data and IP transfers—something not even Alibaba CEO Jack Ma, once Asia's richest man, could do. But for now, as far as Beijing is concerned, Tesla does not own the data that its much-vaunted ve-hicular operating system collects and analyzes in order for its cars to function in the country. In this case, China didn't even need to smug-gle out a thumb drive in order to acquire it. Lawfare was the much easier and more efficient avenue in this instance.

Tesla's apparent quagmire in China is not just an important busi-ness lesson—it's the perfect parable of the Great Heist, boiled down to a single, searing anecdote. A brilliant American company, forged in the furnace of Silicon Valley innovation, armed with cutting-edge technology and a fearless founder, entered the world's largest car mar-ket hoping to maximize shareholder value. In return, China sought to spur greater consumer demand for EVs domestically. But behind the red carpet and factory photo ops, Beijing was already executing the second phase of its plan: to steal the technology underpinning the for-eign vehicles for its own development.

A 2023 article in the *MIT Technology Review* entitled "How Did China Come to Dominate the World of Electric Cars?" tries to explain how Chinese firms like BYD were able to so remarkably capture such market domination in the EV industry. It focuses on China's state subsidies and technological advancement. Completely absent from its explanations is China's modus operandi for the Great Heist. From the moment Tesla set foot in Shanghai, the Chinese state mobilized every lever in its playbook, a truly whole-of-society approach: regu-latory pressure, forced tech transfer, and well-placed insiders whose stolen trade secrets no doubt ultimately made their way to Party-aligned firms. It was industrial warfare waged behind the curtain of open trade. And it worked. Just like with EVs, the public discourse in articles like that from the *MIT Technology Review* around China's "economic miracle" needs to be revisited.

Electric vehicles were a highlight of Xi Jinping's Made in China 2025 strategy, not just as a green energy solution, but as a springboard to leapfrog the West in a critical next-generation industry crucial as a backbone to any modern economy. The strategy established the goal, and PRC collectors, in all their forms, filled the gaps. Back in 2015, the idea of a developing nation dominating the global EV market seemed laughable. But by the end of 2023, the joke was on Detroit—and Palo Alto. China had won. It now commands the heights of the EV battlefield, with sales projected to surge another 20 percent in 2025, topping 12.5 million units. Europe is terrified its own industry will be swamped by cheap EVs from abroad—not from America but China.

It's the same story from the outset of China's entrance in the WTO. American companies—ambitious, aggressive, desperate for scale— saw the Chinese market as the ultimate prize. They knew the risks. But they couldn't resist. And the final twist? The crown jewel of China's EV surge, BYD, was fueled by capital from none other than Warren Buffett—America's oracle of capitalism, financing the very juggernaut now eating its American competitors' lunch.

It's hard to imagine any other scenario than Tesla looking back at its experience in China as nothing other than a failure. While Elon Musk chased headlines, Beijing chased market domination. This wasn't theft in the dead of night. It was daylight plunder, methodical, state-backed, and brutally effective.

The end result?

Another industry in the global economy turned upside down against America's favor.

Others would follow suit.

CHAPTER 7

Chip Spy Wars

IN THE late summer of 2018, Chongji Huang landed a position at one of the most innovative tech start-ups in America. The company, Femtometrix, a California-based firm with a name that sounded equal parts obscure and futuristic, was small but working on big things. For Huang, a young optical engineer who had arrived from the PRC five years earlier and had recently earned both his BS and MS in electrical and electronic engineering from the University of Nebraska–Lincoln, the job was a breakthrough. His résumé boasted some solid experience, including on a project with Boeing, but he was still on the outside looking in. His Femtometrix role, even as a work-for-hire contract, was a promising potential foothold in the industry. He'd be in California, and ideally, his contract gig would turn into a future full-time position with a cutting-edge tech company.

That would be a major achievement for the ambitious engineer—but life wouldn't go all according to plan.

Despite Femtometrix's low profile, the company had millions of dollars in backing from South Korea's two biggest chip manufacturers, Samsung and SK hynix. And with good reason: Femtometrix was building a sophisticated high-tech quality control device designed to save and make huge amounts of money for microchip manufacturers and the vast array of companies that rely on chips—the so-called oil of the twenty-first century—to make their products work.

Huang's new boss was Alon Raphael, who had shepherded Femto-metrix since its gestation in a University of California, Santa Barbara, dorm room. Unlike so many other tech enterprise visionaries, Raphael wasn't a coder or an engineer; he had grown up in Los Angeles, raised by parents who had real estate and design businesses and ran two beloved LA eateries. But Raphael, a philosophy major when he started at college, was an extremely driven, tech-adjacent creative type. In high school, he landed a job at DreamWorks Interactive and cofounded his first start-up, Elumium Network Technologies, which accelerated dial-up speeds. Later he cofounded Tamarisc Diagnostics, a nanobiotechnology-based medical diagnostic company. Those companies helped solidify his skill at taking complex technical concepts, developing their viability and profitability, and bringing them to market.

In 2011, Raphael returned to UC Santa Barbara and fell in with some engineers. His interactions led to a vision: a dynamic tool that would use laser technology to ensure that every new microchip that came out of a foundry would be worthy of its intended job, with no internal or external blemishes. Femtometrix—the first part of the name comes from "femtosecond," one millionth of one billionth of a second—would use femtosecond pulsing lasers to scan sheets of microchips, or wafers, as they came off the fabs and perform surface and subsurface analysis to identify any tears, blemishes, or structural defects of chips that were only a few nanometers thick, thinner than a strand of hair, since a nanometer is one billionth of a meter.[1]

Quality control is essential in the high-stakes race to manufacture the thinnest, smallest, and most complex computer chips. The technical challenges of making ever smaller, ever thinner chips with dense circuitry are daunting. Only a few foundries are capable of continually shrinking the chips while increasing their computing power and capacity. Since nothing is more essential to the global supply chain of technological goods and consumer electronics than microchips, time is of the essence. The longer it takes for malfunctioning chips to be identified, the greater the delays and costs to everyone involved: the company ordering the chips, the foundries making the chips, the shipping companies waiting to deliver the goods, and even the end users, consumers, who ultimately pay for everything—chips, delays, labor, transport.

In the hyperspecialized world of chip manufacturing, the Femtometrix digital quality control system was poised to be a true boon, with applications for every silicon chip everywhere. It could verify the quality of microprocessors at foundries before they were sliced and diced. Such technology could help solidify America's position in the current global war for chip supremacy, as told in Chris Miller's book *Chip War.*

Raphael didn't need a PhD in microengineering to know that the vision seemed ingenious and desirable. But he needed plenty of qualified engineers and optical experts to build out the machines he envisioned. People such as Huang.

The new employee was enthusiastic and focused. He worked closely with Puxi Zhou, another fresh-faced recent graduate with advanced degrees in electrical and electronics engineering, to join the Femtometrix team. Zhou, who had Python programming skills, signed on as a consultant, too. A year later, both men were on staff, with Huang promoted to vice president of system and field and Zhou named senior R&D engineer. They weren't just Raphael's colleagues; he considered them friends. Raphael had even invited Huang to his parents' house for dinner.

Huang also added a second title to his resume. He became a part owner in Femtometrix, investing $100,000 in the company. "He had money from elsewhere, we assume his family," said Alon's sister Shoshana Raphael, who doubles as his lawyer. On his first day of work, she says, Huang showed up in a flashy top-of-the-line Mercedes.[2] Instead of raising internal security and insider threat flags at Femtometrix, Huang's investment did the opposite: it gave him access to company financial data not available to the public. He could see information about other investors, financial statements, P&L reports, and budgets in the company's data ecosystem. According to court papers, he also insisted on seeing secret in-process IP that was in the company pipeline. Despite gaining such access, he was theoretically barred from using any of it. He had signed an "At-Will Employment, Confidential Information, Invention Assignment, and Arbitration Agreement" that contained non-disclosure clauses, according to court documents. Evidently, Raphael and his team believed that the agreement would sufficiently guarantee that Femtometrix trade secrets would remain secrets—or at least offer a measure of protection if, somehow, the company's technology was stolen.[3]

While still employees at Femtometrix, Huang, Zhou, and a third PRC-born engineer, Weiwei Zhao, decided to replicate the company in China. Initially adopting the name Chip Metrology and Detection Cooperation [*sic*], the trio allegedly took Femtometrix's investor pitch deck, substituted their new moniker, and presented it to investors. Eventually they changed the company name—and the name on the pitch deck—to Weichong Semiconductor. According to court papers, the deck was full of proprietary information: graphics, photographs, trade secret product information, and industry reports. It also contained images of Femtometrix's Harmonic F1x product, including telling details that clearly identified the true origin of the source material via the Femtometrix logo and unit name.

Huang quit the company in September 2020, citing issues with his wife's visa as their impetus to move back to China. Shortly after, Huang's colleague Weiwei Zhao also left the company, followed by Puxi Zhou, who now lives in Beijing.

Some months later, Femtometrix investors began contacting Alon Raphael with disturbing news. His former employee Huang, still technically an investor in and co-owner of Femtometrix, had started a rival company in Shanghai and was illegally cloning the California innovator's technology. Not only that, but he had approached Femtometrix backers to ask if they wanted to invest in his rival start-up. *Impossible*, thought CEO Raphael. *This can't be happening.* "I had heard these kinds of stories," he said, "but I said to myself, *No, not that guy, he's my friend.*"[4]

Femtometrix initiated a forensic examination of the company's computer network. Court papers allege multiple violations of the former employees' contracts, including that "Zhou copied the entirety of his work files containing 10 Gigabytes of data from his work computer onto his personal external drive and took the personal external drive with him to Weichong Semiconductor." Even worse, they pointed to the wholesale theft of nine years' worth of Femtometrix work spent developing and building its industry-leading intellectual property. Lawyers sent Huang a cease-and-desist letter on April 14, 2022, and received a classic "deny, deny, deny" response back. It insisted that "All Weichong's design, code, selection, theory, data, etc. are original."[5]

Femtometrix, like Tesla and many other tech firms before them, was learning the hard way about China's unrelenting thirst to acquire technology. They were also learning the frustrating reality that the quest for justice in America took time and there was no guarantee the DOJ could come to the company's aid.

For a small tech start-up in a highly competitive industry, moving with a sense of urgency was an existential necessity. In August 2022, the company filed a civil suit against the three former employees and Weichong Semiconductor, which now operates under the umbrella name Aspiring, a company that claims to offer "nonlinear optical wafer inspection systems."[6]

Raphael estimated that it can cost $20 million to $100 million and eight to ten years to develop and sell what he termed "a novel in-line process control technology" such as the Harmonic F2x that was stolen. In May 2023, he testified before a House of Representatives subcommittee, noting that Weichong had retained a top-shelf British law firm, Orrick, Herrington & Sutcliffe, and "explicitly indicated their intended strategy of waging a legal war of attrition," including multiple motions for dismissal to drive up Femtometrix's legal fees. "It is unclear how a new company like Weichong can afford one of the most expensive law firms in the world," he said, adding, "Small companies do not have the tools or capacity to fight a pattern of systemic theft by foreign entities. Litigation in American courts is inadequate to address incursion, and little support is available."[7]

Weichong's alleged use of the Femtometrix pitch deck seems to have paid instant dividends. Two Chinese venture capital firms, SummitView Capital and Yunqi Partners, invested in the new company. Weichong was also trying to sell its knock-off technology to the same Korean companies, according to Shoshana Raphael. "That was a huge threat," she recalled, noting that it had created a race to get the laser-driven machines into the Korean companies' fabrication centers as fast as possible. "Our machines refine their algorithms by working with chips coming out of the fabs. So getting the equipment into the fab is essential to demonstrate proof of concept."

Despite Weichong's aggressive legal tactics, Alon Raphael had no intention of giving up the fight, later telling members of Congress that he viewed his battle as essential to not just his company's interest but that of the nation. He was "defending what is right because the U.S. cannot afford to lose Femtometrix, as that would critically undermine U.S. semiconductor capabilities and leadership."

That posture and a nimble makeshift legal team led by his sister Shoshana, who specializes in real estate, not international trade violations, began to put pressure on Weichong. A source familiar with the case said that that continued litigation and investigations were pointing to a bigger player behind the Femtometrix ripoff: China's state-owned Semiconductor Manufacturing International Corporation (SMIC). "It just takes time and money. I believe, at the end of the day, the evidence will show that SMIC, at the highest level, was part of this plan to steal this IP."[8]

The damage to Femtometrix was crippling and part and parcel of China's illicit acquisition playbook. "The three guys wind up with an enormous amount of resources to hire lawyers that overwhelm Femtometrix," said the source familiar with the case. "Where did those resources come from? Femtometrix didn't know. Their lawyers didn't know how to figure it out. But you know dadgum well where it came from. So that's another tactic of the Communist Party: You overwhelm the legal defenses of the little guy." The CCP, as noted elsewhere in this book, is not averse to lawfare. In fact, it uses it as a critical and complementary tool to facilitate and enable its espionage activities.

At the end of 2024, Femtometrix reached a settlement with Weichong. The terms remain undisclosed, although a statement from Weichong contended it resolved the dispute "without any payment."[9] Weichong's attempts to cut deals with Femtometrix's partners failed, but the battle continues. Notably, the technology lifted by Weichong is being utilized at Yangtze Memory Technologies Corporation (YMTC) and ChangXin Memory Technologies (CXMT) and other Chinese fabs, yet another example of what appears to be stolen innovative American technology being used against its own critical interests. Microchip technology is one of the core industries targeted by Made in China 2025 in order to reduce China's dependence on foreign technology and bolster national security. In this case, Femtometrix's designs may be deployed in a way the company never dreamed of: as a weapon to defeat the United States in the race for the advanced microchip production. The stakes of this contest are not inconsequential. Microchips are the invisible engines of the modern world—powering everything from smartphones and satellites to fighter jets and financial systems. Whoever controls the design and production of advanced semiconductors holds the keys to economic dominance, technological innovation, and military superiority in the twenty-first century.

Wafer Warfare

If the playbook for obtaining Femtometrix technology sounds familiar, it should. A similar Chinese espionage operation targeting the world's number one supplier of sophisticated microchip design technology had already played out years earlier.

The victim that time was ASML, the Dutch company that dominates the global market in lithography machines, the technology that renders the tiny, intricate patterns of transistors that are printed onto the silicon wafers that are ultimately sliced and diced into chips. As for the perpetrator? ASML's lead attorney, Patrick Ryan, framed the motive for the stolen IP this way: "It's not an accident. It's not anything else . . . it is a plot to get technology for the Chinese government."[10] Once again, the threat would come from an insider working within the company, undoubtedly lured by the lucrative financial and other rewards dangled by the CCP through its myriads of collection organs, including talent recruitment programs and state assistance to domestic start-ups.

Zongchang Yu, an engineer working in ASML's Brion Technologies office in Santa Clara, California, spearheaded the apparent heist. He enlisted the support of several coworkers, including Senior Design Engineer Wanyu Li, who downloaded all 2 million lines of source code for ASML's optical proximity correction (OPC). The software ensures that the microscopic circuits are printed with precision.[11] Two years later, in 2014, the former ASML employee would launch Xtal in a San José office park. A month after that, he opened a second firm, Dongfang Jingyuan Electron, in a Beijing industrial enclave.

Yu was reportedly backed by Jingyuan Han, the chairman and chief executive officer of the steel-manufacturing giant China Oriental Group Company. The CEO is also a CCP party stalwart, with a biography proudly detailing his work serving as a Party representative and at various conferences.[12]

Records produced at a 2018 trial showed that China Oriental owned more than 50 percent of Dongfang, the start-up the former ASML employee founded back in China, often using subsidiaries to mask its investments. While Xtal sought and also received support from South Korean sources, it's worth highlighting that the timing of the company's launch aligned with a CCP strategic initiative rolled out at the very same time: a $35 billion National Semiconductor Fund.[13]

By the time California authorities moved to arrest Yu in May 2019, he had already fled the country. Two of his fellow ASML cronies, Song Lan, who'd become Xtal's vice president of engineering, and Wanyu Li, who was now Xtal's IT director, were also charged. Both men later copped pleas to having taken proprietary company data and received the judicial equivalent of slaps on the wrist: seven months of electronic monitoring for Li and ninety days of community service for Lan. A California court ruled that ASML should receive $845 million in compensation from Xtal. That payout, however, never happened, since XTAL filed for bankruptcy on December 17, 2018.

As for Yu, financial backer of the knock-off company, there have been no repercussions beyond an outstanding warrant for his arrest. In China, he has obtained the status of a hero, hobnobbing with politicians, attending high-profile military parades, and raising significant funds. In 2023, his own company was considering an IPO valued at around $1.2 billion.[14]

In a 2019 statement, ASML's CEO rejected the previous characterization of the events by the company's own lawyer, dismissing the idea that the theft was a PRC-led operation.

"The suggestion that we were somehow a victim of a national conspiracy is wrong," he said. "The facts of the matter are that we were robbed by a handful of our own employees based in Silicon Valley, who had broken the law to enrich themselves."[15]

Why the seemingly logic-defying reversal, which was also reiterated in a formal statement by the ASML board?[16] Business, fear, retribution, and public relations are the obvious suspects. ASML has clients in China that represent billions of dollars in future sales. That massive market share can be cut off at a moment's notice by the CCP in the form of retaliation. So ASML was very likely engaged in damage control. While no direct link may have been uncovered exposing Party directives to steal their technology, the trail from wealthy Party bigwig to stolen IP seems clear and aligns perfectly with the established modus operandi of the Great Heist.

China's relentless campaign of innovation by acquisition has reached a tipping point. The strategic importance of microchip technology has become a national security issue of vital importance for the United States. Microprocessors are omnipresent in the wired world—activating, measuring, and controlling the sensors that power our cars, our devices, and the most sophisticated and lethal military weapons. Much future weaponry will depend on command-and-control technology optimized by chips' ability to perform huge numbers of operations per second. Modern combat jets like the F-35 are flying supercomputers, with microchips critical to enabling everything on the aircraft, from radar systems and stealth capabilities to avionics and targeting. Even the pilot's $400,000 helmet—able to display critical flight data directly onto the visor in real time—is powered by advanced semiconductors that fuse battlefield awareness with machine precision.

Meanwhile, GPU chips, which meld high-speed microprocessors with massive amounts of memory on a silicon wafer the size of a Post-it note, have become the engines of the most sophisticated AI programs in the world, which will also feed into military and surveillance operations in myriad ways, including performing operational analysis to make real-time combat decisions. The fastest, most powerful chips will transmit and receive signals, adapting in midbattle, midflight, and even midbombing. Recognizing this strategic importance, both the Trump and Biden administrations, in a rare gesture of Washington bipartisanship, have placed export controls on such chips and the AI programming functionality to the PRC. The United States has tied these export restrictions to certain technologies and equipment sold by ASML and Nvidia, the global leader in GPU chips. These are welcome moves. But Beijing's interest in chips is not a new development. Decades earlier, the CCP had its eyes (and ears) on a similar US chip giant setting up shop within its borders.

Intel's Inadvertent Surrender

Matt Brazil, a former US Army linguist, spent four years as a commercial officer in the US Embassy in Beijing covering exports and compliance before starting a sixteen-year run at Intel in 1995. He arrived in China "during a period when Western companies, if they had a CCP Party Committee inside the company, it was kind of hush-hush. It wasn't as open as it was starting in the early 2000s." At one point, a senior figure in Intel's China office informed Brazil that two people from the company's CCP committee wanted to interview him. "I was told, 'Just tell them what they want to know,'" Brazil recalled, "'because they're the host country.'"

Brazil met with his two Chinese colleagues/inquisitors—a woman hired to run cyberdefense for Intel and a man in "government relations." Aware that the odd encounter was fraught with potential conflicts of interest, Brazil followed his boss's instructions. "They were particularly focused on TSCM work—technical surveillance countermeasures: finding bugs. At the time, we were about to import into China a set of equipment from the US. It included nonlinear junction detectors that you use to find semiconductors in the walls and telephone equipment that can be used to detect a listening device on the line. And a device that sweeps the radio spectrum, looking for wireless devices. So I gave them the lowdown on that."[17]

The question-and-answer session included an explanation that the new equipment went up to only 30 gigahertz. In other words, it was good for finding basic and low-level devices. But, as Brazil explained, it's not good for finding the kinds of devices above 30 gigahertz that are often used by state-sponsored entities. "So they wrote all that crap down," said Brazil. The CCP inquisitors' interest certainly didn't appear academic.

All these years later, Brazil, the cowriter of the authoritative *Chinese Communist Espionage: An Intelligence Primer*, marvels at the incongruity: The security expert had been instructed to basically tell two CCP members how to successfully bug Intel's office should they so choose.

A few years after delivering his point-by-point bugging tutorial, Brazil was asked to conduct an informal survey of what other foreign businesses were doing regarding TSCM. Only four security officers agreed to discuss company protocol. They were shocked at the idea of deploying bug detection tools, he recalled. "They said, 'If we have something to discuss that we don't want the Chinese side to know about, we just send our people out of the country and have the meeting there.'" The security officers for the foreign firms operating in China understood better than most (often including their own C-suites) the true scale and nature of the threat they were up against.

No doubt such advice seemed like a good idea at the time. But as the incidents at Femtometrix and ASML indicate, without robust, active insider threat protocols, even working outside China affords insufficient protection. As the MSS ruthlessly hunts for insiders by exploiting the borderless digital world, there are no companies impervious to its crosshairs.

Barely thirty years ago, Beijing's best electronics came from reverse engineering circuit boards. Now the same regime is lunging for the summit of the semiconductor mountain—backed by a whole-of-society approach that fuses a war chest measured in trillions of yuan and a playbook that blends subsidies, state decrees, lawfare, and good old-fashioned larceny. Companies such as Huawei and Semiconductor

Manufacturing International Corporation (SMIC), once dismissed as distant followers, are now mass-producing 7-nanometer chips, racing toward even more advanced 5-nanometer nodes despite aggressive US sanctions aimed at stalling their progress. This relentless drive reflects Xi Jinping's determination to end the Middle Kingdom's historical dependence on foreign technologies and claim leadership in the semiconductor sector, a key pillar of his Made in China 2025 manifesto, and an ambition as strategic and geopolitically charged as the nuclear arms races of the Cold War. The chip war's final score is still untallied even as the mega-sized design and supplier of GPUs and system-on-a-chip manufacturer Nvidia builds an R&D facility in Shanghai, but the spy war beneath it is not. Beijing's fusion of intelligence, finance, and manufacturing has already seized a head start, turning stolen schematics into sovereign power—one wafer at a time.

CHAPTER 8

Telecommunications

ONE CHILLY March night in Copenhagen, the glow of the harbor reflected on the glass facade of the Copper Tower, a sleek law office turned impromptu war room for Denmark's leading telecommunication firm. Inside, a crisis had been unfolding for weeks—spreadsheets pored over, devices swept for malware, suspicions and nerves mounting. The security team was on the hunt for a mole within the company who could end up costing millions of dollars in lost contracts to a competing firm. Then, just after 10:00 p.m., a security guard looked up and saw something hovering outside the fifteenth-floor window: a drone. Silent, steady, its lights blinking as it ominously shifted angles, the machine seemed less like a toy and more like an eye—a foreign emissary sent to peer inside. *What was it looking at?*

A whiteboard. On it were scribbled leads and names, as well as Post-it notes, that mapped a corporate case of epic betrayal unfolding in real time. At the center of the storm was Chinese telecom giant Huawei and a sleazy, no-holds-barred quest to win the contract to build Denmark's national 5G infrastructure. The drone's presence confirmed what the team inside had already suspected: They were being watched.

"Grow with Intelligence"—Huawei's Vision Statement

In the global race for technological dominance, 5G telecommunication infrastructure is every bit as contested and strategically significant as microchip supremacy. At stake is nothing less than the nervous system of the future digital economy, a patchwork of high-speed, low-latency networks essential not just for smartphones but for everything from autonomous vehicles to advanced manufacturing, smart cities, and military operations. China, through its flagship telecom giant Huawei, poured billions into rapidly expanding its footprint in this vital sector, aggressively undercutting its rivals to secure contracts across Europe, Africa, and Asia and igniting fears in Washington of unprecedented intelligence-gathering and sabotage capabilities that could follow suit as a result.

In response, the United States tapped into its full arsenal of tools to exert diplomatic and economic pressure, convincing allies to reject Huawei's offerings, and effectively weaponized economic sanctions designed to choke off Chinese access to vital semiconductors. It wasn't merely a competition over market share; it was a high-stakes geopolitical confrontation over the control of the digital highways that underpin twenty-first-century security, economic prosperity, and global influence.

Huawei is a company that turns up with alarming frequency in news reports about telecommunications, national security, and spying. Part of that frequency has to do with the fact that it is the world's largest manufacturer of telecommunication equipment.[1] But it's the company's business methods and reputation that often generate headlines. Founded in 1987 by Ren Zhengfei, a former PLA engineer who rose to deputy director, the company launched with $5,500 and a name—Huawei translates as "Chinese Achievement"—that implied nationalistic ambition from the very get-go.

Investing in telecom infrastructure and hiring seasoned former IBM employees, the company grew at an impressive rate. Beginning in 2000, it began overseas operations and, since then, it has been embroiled in a steady stream of alleged corporate espionage and IP scandals. In 2019, when the company unveiled a new slogan for its cloud business in Hong Kong and the Middle East—"Grow with Intelligence"—it was hard not to wonder if the campaign was more a taunting joke to the rest of the world than a branding play.[2] Huawei certainly would in fact grow with "intelligence."

Some months before the covid pandemic hit in 2020, the glamorous Kobbertårnet building, known as the Copper Tower, in Copenhagen became a focal point in the high-stakes world of winning the global 5G infrastructure battle between the West and China. Huawei naturally was at the center of it. In the spring of 2019, the corner office on the fifteenth floor of the Kobbertårnet, looming over the entrance to Copenhagen harbor and host to the Danish law firm Plesner, underwent an impromptu makeover.[3] The security team of TDC, Denmark's leading telecommunication company (formerly Tele Danmark Communications), had relocated from its offices in areas outside the city to the central office.[4] The team was escalating its security protocols—for good reason. Weeks earlier, TDC had launched a massive internal investigation. The target? A suspected Huawei mole inside the company.

In early March 2019, the company had received final bids from Huawei and the Swedish-owned Ericsson to build and operate Denmark's 5G telecommunication network. The secretive bidding process, however, had been upended when a representative from Huawei suddenly tried to amend the company's best and final offer.

It was a suspicious move. For one thing, Huawei's initial 5G bid had been considerably *higher* than Ericsson's. Now Yang "Jason" Lan, the Huawei account rep who had landed the previous 4G contract with TDC, submitted numbers that undercut Ericsson's by only a few thousand dollars.[5] Also suspicious, the desperate offer arrived more than a week *after* senior management had already tentatively decided to award the contract to the Swedish firm.

Only a handful of TDC executives knew the details of the confidential bids or that Ericsson had emerged as the favorite in the initial survey of TDC executives, according to a blockbuster Bloomberg report documenting the ordeal.[6] TDC's 5G committee was justifiably concerned by the timing and details of the second bid by the Chinese firm; it was impossible not to infer that Huawei had been tipped off and decided to underbid in order to win the contract. And that meant that somehow, TDC's tightly controlled bidding process had been breached.

The weekend after the suspicious bid, TDC's Torsten Juul-Jensen, a balding, bespectacled security specialist who focused on incident responses and forensic analysis, went in to work. A day earlier, his boss, security director Ray Stanton, had told him that there was a suspected leak within the company, possibly involving Huawei and the bid for the new 5G contract. While Juul-Jensen digested the information, Stanton seemed to almost take it in stride; he was scheduled to attend an upcoming security conference in Abu Dhabi and showed no inclination to change his plans in response to the serious allegations being made.

For Juul-Jensen, however, the security implications were frightening. He was not alone in sharing such sentiments. Sitting in the bunker-like office that served as TDC's security command center, he received a text from Jens Aaløse, the executive who had received Huawei's last-second altered bid and met with Jason Lan. Aaløse was in the office, too, and he asked Juul-Jenson to come upstairs. There, he told Juul-Jenson about the timeline of the bids and his suspicions about Huawei's representative, Lan, saying that he seemed inexplicably cocky and confident during a brief encounter with Aaløse after the new bid's submission.

In response, the executive described the events that were unfolding as "by far the most important in TDC's history ever" and told Juul-Jensen to "do what it takes" to find out how Huawei had gotten its insider information, as reported by Bloomberg.[7] Juul-Jenson got to work.

The next week, TDC's 5G team voted to accept Ericsson's offer. When Allison Kirkby, TDC's CEO, notified Lan of the decision, the Huawei representative didn't take it well, complaining that the decision would negatively affect him personally. Other Huawei managers at the meeting were less direct. Threats were made, insinuating that the decision would hurt other Danish companies doing business with China in the future. A retaliatory threat if not explicitly made, then at least implied.

TDC executives remained unmoved, and the security team supervised by Juul-Jensen collected every phone, computer, and tablet from senior management within the company to scan them for
malware. They turned up nothing—no viruses, no phishing emails,
no backdoor installations. Juul-Jensen reasoned that if the security
breach hadn't come from an outside cyber-intrusion, it had to have
originated from someone inside the company. He ordered his team
to sweep the network for any correspondence with Jason Lan, the
Huawei rep. A potential suspect emerged—a senior executive whose
calendar revealed that he had met repeatedly with Lan, including for
meals at the restaurant in Copenhagen's ultrapricey five-star Hotel
d'Angleterre. There was a slight problem, however, for Juul-Jensen:
The person of interest was none other than his boss, TDC security
director Ray Stanton.

Aaløse, apprised of the social engagements between his security director and Lan, arranged for a security team to join him at
the airport to confront Stanton on his return from the conference
he attended in Abu Dhabi. The welcome party escorted Stanton to a
private room at the airport, where he tried to explain that he and Lan
were merely friends, so much so that he had even once gifted him a
Garmin wristwatch.[8] Asked to turn over his computer and phone,
Stanton produced four separate phones, including a Huawei model.[9]
Although Stanton was later exonerated of any wrongdoing, he was,
according to the Danish podcast *Operation Pelligrino*, temporarily
suspended by TDC. In turn, Juul-Jensen was appointed to lead TDC's
Huawei investigation full-time.[10]

Examining Stanton's hardware—and that of everyone else in
the TDC universe—the security team worked to determine who
had accessed the document that contained the Ericsson bid or had
somehow been sent a copy of it. They examined the users who had
shared access or had been sent the file. A forensic examination determined that Stanton did not have access to the bid document until *after*
the leak, a sequence of events that exonerated him as the mole. But a
new suspect emerged. A sweep of phone records showed that Dov
Goldstein, TDC's head of special projects and cost optimization initiatives, who reported to CFO Stig Pastwa, *had* exchanged numerous

calls and texts with Lan. The duo had also met for dinners at Hotel d'Angleterre.

While the TDC security team investigated possible links between Goldstein and Lan, they began to wonder about the resilience of their security protocols. During a companywide electronics sweep, they discovered unfamiliar, powerful microphones clandestinely burrowed in the company boardroom. They had no idea how the recording devices made it there. Fearing that the division itself might be compromised, the security team relocated to a new site: the Copper Tower, the home of the company's law firm.

Taking refuge on the fifteenth floor of a well-secured building seemed like a prudent move—until the law firm's servers were hit with a denial-of-service attack, limiting the TDC team's access to its data, email, and web resources. From there, as Bloomberg reported, things got even more bizarre. Members of the TDC security team noticed that they were being photographed in public after leaving the office. Aaløse's summer home was also later burgled.

Things soon kicked into high gear. To elaborate on the length to which Huawei appears to have gone to obtain a competitive advantage, on March 20, 2019, a large drone was hovering close to the Copper Tower, shifting into different positions outside the fifteenth floor but always facing the window, with its probing light honed in on the building. After several long minutes, it flew away. A security guard on duty reported his close encounter, and the next morning, Juul-Jensen and the TDC security team got to work trying to figure out what exactly was being targeted by the suspicious craft. The group kept a long list of its leads on a large whiteboard that faced the office windows. It was dotted with Post-its bearing categories such as "suspects" and "leakage," along with corresponding details.[11] As it turned out, they had forgotten to pull the shades down.

Whatever intel the drone might have gleaned, it was unlikely to help the suspected TDC mole Goldstein. Investigators unearthed several connections between Goldstein and the Huawei representative Lan. The day after the 5G team had decided to accept Ericsson's bid, Goldstein had called the Huawei executive twice, according to call logs cited by Bloomberg, and via email arranged a meeting. Video footage captured Goldstein leaving around the time of the meetup with a laptop in tow. The TDC investigators concluded Goldstein had taken his work laptop and showed Lan the PowerPoint document with Ericsson's bid.[12]

The day after Goldstein and Lan met, the Huawei rep had submitted his company's new, lower offer. Huawei, China's telecommunications champion and the CCP's ticket to controlling the global highways of information, was intent on capturing another 5G market in Europe with no qualms about how such a feat was accomplished.

The preponderance of evidence indicating that Goldstein was the mole was compelling. But TDC ultimately didn't contact the police. Neither Lan nor Goldstein has ever been charged with a crime and all allegations against them remain unproven. Evidently, the company preferred to see the suspects go away quietly. Pastwa stepped down at the end of March. Goldstein followed about two months later, announcing on LinkedIn that he was "ready for new challenges." Given his reportedly caffeinated final meeting with Lan, the last sentence of his farewell announcement, cynics would be forgiven for reading as nothing less than a subtle taunt: "Feel free to reach out—I'm ready for a cup of coffee 👍"[13]

As for Stanton, the former security chief, he resigned, citing the company's change in direction.[14] Huawei also publicly insisted that it had done nothing wrong. It also reiterated its claims that the company is completely autonomous from the CCP. However, just a few months after losing the TDC contract, a news report surfaced of an alleged recording wherein the Chinese ambassador to Denmark allegedly made threats that a trade deal between China and the Farøe Islands, an independent territory that is part of the Kingdom of Denmark, would be dropped if Huawei was not able to secure contracts for the rollout of 5G on the island. A judge issued an injunction against publishing or broadcasting the recording.[15] Nonetheless its revelation further underscored just how aggressively, and to what extent, the Chinese were willing to go to in order to make sure its wiring controlled the world's communication and data flows.

Days later, the CEO of Huawei Denmark sent a personal letter to Danish Prime Minister Mette Frederiksen that downplayed the idea that the CCP might have helped Huawei: "Our relationship with the Chinese government is no different from normal business-government relations for private companies in other countries."[16] The Danes were not reassured. In 2021, the Farøe Islands awarded their business to Ericsson.[17] The CCP's recognition of just how important such telecommunications infrastructure could be had a long history behind it.

Weaponized Communication and Disconnection

In 1999, eight years before the release of the first iPhone, two PLA colonels published *Unrestricted Warfare: Two Air Force Senior Colonels on Scenarios for War and the Operational Art in an Era of Globalization.* The treatise on military strategy asserted that "modern information technology" is the "bonding agent" that will supplant military power as the ultimate weapon of control.

> We can say with certainty that this is the most important revolution in the history of technology. Its revolutionary significance is not merely in that it is a brand new technology itself, but more in that it is a kind of bonding agent which can lightly penetrate the layers of barriers between technologies and link various technologies which appear to be totally unrelated.[18]

Modern information technology—the internet, digital networks, cell phones—transmits the data that run the world. Telecommunication systems link those data, enabling the monitoring of what people (military leaders, CEOs, government officials, inventors, anyone) say, where they say it, and whom they say it to. This makes the telecommunication industry like no other sector in the global economy.

Sure, the players in this sector are concerned with market penetration, sales, and ultimately profits, just like those in any other traditional business industry. But from a geopolitical and military point of view, the inherent strategic significance of telecommunications stands out. Telecom networks and devices are essential to establishing espionage entry points, for instance, gaining access to all forms of data and conducting surveillance operations. In 1979, AT&T, the leading American telecom, launched a marketing campaign advising audiences to "Reach out and touch someone." Controlling a national network enables hostile actors to reach out and secretly track anyone—or steal their information.

The modern telecom infrastructure operates as the circulatory system, or information superhighway, of the twenty-first century. It ferries or links data from sender to recipient via copper wires, fiber-optic cables, radio waves, and satellite links. Phone calls are just a fraction of what telecom companies transmit and track. An individual's personal data—whom they call, what websites and apps they use, the emails and attachments they send—all travel through telecom networks. Valuable business or personal data or potentially damaging information can be accessed and weaponized. It is conceivable that embarrassing or compromising files could also be injected into accounts. Or that someone might send misinformation from a user account.

While the full extent of such surveillance implications are ominous, they're not even the biggest threat posed by telecom vulnerabilities. Telecoms, quite simply, allow society to function. Never mind the ability to watch Netflix or send emails; corporations rely on these networks to communicate, plan, trade, and conduct business transactions. So do our government and military. The most efficient way to defeat an army is to shut down its ability to communicate. Make even the most formidable foe blind and deaf on the battlefield and they can be defeated. As Sun Tzu wrote over 2,500 years ago, "The skillful leader subdues the enemy's troops without any fighting."[19]

While the internet is built on the principle of multiple pathways of connectivity, once inside a telecom network, hackers can wreak havoc in untold ways that interrupt or deny service. Code can be rewritten or inserted to interfere with transmissions. Viruses can be uploaded. Key nodes can be pinpointed for denial-of-service attacks. Switching stations, which distribute packets of data at lightning speed, can be shuttered. China's strategic focus on this sector as a priority target for intelligence for its vast whole-of-society collection apparatus is not an accident. In fact, unsurprisingly, it too was identified by

Made in China 2025 as one of its ten strategic sectors. Nothing less than positioning China as the world leader in digital infrastructure to maximize geopolitical influence was the goal. Naturally, promoting Huawei as a national champion to achieve these aims by helping them compete globally would also be necessary for Xi to achieve his grand vision.

Chinese Achievement

One person who clearly understands the importance of the telecommunications industry to national security is Huawei founder Ren Zhengfei. Ren applied to join the CCP early in his career and was initially rejected. His service, however, with the PLA engineers earned him endorsements from the PLA Party branch that eventually won him membership.[20] Huawei's global 5G market grab—with the goal of stringing its gear through one nation's telecom infrastructure after another—tracks perfectly with Beijing's playbook for SIGINT collection to enable the Ministry of State Security to widen its reach. While Huawei predictably denied any links to the alleged corporate telecom espionage in Copenhagen, it was hardly the first time charges of wrongdoing have surfaced against the company—or that it has vociferously denied them.

The history of Ren Zhengfei's strategic focus and quest to dominate the telecom industry suggests that he has no limits in terms of spending, stealing, or violating agreed-upon ethics when it comes to trying to achieve his ambitions. The list of his company's alleged abuses is as disturbing as it is long. In 2007, Ren was interviewed in New York by the FBI about suspicions Huawei was circumventing federal embargos on the sale of American technology to Iran. During the exchange, Ren "falsely stated" that Huawei had not violated US export laws and had not dealt directly with any Iranian company, according to a 2019 indictment file against Ren's daughter, Wanzhou Meng. Lying to an FBI agent is a crime, but the FBI did not arrest Ren for his apparent false statements. As troves of accumulated evidence listed in a future indictment would later demonstrate, his company had funneled banned US technology to Iran using Skycom, a Hong

Kong–based company once wholly owned by Huawei, and convinced several financial institutions operating in the United States to move millions of dollars in secret payments tied to Iran.[21]

Apparently undaunted by that encounter with US law enforcement, Ren immediately embarked on a series of personal overtures to highly specialized technical experts at prominent US universities. A source familiar with Ren told us the CEO volunteered to support those researchers and their labs financially in exchange for having all the experts' resulting IP filed and patented by Huawei.[22] Ren's unnerving offer, which at least one potential recipient refused, would have added up to tens of millions of dollars over the years. It would not be the last time Huawei targeted the cutting-edge IP being developed in American universities.

Meanwhile, the company was diversifying how it went about acquiring such IP. In 2012, Huawei, then the third largest phone manufacturer after Samsung and Apple, wanted to increase the speed of its quality control division. The rival American telecom T-Mobile had developed a phone-testing robot called "Tappy" in its Bellevue, Washington, factory. More a high-tech series of moving, electrical arms than a full-bodied assembly line android, Tappy's robotic tentacles could touch device screens, test phones, and identify software errors while measuring each device's operating speed and battery efficiency. Such data was critical to bringing the best possible product to the market and ensuring consumer preferences were met in order to maximize sales (and the bottom line).

Huawei, which sold its phones to T-Mobile and was reportedly attempting to build its own testing robot, arranged for its engineers to visit the T-Mobile laboratory and test trial Tappy after signing nondisclosure and confidentiality agreements that forbade them to take photos or videos of the device. Additionally, Huawei (and its subsidiaries) agreed not to ever attempt to reverse engineer Tappy.[23]

Demonstrating their singular appreciation for T-Mobile's hospitality, the Huawei engineers were promptly caught taking photos and measurements of Tappy. In a stunningly detailed federal indictment, investigators produced emails sent by Huawei engineers in China, repeatedly demanding the acquisition of "information we need to build our own robot system" and sending a wish list of specifications concerning Tappy robot hardware components and software systems.

At one point, two US-based Huawei engineers with clearance privileges helped another unauthorized Huawei engineer enter T-Mobile facilities. Nervously scanning around, one of them broke off one of Tappy's robot arms and smuggled it into a bag before later being caught.[24] Contacted by T-Mobile security, the engineer denied taking the robot arm, only to later change his story. With zero shame, he claimed that he had found the missing part in his bag, calling the incident a "mistake" and offering to return it.

If this culture of corporate theft seems like a mistake, it isn't. The Huawei Tappy indictment laid out an extraordinarily damning sequence of emails from Huawei's China and US headquarters relating to a July 2013 corporate bonus plan to reward "employees based on the value of information they stole from other companies around the world and provided to Huawei via an encrypted email address."[25] A "competition management group" would review individual submissions and additionally bestow awards to the top three regions that provided the most valuable information. With the ease of a simple email, thousands of Huawei employees around the world were suddenly transformed into, in effect, potential intelligence collectors. This fusing of private sector resources to Chinese government strategic priorities, and the previously unseen and exponential scale it resulted in for MSS collection reach around the world, would prove to be a unique feature of the Great Heist and one that other countries could hardly fathom pulling off.

Codifying a corporate culture of theft poses problems almost anywhere in the world. In the West, like most of the world, industrial espionage is against the law and can result in fines and/or imprisonment for companies operating there, Chinese or otherwise. Promoting theft also seems like a bad policy move by a company that had just denied any wrongdoing in the Tappy technology theft case with T-Mobile. Like many other CCP-backed national flagship corporations, Huawei has few qualms, however, about playing by a different set of rules. Still, the pure brazenness of the theft policy compelled the executive director of human resources at Huawei USA to email staff members, advising that despite the home office's encouraging trade secret theft, "here in the U.S.A. we do not condone nor engage in such activities and such a behavior is expressly prohibited by [Huawei USA's] company policies."[26]

Ultimately, Huawei claimed it fired two engineers for inappropriate actions, but it disputed accusations of trade theft. In 2017, a federal jury found Huawei misappropriated T-Mobile trade secrets, but did not award damages for that aspect of the suit, holding the violation wasn't "willful."[27]

There have been several other well-documented corporate espionage cases lodged against Huawei. One dates back as far as 2001, when CEO Ren met with Shaowei Pan in Beijing, according to a trade secrets complaint filed by Motorola. Pan, whom *The Wall Street Journal* reported is a relative of the Huawei founder, was then a senior software engineer at Motorola, where he would later become the director of architecture. At some point, Pan pitched Huawei a plan to start a rival company, Lemko, which would develop wireless technology based on Motorola's research. In March 2003, Pan, allegedly acting at Huawei's request, transmitted confidential specifications for the Motorola SC300 base station to Ren Zhengfei. According to court papers, Pan was not alone. In 2007, a fellow Motorola engineer named Hanjuan Jin was nabbed at Chicago O'Hare International Airport with $30,000 in cash; more than a thousand documents, many marked "confidential and proprietary"; and a one-way ticket to Beijing. Although Jin claimed in a subsequent interview that the authorities "made a mistake" (she also said she had "TB and meningitis"), she was convicted of stealing trade secrets and sentenced to four years in prison.[28]

At least four other Motorola employees were also named in the company's lawsuit against Huawei, Lemko, Pan, and Jin.[29] The suit was settled out of court,[30] and all these years later, Pan, who was never charged with any wrongdoing, is still listed on LinkedIn as the CTO of Lemko, based in Illinois.

Huawei launched other attempted corporate raids against key competitors around this same time. Versatile Routing Platform routers had caught the eye of Huawei developers as essential technology to manage and direct internet traffic in a fast, efficient manner.[31] In 2004, Cisco sued Huawei for "direct, verbatim copying of our source code, to say nothing of our command line interface, our help screens, our copyrighted manuals and other elements of our products," wrote Cisco chief legal officer Mark Chandler, who added that a "Neutral Expert" had issued a final report on the case. Chandler shared highlights of the programmer's decoding. Among the findings surfaced were that Huawei had access to the Cisco code which was "electronically copied" and that Cisco's source code was directly used in Huawei's version.[32] Despite the apparently clear evidence of corporate malfeasance, Cisco later dropped its case after Huawei agreed to stop selling the disputed routers and related products.[33]

Bad Optics

Huawei's drive to obtain American IP in the face of US countermeasures to have their products banned or blocked in markets around the world persists. In 2021, Huawei joined Optica, the rebranded name of the 108-year-old professional group the Optical Society of America, to offer a $10 million deal to sponsor a research competition via the Optica Foundation, a bombshell Bloomberg article reported. Optica is devoted to the science of light. In the twenty-first century, applications involving light are at the forefront of laser technology, space exploration, biomedical diagnostics and therapies, and, of course, telecommunications.

The plan to distribute $1 million a year in total prize money from Huawei was never supposed to see the light of day. Documents viewed by the Bloomberg reporter specified that Optica would not have to identify "Huawei as the funding source or program sponsor" of the competition. The report also unearthed apparently clear attempts to keep the relationship clandestine: "The existence and content of this Agreement and the relationship between the Parties shall also be considered Confidential Information."[34]

The language makes clear what Optica was signing on to do; it was effectively taking funding from Huawei, a pariah in American academic circles, to drive optics research. In return, the foundation allowed Huawei to gain access to new leading optics technology in bulk. To be clear, Huawei's money allegedly came with very specific strings attached. One of the members of the selection committee for the prize was a Huawei executive, Xiang Liu, Huawei's chief optical standards expert, who would presumably see all contest submissions. "Optica was obviously laundering the research for Huawei," a member of the organization who is familiar with Huawei's aggressive acquisition strategies told us.[35]

Confronted by the reporter who had broken the news, Huawei and Optica's leaders adopted a nothing-to-see-here attitude, essentially trying to rebuff any suggestion of laundering or helping Huawei. A corporate spokesman insisted that Huawei had simply wanted anonymity so it wouldn't be "seen as promotional." Optica CEO Liz Rogan said that anonymity is normal in the donation game and "there is nothing unusual about this practice."[36]

Disturbed by the Optica report, Representative Frank Lucas, the chair of the House of Representatives Committee on Science, Space, & Technology, and ranking committee member Representative Zoe Lofgren issued a letter asking additional questions. The congressional letter was likely prompted by the Bloomberg report. Optica responded that it had decided to return Huawei's funds but also divulged that it had received two other donations from Huawei. This led to even further questioning by American lawmakers.[37] CEO Rogan and her counterpart at the Optica Foundation both reportedly left the organization after the scandal broke. As underscored by this example, China is rewriting the rules of what "traditional" espionage entails and creating novel and unconventional avenues to obtain the information it needs to ensure it comes out on top in its grand struggle against America.

Danger: High Voltage

Recognizing the geostrategic significance of the industry, since 2017, the US government has imposed trade restrictions on Huawei, progressively banning the use of the company's telecommunications equipment within government agencies.

On April 17, 2019, "Who Owns Huawei?," a paper published by

Christopher Balding, a professor at New Kite Data Labs, and Donald C. Clarke, a professor at George Washington University Law School, reported that a holding company owned 100 percent of Huawei. Ren Zhengfei owned 1 percent of the company, with the remaining 99 percent held by "an entity called a 'trade union committee' for the holding company. The scholars concluded, "Given the public nature of trade unions in China, if the ownership stake of the trade union committee is genuine, and if the trade union and its committee function as trade unions generally function in China, then Huawei may be deemed effectively state-owned."[38] In May 2019, the US Department of Commerce blacklisted Huawei, requiring it to get US government approval to buy American technology. That same day, government agencies were empowered to ban US companies from using telecommunications equipment produced by Huawei and other firms that were found to pose national security risks. In 2021, the Federal Communications Commission (FCC) ordered US telecom companies to remove all equipment made by Huawei and fellow Chinese manufacturer ZTE from their networks and agreed to fund the replacement costs.

The US legislation in the name of national security and protecting and hardening our telecommunication infrastructure may be too little, too late. The ideas espoused in the PLA colonels' strategic bible *Unrestricted Warfare* about controlling "modern information technology" seems to remain highly relevant to influencing and shaping China's commercial and government pursuits in this industry.

Things would soon be taken up a notch, moving well beyond fears about surveillance. On May 24, 2023, Microsoft Threat Intelligence announced that it had detected a Chinese state-sponsored hacking assault targeting US infrastructure on Guam, where strategic US military bases are located, and elsewhere in America. Dubbed Volt Typhoon—"Typhoon" is Microsoft's internal code name for China-based bad actors, as opposed to, say, Russian cybergangs—the hackers had used sophisticated "Sharpshooter" exploits known metaphorically as "living off the land."

That is, the hackers used a complex script that tricks an operating system into triggering access to a network and loading information-stealing instructions into memory. It's in effect an invisible heist that leaves behind no resident code or virus.[39] While Microsoft noted that such hacks typically focus on espionage and information gathering, the company speculated that China was "pursuing development of capabilities that could disrupt critical communications infrastructure between the United States and Asia region during future crises."[40] Curiously, and perhaps coincidentally, investigators tied the incursions to hacks of older Cisco routers[41]—the same sphere of technology that Huawei had been accused of copying from Cisco two decades earlier.

Fifteen months later, in September 2024, a new, equally ominous threat emerged: Salt Typhoon. Early reports revealed that CCP-backed hackers were targeting internet providers and gaining access to cable and broadband provider infrastructure. The implications were both terrifying and hard to miss: hacked telecommunication companies might be susceptible to disruption, and their data—not to mention the data of customers, such as emails and contacts—might have been accessed.

The reality was worse. At least eight US telecommunication firms had been breached. Among those hit were the United States' leading telecoms, Verizon, AT&T, T-Mobile, and Lumen Technologies.[42] Reports surfaced that the hackers had accessed the metadata of millions of Americans and targeted the phones of then presidential candidate Donald Trump and members of Kamala Harris's campaign.

"This is an ongoing effort by China to infiltrate telecom systems around the world, to exfiltrate huge amounts of data," Sen. Mark R. Warner (D–Virginia), chairman of the Senate Intelligence Committee, charged. Warner called the attack the "worst telecom hack in our nation's history—by far."[43] He wasn't exaggerating. As we've suggested, protecting the integrity and reliability of our telecom companies is or should be near the top of America's greatest national security priorities. Noting that the networks were still compromised, Warner added that securing telecom infrastructure would involve replacing "literally thousands and thousands and thousands of pieces of equipment across the country." America's complacency toward this issue would result in very serious costs.

US telecoms dragged their feet with regard to the FCC requirement to remove all Huawei and ZTE equipment because Congress had previously approved only $1.9 billion for the projected $5 billion plan. In December 2024, Warner's colleagues in the House of Representatives approved $3 billion.[44] After dragging its feet for years the United States was finally beginning to give the telecom threat the attention and resources it deserved.

As important as telecommunications is there are even more critical technologies being targeted by China, which have almost incalculable implications for capturing and redefining the commanding heights of economic and military power in the decades to come.

Foremost among them: AI.

CHAPTER 9

Artificially Subsidized Intelligence

IF THE criminal indictment against Linwei "Leon" Ding is to be believed—and the evidence against him seems quite compelling—it's easy to imagine the engineer closing his MacBook laptop at his workstation at the Googleplex in Mountain View, California, and fighting back a smile, reminding himself he needed to stay cool and remain in the moment.

Given what investigators found, Ding must have been all business. It was in the thirty-seven-year-old programmer's best interest to keep up appearances. And that didn't mean just wearing thick-rimmed, rectangular hipster spectacles. Staying in character as a talented, dedicated engineer devoted to the hottest segment of computer programming would have been key.

Still, who could blame him if he had smiled? The irony was hard to miss: Google itself, from a certain perspective, had helped Ding. The company had *given* him the laptop, and, as investigators charged, he'd used the Apple Notes function on that computer to save hundreds of Google source files and scripts containing the tech giant's artificial intelligence trade secrets. Then he'd saved the Apple Notes files as PDF documents on the laptop. Last, he then uploaded the documents to his own Google cloud account.[1] The company that paid him handsomely, that had helped him vastly increase his knowledge of AI, and that had introduced a series of rigorous security protocols to prevent the transfer of its billion-dollar intellectual property had conveniently, if unwittingly, provided him with the tools for illicit extraction, according to the indictment details.

Ding put his laptop in his bag, hoisted it over his shoulder, and slipped out into the cool Northern California evening. Heading home, he walked through the Googleplex, with its beach volleyball courts and continually catered workdays—a campus concocted for tech world elite.

Did he preen a little? Again, it's easy to imagine. For months, according to the indictment, Ding had been executing an operation that had global power implications and might actually change the fate of the world. Didn't that mean he had outfoxed a tech giant? Perhaps Ding allowed himself a sneering joke: Given everything he'd achieved, Google's corporate and security intelligence might be viewed as truly artificial.

Linwei Ding was hired at Google in 2019 to work on the platform that powered the company's network of supercomputing data centers. One of his primary responsibilities included coding to ensure that graphics processing units (GPUs), the sophisticated semiconductor chips that make so many complex operations possible via parallel processing, powering everything from 3D video games to computer monitors to credit card approvals, could be used efficiently for a variety of tasks, including machine learning and AI applications. To do his job well, he needed access to the code and hardware infrastructure that drove the software platform, as well as the AI models and applications it supported.

Naturally, Ding had been granted that access. And why not? He had signed Google's Code of Conduct, promising to "take steps to keep our trade secrets and other confidential intellectual property secret."

Google's company mission is "to organize the world's information and make it universally accessible and useful."[2] But that openness did not extend to the company's own technology and search secrets. Google has a remarkable array of protocols and procedures to ensure that its property is kept secure. Video cameras focus on building entrances. Entry to buildings is gained via badge access, and within the buildings on the vast compound, certain areas or floors even require special access permissions. To protect information on the private company network, a monitoring system logged data transfers to and from Google's network, and only registered devices could gain entry to the corporate network. All Google employees were required to use two-factor authentication for their work-related Google accounts. Employee activity on Google's network was logged, including file transfers to platforms such as Google Drive.

The Google employment agreement Ding had signed in 2019 was filled with still more pledges, including holding company trade secrets "in strict confidence" and using confidential Google information only for "the benefit of Google" during his employment. He also promised not to "retain any documents or materials or copies thereof containing any Google Confidential Information" upon termination from Google, and avoid any future or other employment or business activity that "directly relates to the business in which Google is now involved, becomes involved, or . . . otherwise conflicts with Google's business interests."[3]

In May 2022, according to court records, Ding began breaking his security vows. Over the next twelve months, he allegedly transferred files containing protected trade secrets to his personal Google account. He worked slowly and methodically, converting and cloaking smaller batches of files as PDFs, evidently hoping not to trigger Google's internal monitoring system that tracked file transfers. Evading detection, he continued his operation, investigators found, and ultimately exported over a thousand files.

Ding's file-swiping operation was allegedly part of a larger plan: He would use his access to create new opportunities in his native China with the sensitive information he pilfered. That June, he received a job offer from Yuan Ye, the CEO of Beijing Rongshu Lianzhi Technology Company, which was developing a learning platform to train AI models and was interested in developing machine learning software using GPU chips. It was quite an offer: chief technology officer, not bad for someone with limited managerial experience. The perks were good, too: a $177,600 salary, an annual bonus, and company stock.

On subsequent trips to China, Ding appeared at investor meetings to raise money for Rongshu. At an April 17, 2023, meeting, CEO Ye publicly stated that Ding was now Rongshu's CTO.

Working for two companies at the same time was not enough for Ding. In May 2023, he allegedly started a third gig, founding the Shanghai Zhisuan Technology Company to develop a cluster management system (CMS) to accelerate machine learning tasks, including training large AI models powered by supercomputing chips. That month he sent an application for the company to a start-up incubation program called MiraclePlus. In November, he granted 7 percent ownership to a MiraclePlus company in exchange for a capital investment. Days later, after appearing at a MiraclePlus venture capital investor conference in Beijing, he circulated a document to a Shanghai Zhisuan WeChat group with a brazen pitch: "We have experience with Google's ten-thousand-card computational power platform; we just need to replicate and upgrade it—and then further develop a computational power platform suited to China's national conditions."[4]

That sentence was a tacit admission of his intentions: Ding planned to duplicate and optimize Google's computational power using stolen trade secrets. That was bad enough. But it was the last phrase of the sentence—"Suited to China's national conditions"—that was most ominous. Artificial intelligence and machine learning can be used to mine and analyze billions of points of data at blazing speed. Google, which first spearheaded the creation of large language models that drive AI platforms such as ChatGPT and its own Gemini, has been a market leader in data and analytics and delivering the right programmatic response to a given query. Its core business involves answering functional, informational, or utilitarian questions. But what if "national conditions" demand questions that are meant to skirt or break international law?

If there was ever any doubt about whether Ding's theft of Google documents was a national security issue, the answer was crystal clear. A presentation circulated to potential Shanghai Zhisuan investors cited a document issued by the State Council, which was unambiguous in its stated goals: "State Council Notice on the Issuance of the Next Generation Artificial Intelligence Development Plan," issued by the guiding force of the CCP, explicitly called for the development of high-performance computing infrastructure. It also alluded to another CCP document, "Interim Measures for the Management of Generative AI Services," that specified strategic measures to "encourage independent innovation in basic technologies such as generative ratification intelligence algorithms, chips, and supporting software platforms."[5] China's government was making clear its intention to dominate the AI industry.

Targeting Practice

Ding's pitches aligned with CCP documents for a reason: Although Made in China 2025 does not specifically mention AI, the plan lists the IT industry as one of its top strategic priorities.[6] AI has become arguably *the* most important critical technology for the PRC, as its potential to act as a force multiplier for effectively all other industries is nearly boundless. When US intelligence officials analyzed how the PRC might use AI, they gamed out various scenarios. Military usage was an obvious concern. AI can be used to make "smart" weapons smarter and more efficient by evaluating rival troop movements, optimizing shooting trajectories, and syncing with command-and-control systems to adjust the deployment of weapons in midflight.

As scary as those scenarios are, FBI analysts believe that the vast troves of personal data that PLA and MSS hacks obtained from private companies such as Equifax, Marriott, and Anthem, as well as government agencies including the Office of Personnel Management (OPM), could also prove vital to targeting operations for recruiting future spies, enabling massive cyberhacks, and/or other forms of malign strategic influence campaigns. In October 2023, while Ding was busy expanding his AI portfolio, FBI Director Christopher Wray described AI as "an amplifier for all sorts of misconduct. . . .

The Chinese are keenly interested in stealing our A.I. And, so then, when you come back to China, it's sort of the convergence of those two things together: the theft, but then, the ability to misuse it. And in their case, AI—since they have stolen more personal and corporate data than any other nation by orders of magnitude—if you then think about what AI can do to help leverage that data—to take what's already the largest hacking program in the world by a country mile and make it that much more effective—that's what we worry about."[7]

At one point, US officials wondered if CCP's hackers had collected *too much* information, creating a scale of collected data that was unmanageable and therefore, in practice, meaningless. But AI's incredible ability to parse and sort, to find logic, and to deduce patterns within apparent data chaos means that the troves of data can be weaponized on an exponential scale once thought impossible.

Finding out that a biotech CEO is in financial debt, for example, might make that executive a potential target for a recruitment pitch by MSS officers; discovering that same CEO has a partner whose mother has stage 4 cancer in Shanghai might make that CEO even more of a target.

Microsoft Vice Chairman and President Brad Smith believes that such scenarios are not far off. "Initially the big question was: did anyone, including the Chinese, have the capacity to use machine learning and fundamentally AI to federate these data sets and then use them for targeting," he said in a *Wall Street Journal* interview. "In the last two years we've seen evidence that that, in fact, has happened." He cited a 2021 attack targeting thousands of systems using Microsoft Exchange Server messaging and collaboration software as an example of AI's analyzing and parsing data to wreak havoc. "We saw clear indications of very specific targeting," he said. "I think we should assume that AI will be used to continue to refine and improve targeting, among other things."[8]

AI becomes a particularly effective espionage targeting tool when it can identify useful intelligence out of vast troves of data and connect that data with other disparate sources. Combining fact A with fact B may yield opportunity C to accrue more information, more wealth, more power, or all three. But first you need to identify the facts. For example, an American nuclear engineer with access to top secret technology might be a person of interest, a valuable potential source of information, to the MSS. But extracting that information is going to be difficult. If the MSS can access the engineer's personal data via stolen financial and medical records or emails, it might be able to uncover information that would compel the engineer to share secrets. Spy handlers use all kinds of intel as levers of influence: Is the target buried by mounting debts? Going through a divorce? Dealing with a spoiled son who is gambling and missing payments on his luxury sports car? A mosaic profile of a potential intelligence source built from all these different sources can prove highly effective in the hands of a good case officer.

Identifying technical experts working on specific technologies or highly specialized areas throughout the world has never been easier, thanks to LinkedIn and the advanced search technology that enables mass probes of scientific publications. But the challenge of finding more specific and more personal information required to manipulate such a target can be significantly reduced by AI.

>1,000 Files

In December 2023, Ding's alleged plans to supercharge his career and China's AI industry with stolen Google IP looked pretty good. At that point, per investigators, he had seven months' worth of files containing stolen trade secrets, a significantly increased income, and promising business development deals poised to make him a tech lord in Shanghai. Ever aggressive, he appeared to still be trolling for more funds for his start-up and hyping his firm's patriotic intent. That same month, he submitted an application to a Shanghai-based talent program, extolling Zhisuan's mission to "help China to have computing power infrastructure capabilities that are on par with the international level," court papers revealed.[9]

Then he got a shock. The defense system he thought he had outfoxed suddenly came to life. Working remotely in China on December 2, 2023, he uploaded additional files from the Google network to one of his Google Drive accounts. On December 8, Google security detected his activity. Ding was soon thereafter approached by a company investigator.

Confronted with possible evidence of his criminal activity, Ding lied, prosecutors say. He told the investigator that it had been an innocent mistake, a dumb decision. He had stored the files as a form of keepsake, evidence of some of his work at Google. Clearly Ding's spur-of-the-moment statement was far-fetched. Buried in his story was an obvious implication that the investigator really wanted to know more about: Was Ding thinking of leaving the company? No, Ding insisted, according to court papers. He had no intention of doing so.

To demonstrate his innocence and good faith, he signed a Self-Deletion Affidavit, a somewhat naively named document in which he asserted that he had "permanently deleted and/or destroyed all copies" of any nonpublic information gained from his job. "As a result, I no longer have access to such information outside the scope of my employment," he self-attested.[10]

Less than a week after declaring that he had no intention of leaving Google, Ding bought a one-way ticket from San Francisco to Beijing. Perhaps he planned an open-ended trip with an unknown return date to the United States. But his next move made that highly unlikely: He emailed his resignation to his manager at Google. His last day at work would be January 5, 2024.

Ding's sudden departure plans, combined with his recent file-sharing activity, set off alarm bells in Mountain View. The company discovered his November appearance as the CEO of Shanghai Zhisuan at the MiraclePlus investor conference in Beijing. Soon after, Google halted Ding's network access and locked his laptop remotely. A subsequent search of Ding's network activity discovered a thousand unauthorized uploads of Google documents from May 2022 through May 2023.

As they reviewed Ding's activity, Google investigators accessed the surveillance video footage monitoring the entry to Ding's office building on the Google campus. On three separate days, a Google employee had been filmed scanning Ding's access badge. Questioned by security, the employee claimed that Ding had requested a favor: to scan Ding's badge while he was traveling to apparently show like he was dutifully headed into work. The ruse, according to the accomplice, was simply to make it seem as if Ding was working from his office.[11]

Time, it seemed, was running out on Ding. Google contacted the FBI, which started working on a warrant application to search Ding's residence. Google security personnel got to the house first, however, and stripped Ding of his company laptop and phone. Two days later, on January 6, 2024, one day before Ding was scheduled to fly to China, the FBI moved in, raiding Ding's home and seizing his personal electronic devices and other evidence.

Watching the federal agents enter his house, the software engineer was about to become a convicted spy. His actions regarding the trade secrets were on his devices and his Google accounts. Incriminating emails and documents filled his devices and accounts. As a programmer who had helped create and manage networks, he had to know that his activities could be tracked and ultimately accessed. The FBI told him not to leave the country, and the following week he was hit with a second search warrant giving investigators access to his two Google Drive accounts. One of the accounts contained more than a thousand unique files containing Google confidential information, including designated trade secrets.

On the morning of March 6, 2024, the FBI arrested Linwei Ding at his home in Newport, California. When announcing the bust, Special Agent in Charge Jeff Fields credited "early collaboration with Google," which had allowed the Bureau "to surge resources and accelerate this investigation to prevent Linwei Ding from causing further damage."[12]

Exactly how much damage Ding caused the company remains unknown. Did he transport Google's proprietary files on his many trips to the PRC? Did he share their content with engineers at both Beijing Rongshu Lianzhi Technology Company and his start-up Shanghai Zhisuan? Perhaps he had provided a treasure trove of Google's commercial secrets to an MSS agent handler while in the country? Had the investors and talent programs required proof of concept details? The answers remain unknown, and it seems likely that Ding will provide some of them as part of a plea deal. If Ding did in fact have a relationship with the MSS, something not confirmed by court records, it certainly could have been masked and kept out of the public light by the agency's effective use of tradecraft, the measures taken to keep an illicit relationship hidden from the world. As of early 2025, his case had not yet come to trial. But among the fourteen counts listed in the indictment, the charges of economic espionage and trade secret theft could carry up to fifteen years in prison plus a $5 million fine per count and up to ten years in prison plus a $250,000 fine per count, respectively. The theft for stealing America's trade secrets—on paper at least—appear severe. Even so, how does a $5 million fine stack up to the potentially exponential advantage, and opportunity costs, of allowing your greatest geopolitical rival to obtain critical information about one of the world's most redefining technologies?

Artificial General Intelligence

While Ding was busy with orchestrating his theft of Google's cutting-edge AI research, events in Beijing in early March 2023 may have prodded him to keep going, implanting visions of wealth and heroism in his eyes. It was the Two Sessions season, the gathering of two major CCP confabulations: the National People's Congress (NPC) and the Chinese People's Political Consultative Conference (CPPCC). Zhu Songchun, the dean of the Institute for Artificial Intelligence and the School of Intelligence Science at Peking University and the founder of the Beijing Institute for General Artificial Intelligence (BIGAI), was one of the featured speakers at the CPPCC. His speech was hotly anticipated, and for good measure.

Zhu had spent decades establishing himself as one of the world's foremost AI scientists. For eighteen years, from 2002 to 2020, he had been a professor at UCLA, and starting in 2010, he had served as the director of the university's Center for Vision, Cognition, Learning, and Autonomy. In addition to being an employee of the state of California, he also worked for the US government on high-level security issues.

The side-parted hairstyle of Zhu, a citizen of the PRC and a legal resident of the United States, made him look more like a friendly Rotary Club member than a shrewdly calculating scientist. Evidently his affability, expertise, and relatively benign profile worked to his advantage. Over the years, he had been handed an estimated $30 million to conduct computer research for the US military and other American institutions.

In 2021, after having taken a leave of absence from UCLA a year earlier to return to China, the Department of Defense awarded him $699,938 to develop "robot autonomy" by researching the use of autonomous drones for search and rescue missions. That same year, the Office of Naval Research gave him another grant, for $520,811, to work on "cognitive robot platforms" for "intelligence and surveillance systems via ground and aerial sensors."[13] The Pentagon was entrusting Zhu with some of its most sensitive R&D projects.

Pretty good gigs for a man who now lived and worked full-time in the PRC. But Zhu was one of many Chinese scholars who had been raiding the halls of the American academy and federal funding channels for years. And judging by several well-publicized instances related to such cases, it was clear that the US technology grant and research system had yet to establish a mechanism for sufficiently policing its grants or grantees. Not that Zhu was doing anything explicitly illegal, of course.

In Beijing's Great Hall of the People, Zhu addressed over two thousand political movers and shakers who filled the three tiers of the conference center clad in suits, dresses, and surgical masks. His goal, judging from his speech, was to try to encapsulate the vast importance of artificial intelligence. And he chose a truly explosive metaphor to get that idea across.

"Artificial general intelligence [AGI]," he said, "is the strategic high ground of international scientific and technological competition in the next ten to twenty years, and its influence is equivalent to the 'atomic bomb' in the field of information technology."[14]

Did Ding hear Zhu's call in the reports that followed the event? It seems highly likely. Both men had ties to the California university system and were obsessed with AI. It's possible Ding was emboldened by Zhu's message; it would be reasonable to presume, after such an explosive speech, about both the national and commercial value of the cutting-edge AI files the Google employee had access to at work.

After his keynote address in the Great Hall, Zhu continued to beat the AI drum, appearing at the 26th Peking University Guanghua New Year Forum in the Centennial Lecture Hall of Peking University later in January 2025. Zhu was morphing from a scientist into a political thinker intent on tying AI to geopolitical issues. Despite the decades of technological knowledge reaped in the United States, and with grant funding by the US military and government, Zhu used overtly nationalist language when staking out the necessity for Chinese superiority in the AI space: "The development of general purpose artificial intelligence depends on Big Data, computing power (compute), and chip technology. In the background, however, [it] is not merely about competition in technological capabilities but, even more so, it is a struggle for global confidence and for control of the narrative."[5]

By "narrative," Zhu seemed to be saying the United States was perceived as the present leader in the space. "Our goal, and our responsibility," he said later in the speech, "is to create world-class technology through Chinese thought. China is fully capable of seizing the initiative in the era of general AI." He was making clear where his true loyalties lay.

Zhu's words about creating world-class technology did not entirely agree with the way the scientist had obtained his knowledge, much of which had been gleaned in the US with the fruits of investments made in US dollars not Chinese yuan. He, like so many other potentially MSS-influenced operators, gamed the American system, continually seeking financial support in the United States while also contracting with parallel programs back in the PRC. Investigations by *Newsweek* and the Congressional Select Committee on the CCP dug deep into Zhu's résumé, uncovering a string of potentially troubling connections and events. According to *Newsweek*, while working at UCLA and receiving US funds, Zhu launched an AI "institute near Wuhan, took a position at a Beijing university whose primary goal is to support Chinese military research, and joined a Chinese Communist Party 'talent plan,' whose members are tasked with transferring knowledge and technology to China."[16] These red flags were apparently missed by any screening measures put in place before the scientist received US government and DOD grants.

In early 2025, the media were flooded with reports suggesting that Zhu's vision of China dominating AI was beginning to materialize. DeepSeek, an AI start-up backed by a relatively small and mysterious Chinese hedge fund, unveiled its new AI paradigm, R1, which didn't rely on superior US microchips, was built for a fraction of the cost that American AI platforms, used far less energy, and was open source and free. It also made use of something called reinforcement learning, essentially writing programs to rate its responses, thereby fine-tuning its results via machines instead of humans. Although programmed differently than the AGI of Zhu's dreams, the impact and potential aligned with the "narrative" shift the scientist had said was so critical to the future balance of power in the space.

In our speculative, tech investor–driven world, DeepSeek shook up the markets, with AI chip leader Nvidia plummeting $600 million in valuation in one day amid breathless statements from tech investors.[17] Marc Andreessen, a venture capitalist and AI true believer, posted on X, "DeepSeek R1 is one of the most amazing and impressive breakthroughs I've ever seen."[18]

But one week after its January 20, 2025, unveiling, it was hard to discern the innovation from the hype. Industry leader OpenAI announced suspicions that its data was being used by DeepSeek to "distill" or train R1, a violation of OpenAI's terms of service. Microsoft, a billion-dollar investor in OpenAI, reportedly believed that DeepSeek was linked to large amounts of data it had detected being exfiltrated through OpenAI developer accounts in late 2024.[19] Reports surfaced that banned high-tech American chips were available in Chinese markets and that DeepSeek relied on tens of thousands of Nvidia chips.

Meanwhile, rival AI firms were already incorporating reinforcement learning into their systems. In fact, two weeks before DeepSeek's debut, Microsoft Asia announced a model called rStar-Math, which used similar training, and one week after the R1 release, the Allen Institute for AI unveiled Tülu3–405B, another open-source AI mode that used reinforcement learning techniques and claimed to outperform DeepSeek.[20]

While no legal charges have been brought against DeepSeek, the timing and techniques of its R1 debut raise inevitable questions, given so many years of the PRC's acquisition-by-theft strategy. Was R1 the result of indigenous innovation, the culmination of years of Zhu's focus? Or did the technology appear through other means, perhaps involving Ding's methodology? Given the opacity and black hole of the Chinese economic and legal systems, circumstantial evidence is likely all that we'll ever have to make our evaluations.

Then there was the issue of surveillance: DeepSeek eagerly shared R1 with the world, but per its privacy policy, the application collects personal information, IP addresses, and keystrokes in the PRC, where the CCP effectively owns all such data.[21] This is a reminder of what may be AI's most dangerous application outside of its military uses: Anytime users ask R1 to integrate or aggregate data files, their queries will be sent to China, where likely an AI system of the future, if not already today, will mine any and all available data points, including who made the query, where they were, and what the query was, in order to drive even more targeted operations against the United States and the West.

While sophisticated machine learning and general AI loom as potential command-and-control operating systems for combat with frightening efficiencies, their real-world uses to conduct espionage and theft will likely grow exponentially. Former CIA operations officer Charles Finfrock, today the CEO of Vigilance, envisions human-seeming bots named Svetlana or Little Me engaging with US military adversaries on the battlefield to mine intelligence or troop locations. "They would collect all their bio. It would be the intel you can do to scale. Imagine if the Tinder profile is not only not real, but the Tinder profile is actually a setup itself."[22]

Tomorrow's breakthroughs in AGI will undoubtedly supercharge the spy game. Beijing already sits on warehouses of US data, much of it still locked behind today's encryption. The MSS is likely biding its time: When AGI finally reaches its predicted full potential, you can bet China's intelligence directorates will use it in new and very powerful ways to further pilfer American research and secrets. This won't stay limited to the civilian theater, either. The information stolen will flow straight into the PLA's arsenal, helping transform ones and zeros into kinetic effect at machine speed. The groundwork for doing so has already been laid from decades of similar theft cases targeting America's military might.

CHAPTER 10

Sneak Attacks on the
Department of Defense

IN MARCH 1996, two US aircraft carriers appeared off China's coast—and Beijing blinked.

The Third Taiwan Strait Crisis had reached its boiling point. China had been firing missiles into the waters near Taiwan in a show of force ahead of the island's first democratic presidential election. The message was unmistakable: Pursuit of self-determination would be punished by force if necessary.

But Washington had a message of its own. In a matter of days, the Clinton administration deployed the USS *Independence* and USS *Nimitz* battle groups into the region. Carrier-based aircraft began patrols. Submarines moved into the launch position. The world nervously watched. Beijing watched, too. And then, quietly, it stepped back.

The missiles stopped crashing into the tropical Pacific waters. The political rhetoric softened. Taiwan proceeded with holding its election. And the Chinese leadership, humiliated on the global stage, came to terms with one unavoidable truth: The United States could project power; China could not.

This incident was a turning point for China's high command. What followed was a decades-long CCP campaign to ensure that such an event would never happen again. Inside the halls of the Central Military Commission, in the war colleges of the PLA, and in the high-tech laboratories of China's rapidly expanding defense sector, a single strategic objective began to take shape: In the next crisis over the Taiwan Strait, Beijing, not Washington, would be the one dictating events.

The 1996 humiliation was studied, modeled, and in essence reverse engineered. Chinese military planners didn't just watch US warships, they dissected them. Aircraft carrier groups became symbols of US dominance but also floating targets. If the PLA could not match US power symmetrically, at least for the time being, it would counter it asymmetrically.

What emerged was a blueprint for the twenty-first-century battlefield tailored for the Asia Pacific: long-range missile barrages, space-based surveillance, cyberattacks, anti-access/area denial (A2/AD) strategies, and, perhaps most dangerously, the development of hypersonic weapons capable of hitting US assets across the region at indefensible speeds, rendering traditional air defense systems useless.

With the advent of such weaponry, by 2025 the Chinese military no longer needed to fire warning shots. It could target US bases in Japan, Guam, or the Philippines with precision and speed. Carrier strike groups that once operated with impunity now risked becoming high-value targets within minutes of a conflict's outbreak.

For the United States, the lesson of 1996 was simple: Deterrence works. For China, the lesson was far more profound: *It needed a total military rejuvenation.* Parity with American forces was insufficient. Domination of the Asia Pacific was the only option. Today, when the US Seventh Fleet sails toward the Taiwan Strait, it does so under satellite surveillance, within missile range, and potentially, one day in the not-too-distant future, into the path of a hypersonic strike by the PLA's Rocket Force. What began as a crisis over an island's election decades ago became the origin story of a strategic pivot that would carry major ramifications for the global balance of power for many years to come.

The American carriers came. They left. But the memory—at least in Beijing—never did. The MSS got to work.

———————

NEARLY TWO decades later, in 2024, the Pentagon's 182-page report to Congress on the PRC's military and security developments outlined China's ambitious and breakneck efforts to acquire highly sensitive technology and military plans, everything from aviation technologies to accelerometers, gyroscopes, signal decoders, space communications, and syntactic foam.

The report is an alarming distillation of the emerging battlefield of the future. Disturbing scenarios abound, from intercontinental nuclear attacks to targeting Taiwan with a mass amphibious naval invasion. Perhaps most daunting is a new PLA strategy of Multi-Domain Precision Warfare (MDPW) that augments command-and-control networks by utilizing Big Data and AI to synchronize PLA communications, computer, intelligence, surveillance, and reconnaissance divisions. This network, the report projects, might "rapidly identify key vulnerabilities in the U.S. operational system and then combine joint forces across domains to launch precision strikes against those vulnerabilities."[1] AI and raw military power, in other words, combined for lethal effect.

China's rapid development of such advanced technology did not happen organically. Over the past three decades China has orchestrated a staggering number of intelligence penetrations of America's military industrial complex. The Pentagon report highlights the recent arrests of a former US service member who attempted to deliver a device that would enable the PRC to access US secure military computer networks; two US service members who transmitted sensitive information to the PRC regarding naval warships' weapons, propulsion, and desalination systems; and a US Army intelligence analyst who shared manuals for the HH-60W helicopter, the F-22-A Raptor stealth fighter, ICBMs, and DOD Operation Plans (OPLAN) during a Taiwan invasion. And this small sampling are only the ones who were caught . . .

The scope of these espionage operations is truly astounding, offering endless variations on a relentless theme of acquisition, acquisition, and more acquisition by the Chinese collection apparatus in order to achieve Xi's strategic ambitions of military domination in Asia. Two such penetration cases in particular—attacks from insiders and outsiders, some positioned for years and able to wait patiently to strike—underscore the incredible damage and incalculable losses to American military might as a result of the Great Heist.

A Low-Flying Mole

Riyadh, February 2024
The Arabian sun was glaring outside as visitors gathered at the World Defense Show. Inside a purpose-built venue just outside the city, over 100,000 visitors from seventy-six countries discussed oil money, firepower, and global ambition. Saudi Arabia was hosting the future of war: Drones, missile defense systems, and augmented reality helmets were on display to visiting delegates and generals to preview tomorrow's battlefield and the tools that would determine victors and losers. Weapons systems were displayed across the showroom floors—including full-scale armored vehicles painted in desert camo. No doubt intimidating. But it was at the booths for Chinese arms firms, in particular, that drew major concern from visiting American representatives.

The aircraft on display was just a model—but one that looked eerily familiar. Sleek and coated in radar-absorbing gray, with sharp angles and sawtooth edges. A faceted cockpit. Engine nacelles sunk just so. To the untrained eye it looked like America's own F-35, its advanced multipurpose fighter designed to ensure air supremacy for decades to come and with a program life cycle exceeding $2 trillion. But the label on the model display was as clear as day: FC-31. And the flag beside it wasn't the Stars and Stripes. It was red, with five yellow stars.

Any American defense official seeing such a display couldn't help but get a knot tightening in their gut. How was the PRC able to develop such predatory aircraft so quickly and with such advanced technology—something that had been in development at Lockheed Martin since the mid-1990s? Their thoughts inevitably must have turned to the American pilots who one day might have to face down such crafts in dogfights over the Pacific.

IN 2006, Su Bin, aka Stephen Su, a Chinese national and permanent resident of Canada, launched Lode-Tech, an aircraft cable harness firm with offices in both Beijing and Vancouver. Su, an aerospace engineer and self-described multimillionaire who lived in a $2 million home near Vancouver International Airport,[2] had a genial demeanor accentuated by a chunky, rounded face that swelled from under a close-cropped haircut. He had a frank, enthusiastic manner, the kind of upbeat personality you might expect from a salesman of a small start-up. And that's how he presented himself: as a top seller of insulated custom electrical cables filled with the wires that help make up an airplane's nervous system. And if there were other ways to build networks, whether you needed intercom systems, radio support, or wiring for transponders, he was interested in those, too. His keen interest in all things aviation—who knew whom, who sourced what—seemed like normal behavior to many in the aviation industry. It's what salesmen did.

In reality it was also an old-school spy method of intelligence gathering. And Su's business persona, according to Bob Anderson, a former assistant director of the FBI's Counterintelligence Division, was in large part a cover for an elaborate multipronged military aviation intelligence-gathering operation that would, ultimately, have major ramifications for American air superiority.

"People liked him," Anderson told a CNN reporter. "They didn't think he was an ass**** and I know that sounds stupid, but people are people and that's how it started."[3]

Despite his Canadian business, Su still had deep roots in Beijing. Interviewed for a *Wall Street Journal* article in 2012 about wealthy Chinese moving to the West, Su portrayed himself as a millionaire engineer getting ready to leave Beijing permanently, in part because he was critical of the CCP. "The government has too much power," he said. "Regulations here mean that businessmen have to do a lot of illegal things. That gives people a real sense of insecurity."[4] Professing such ideological disdain for the Communist Party in Beijing, it now appears with hindsight, seems to have only been a ruse to throw any potential investigators off his tracks.

Indeed, Su's harness business may have been legitimate, but it also provided a front—an entry point—into the world of American and Canadian aviation manufacturing to do the very "illegal things" he was supposedly so uncomfortable with. Su's business networking for the relatively benign industry was in reality a way to map out the contractors, design firms, and corporate divisions of companies that worked on cargo planes. But his eventual target, the biggest prizes of all, were America's high-tech flying machines, including the C-17 and the F-22 and F-35 stealth fighter jets.

In 2008, when the PLA's air force announced plans for Project 718 to develop a stealth jet built by Chengdu Aircraft Corporation, Su was in the right place at the right time, ideally positioned to help co-ordinate the acquisition of key technology plans to build the sophisti-cated, radar-eluding supersonic flying machines.

In the summer of 2009, court papers reveal, Su began working with two hackers based in China. He emailed them lists of aero-space companies for the two hackers to evaluate and target for computer intrusions. The communications were often astonish-ingly granular, including a password-protected file listing email addresses, telephone contact information, and roles of program personnel, including members of the US government working on a military development project, according to court papers.

The two hackers then unleashed a slew of phishing exploits to access the critical platforms recommended by Su based upon his ex-tensive network-driven targeting. The first year, they breached the Pentagon's multibillion-dollar Joint Strike Fighter project via a hack of Lockheed Martin. To hide their tracks, the hackers encrypted the downloaded information to mask what they had stolen.[5]

Su also exchanged emails that shed light on the Chinese trio's motivations and methods. According to FBI Special Agent Noel

Neeman, who accessed emails between Su and his coconspirators, the hackers began targeting Boeing's computer network as early as 2009. By 2010, Su and the hackers were exchanging emails about specific files and directories relating to the C-17, Boeing's sophisticated transport vehicle. As Neeman reported, one 2010 email contained a 1,467-page document with a "directory structure and list of approximately 50,000 files related to the production, performance, or testing of the C-17" with 142 files highlighted in yellow. This included PDFs on hangar requirements, load testing, wiring failures, and other C-17 production details.[6] In case there was any ambiguity surrounding the group's mission, the FBI also captured exchanges in which the men had discussed selling the documents to leading Chinese aviation companies.

Among the documents Neeman uncovered was an attachment that clearly described the care for how such hacked military and industrial intelligence was transferred to PRC. Neeman didn't specify the organization, but it bears several hallmarks of previous MSS operations: specifying the involvement of a Chinese intelligence officer, coordinating operations with the Ministry of Science and Technology, and employing tradecraft to physically transport the intelligence into China to avoid telltale detection of the illegal activity. The document also outlined elaborate and expensive protocols that would be beyond the abilities or expense lines of normal aviation firms. Su's email below, complete with Neeman's comments in brackets, underscores this point.

First, we use the surveillance means which combines espionage work and technology(s) to accommodate the demands of S&T [likely Science and Technology] development.

Second, we have gradually established technology bases outside China for the sake of security/safety and stability. So far, jump servers [likely hop points] have been set up in the U.S., Korea, Singapore and etc. The rotations/switches/changes are made on them irregularly based on the security/safety variations of the environment.

Third, machine rooms are set up in the surrounding areas/regions for work convenience. Our machine rooms have been set up in Hong Kong and Macao respectively with legal status.

Fourth, in order to avoid diplomatic and legal complications, surveillance work and intelligence collection are done outside China. The
collected intelligence will be sent first by an intelligence officer via
a pre-ordered temporary server placed outside China or via a jump
server that is placed in a third country before it finally gets to the
surrounding regions/areas or a work station located in Hong Kong.[7]

The document also contained a brief, awkwardly worded but chilling summary of previous espionage and theft campaigns:

In recent years, we, with relentless work and through multiple
channels, have obtains respectively a series of military industrial technology data including F-35, C-17, [additional identified U.S. military
technologies] as well as the Taiwanese military maneuvers, warfare
operation plans, strategic targets, espionage activities and so forth.[8]

Su's spree of stolen military secrets, dubbed Byzantine Hades by
US investigators, continued while FBI investigators studied swaths
of emails and examined attachments of stolen files, trying to match
them with data housed by Boeing and other targets in order to con-
firm other intrusions.

Emails revealed that the C-17 was one of three high-value targets.
Su's hacker pals had also obtained plans for two of the US Air Force's
(USAF) premier weapons, the F-22 Raptor and the F-35, including
the latter jet's flight test plans. All told, they stole 630,000 C-17 files
and reams of files on the other jets. Su's emails to his conspirators
indicated that he had looked at every byte sent to him, evaluating acquired material to direct further attacks and translating the English
plans for the PLA. In June 2014, as the incontrovertible evidence piled
up, US law enforcement agencies learned that Su was in Canada and
planning to depart for Beijing imminently. They promptly issued an
extradition request to Canadian authorities, and the Royal Mounties
snatched him before he could escape to Chinese soil.

Days after Su's arrest, the world got a taste of China's spycraft fusing with statecraft and lawfare. The CCP decided to send a message
to the Ottawa government, as the Chinese authorities, likely with

MSS input if not explicit direction, engineered the arrest of Kevin and Julia Garratt, two Canadian citizens who had emigrated to China in 1984 to teach English and operated a café in Dandong on the North Korean border. The devout Christian couple were given absurd charges similar to those facing Su. According to their lawyer, "The Chinese made it clear that the Garratt case was designed to pressure Canada to block Su Bin's extradition to the US."

For well over a year, the extradition case involving Su crawled along, as did the fate of the Garratts. While Julia was released after six months in prison, Kevin was indicted on charges of stealing state secrets. But Beijing's trumped-up retaliation backfired when a lawyer explained to Su that the extradition battle might go on for years—longer than the probable US prison sentence Su might face. The accused aviation spy agreed to be extradited. The manufactured case against Kevin Garratt subsequently collapsed. He was released on bail and returned to Canada in September 2016 to join his wife.[9]

On March 23, 2016, Su Bin pled guilty to violating the Computer Fraud and Abuse Act of 1986 and the Arms Export Control Act of 1976 and was sentenced to five years in prison. He was released in October 2017 due to time served. His hacker pals remain at large in the PRC. China denies any wrongdoing, insisting that cybercrime is hard to trace.

Military aviation experts say that there is no question the PLA/AVIC J-20 and J-31 stealth jets are clones of F-17 and F-35 designs. As for the Y-20 military transport plane, which debuted in 2014, one aviation site noted its "uncanny similarity" to Boeing's C-17 Globemaster III in terms of design, "overall size and weight plus cargo capacity."[10]

A Sleeper Agent

In late October 2005, a mild-mannered sixty-four-year-old engineer based in California named Chi Mak finalized plans to make good on twenty-odd years of spycraft, delivering a payload of top secret naval technology to Beijing. Mak had stealthily assembled key blueprints and specifications for one of the world's most sophisticated submarine engines. The product of decades of American research and millions of taxpayer dollars, the cutting-edge technology had the potential to transform the balance of military power in the Asia Pacific.

Mak, who had immigrated to the United States from Hong Kong in the late 1970s, was a bespectacled, short, even-keeled presence at Power Paragon, an Anaheim-based leader in military-grade power distribution systems. He impressed his bosses with his hard work and enthusiasm and in 1996, after eight years at the firm, was granted a "Secret" level security clearance. Eventually, he was assigned to work on silent propulsion systems, a critical and sensitive technology used by the US Navy to enable American submarines to avoid detection by adversaries. This ability of submarines to remain unseen and unheard is essential to maintaining America's strategic nuclear deterrence across the globe's frigid oceans.

In 2003, the FBI received a tip that Mak might be a person of interest. Teaming up with Naval Criminal Investigative Service (NCIS) agents, the Bureau began digging into his background and discovered that he had previously worked for the MSS tracking US military ship movements during the final days of the Vietnam War. After eavesdropping on earnest political conversations between Mak and his wife, in which they expressed devotion to none other than Mao Zedong himself, agents concluded that Mak had been directed by MSS to come to the United States with one mission: to burrow his way into the American military industrial complex and steal military secrets for the CCP.

Now investigators had to prove that he was doing just that. For eighteen months, they tailed Mak and his wife, Rebecca Chiu, as they shopped, played tennis, and frequently drove to a local store that offered free coffee. The agents also sorted through the couple's garbage, monitored their phone calls, and eventually staged an elaborate midnight break-in. Inside the Mak home, they discovered and photographed purloined naval propulsion plans, as well as documents identifying other Chinese operatives and MSS "task lists" that requested specific defense information. They also found another shocking detail: Mak was not working alone. Spying for Communist China was apparently a family business for the Maks.

Mak had photographed and collated Power Paragon's plans onto

CD-ROMs at home in Downey, California, and provided the discs to his younger brother, Tai Mak, who worked for Phoenix TV, a satellite TV firm backed by the Chinese government. Investigators learned that Tai Mak and his wife, Fuk Li, were traveling to China and that Tai had enlisted their son, Yui "Billy" Mak, to encrypt the defense data and back it up onto a CD-ROM disk. The married couple then planned to smuggle CD-ROMs containing the information on the highly sensitive propulsion technology out of the country by inserting them into children's books.

As the couple tried to make their way onto their flight, airport security at Los Angeles International Airport searched the bags of Tai Mak and Fuk Li and located the hidden CD-ROMs. An FBI surveillance team videotaped the search and the ensuing arrest of Tai and Fuk.

But as they did, the agents scanning the busy airport terminal soon learned that they were not alone. A group of Asians were filming *them.*

The FBI team was perplexed. Were the Chinese spies being spied on by other Chinese spies? Was the MSS trying to turn a disaster into a positive by identifying FBI agents for future use?

The Chinese film crew was detained and its camera was confiscated, recalled one of the FBI agents, who envisioned a whole new line of investigations opening up. "The United States Attorney's Office said we didn't have enough evidence and that 'You gotta release them.' So we did, but we kept the camera and the film."[11]

If the Chinese surveillance team got away, the Maks did not. Coordinated with the airport bust, the joint FBI and NCIS team arrested Chi Mak and his wife, Rebecca, at their California home in front of bewildered neighbors. The FBI's investigation had nailed the sleeper agent.

Chi Mak was sentenced to twenty-four and a half years in prison on charges of conspiring to export US military technology to China and acting as an unregistered agent of a foreign government. His wife, Rebecca Chui, pleaded guilty to acting as an agent of the People's Republic of China, served three years, agreed to give up her US citizenship, and was eventually deported. Tai Mak was sentenced to ten years after entering a guilty plea for violating export control laws. His wife, Fuk, and their son, Billy, who pled guilty to aiding and abetting Tai, were sentenced to probation and a year in prison, respectively.[12]

"We will never know the full extent of the damage that Mr. Mak has done to our national security," Judge Cormac J. Carney wrote, explaining the reasoning behind Chi Mak's long sentence. "A high-end . . . sentence will provide a strong deterrent to the PRC not to send its agents here to steal American military secrets."[13] The aspiration for the sentencing was noble but would alas prove futile. Chinese agents would continue to target American secrets undeterred.

Judge Carney, sadly, has been a rarity in the judicial branch when it comes to sentencing CCP agents. Many cases involving CCP agents often result in slap-on-the-wrist plea bargains. This enables the Department of Justice to close lengthy cases quickly and save limited resources for other prosecutions. But it's a problematic trade-off: expedience versus deterrence. There's a strong argument to be made that a quick, toothless sentence emboldens bad actors instead of deterring them—even if more prosecutions are successful. The CCP's and MSS's cavalier attitudes toward the fate of their agents further complicate the issue. Under Xi Jinping, state power always trumps the individual, who essentially has no rights. In 99.9 percent of US prosecutions of CCP agents, Beijing has rejected any suggestion of wrongdoing.

From all appearances, no one at the MSS or the CCP Central Committee cared less about Chi Mak, who died in prison on October 31, 2022, alone, in a barren prison cell as a traitor. He was eighty-two years old. Given that his arrest tipped US investigators off to a second major spy initiative at NASA, it's probable that they were furious with him. That tip-off, which led to the arrest of Boeing contractor Dong-fang "Greg" Chung for collecting space shuttle trade secrets, was no doubt just as embarrassing to China. Chung was sentenced to fifteen years in prison as the first person convicted under the Economic Espionage Act of 1996.[14]

In addition to sensitive data on the space shuttle, Chung also stole classified designs for the Delta IV rocket for his MSS handlers, an event that should have raised more urgency in the United States counterintelligence circles about the priority Beijing had placed on stealing advanced rocket systems and NASA-related programs. The likely implications of such thefts in terms of advancing China's ballistic missile program (and therefore its ability to potentially strike the US homeland with nuclear warheads) and its ability to project power in space (a critical future domain of warfare) is truly sobering to consider. At the very least, it should have triggered more heightened safeguards for related high-valued collection targets that could tip the balance of military power—programs such as hypersonic technology.

Unfortunately, that didn't happen.

CHAPTER 11

Hard Lessons in Hypersonics and National Security

IT BEGAN with a Toyota RAV4, idling on a quiet street in Manila. The air was humid, and the city buzzed with activity. Inside were three men. One, Deng Yuanqing, was a Chinese national and the others were Filipino, posing as surveyors. On the dashboard: a mounted tablet, connected to a Global Navigation Satellite System. In the back seat: a high-powered imaging drone and a custom-built data relay antenna. They weren't lost, nor were they tourists. They were closely observing a sensitive US military base. And they were mapping it in meticulous detail.

On January 17, 2025, Philippine security forces moved in. Deng and his team were arrested in Makati, the country's financial district. Days later, five more Chinese nationals, claiming to be Taiwanese tourists, were detained on the island of Palawan, just miles from key Philippine naval outposts and US rotational facilities.[1] Each arrest unraveled another layer of a chilling reality: China wasn't interested in using its agents to map the region just for the sake of it. Rather the targets of the motley surveillance crews were airstrips, fuel depots, radar towers, and ammunition storage sites, everything that would need to be hit first in the event of war between China and the United States.

Those operations in the Philippines, which have yet to come to trial as of June 2025, were pieces of a global mosaic of espionage, part of a larger intelligence architecture designed to make one of the most dangerous weapons on Earth—China's hypersonic missile force— even deadlier and more accurate.

With speeds exceeding Mach 5, maneuverability that defeats conventional missile defense systems, and precision guidance that depends on exact geolocation data, hypersonic weapons are not designed for forewarnings. They're designed for preemption and lethality. And the most vulnerable targets are the forward bases that provide the US military its reach across the Pacific: Guam, Okinawa, Palawan, Subic Bay. The hypersonic missile force relies on having every hangar mapped, every fuel depot logged, every flight line measured—data fed into fire control systems thousands of miles away.

The People's Liberation Army Rocket Force (PLARF) doesn't need to land troops on US soil to cripple this country's defenses in the event of war; it only needs to hit hard, first, and with precision. Such a strike, Chinese military planners no doubt consider, could be enough to deter America from coming to Taiwan's assistance in a PRC–Taiwan-armed conflict. The idea would be to strike with "shock and awe" and break, from the very outset, the American will for any such war by giving them a heavy taste of the costs they would have to bear. At hypersonic speeds, any such first strike on US bases could be over before the first alert reaches a command post or triggers air defense systems. For decades, the United States bet on distance as a form of defense in depth—on deep supply lines, secure bases, and technological overmatch. But hypersonic weapons make distance significantly less relevant. Geography no longer protects us. And in a world in which minutes separate detection from destruction, there is no room for error.

The spy ring in the Philippines wasn't gathering intelligence for trivial matters. It was drawing a kill list, a system of first-strike capability, powered by espionage, precision technology, and the ruthless logic of deterrence through dominance.

WHEN AIR Force Secretary Frank Kendall III delivered his address at the Air & Space Forces Association's Air, Space & Cyber Conference in September 2021, he had been in office only two months. A graduate of West Point with a master's degree in aerospace engineering from the California Institute of Technology and a law degree from Georgetown University, he had spent years in the private sector. But with previous stints directing tactical warfare programs and acquisition, technology, and logistics at the Pentagon, he was quick to learn. He needed to be. In his first month in office, his troops executed what he called "the largest evacuation of people in US history" in Afghanistan following the Biden administration's disastrous pullout from the country. In his spare time, he had received plenty of updates on China's military strength, which, in oblique terms, he shared with the packed conference crowd. His principal focus, as he explained in his address, was China and the threat its rapid military rise posed to the United States and the world at large. His number one concern was China's increasing capabilities to effectively deploy precision weapons. "For about 20 years," he said, "I've watched the range and target set for these weapons, their sophistication, and their inventories, increase.

"They have now gone from a few hundred miles to thousands to literally around the globe. They have gone from a few high value assets near China's shores to the second and third island chains, and most recently to intercontinental ranges and even to the potential for global strikes . . . strikes from space even."[2]

Kendall didn't give any specifics. That sort of information would undoubtedly have been classified. But intelligence sources soon began filling in the details about China's ability to strike from space. Two months after Kendall assumed command of the US Air Force, the People's Liberation Army's Rocket Force (PLARF) staged a critical test of groundbreaking weapons technology. It launched a

Long March rocket carrying a hypersonic glide vehicle (HGV) loaded with a live missile. About five hundred miles above the earth's surface, the zone scientists call low Earth orbit, where many satellites reside, the HGV was released. Traveling at an estimated seven thousand miles an hour, it circumnavigated most of the globe at altitudes beyond the detection of radar and early warning systems before re-entering the atmosphere.

As the HGV descended near China—part of a flight plan designed to deter monitoring by the West—its outer shell, experts estimate, increased to temperatures between three thousand and five thousand degrees Fahrenheit, the unavoidable result of friction at such supersonic speeds. Such blistering temperatures pose huge technical and engineering challenges to scientists working on hypersonics, forcing them to search for more stable materials and sleeker designs to ensure both structural and operational stability. The HGV did not melt or explode. It continued at a low trajectory, heading toward its target and releasing its payload.

That first demonstration of a long-range hypersonic bombing expedition wasn't 100 percent successful—such experimental tests rarely are. American and Asian intelligence sources reported that the missile had landed about twenty-five miles from its intended destination. In a combat situation, that might have been a misfire. To those in scientific, military, and intelligence circles, however, the result was anything but a failure; on the contrary, it was an astonishing achievement. Most importantly, China was learning—and learning quickly. Soon they would master their craft.

Buttressing USAF Secretary Kendall's remarks in September 2021, one baffled American intelligence source struggled to put these tests into perspective, making the demonstration sound, perhaps, nearly miraculous: "We have no idea how they did this."[3]

China's rapid development of this critical emerging technology wasn't an accident. It was the fruits of a meticulously executed campaign of targeted espionage extensively planned years before. The world's greatest superpower had stood by as its foremost strategic rival had brazenly stolen one of the technologies behind a critical new weapons system that could wreak havoc on future battlefields.

A Hypersonic Acquisition Primer

The precise details of how the PLA built its test hypersonic glide vehicle and fine-tuned what one analyst has termed an orbital glider
release system (OGRS)[4] remain largely unknown in the West. (A
spokesperson with the Chinese Ministry of Foreign Affairs later denied that the test had happened, insisting that the rocket launch had
been conducted merely to verify spacecraft reusability.[5]) But the way
the PLA amassed the knowledge and skill to leapfrog over American
hypersonic development so quickly should come as no surprise to
intelligence insiders.

The CCP's obsession with obtaining the plans for state-of-the-art
Department of Defense initiatives through sophisticated pairings of
HUMINT and cyberhacking operations, and pervasive cash-driven
talent acquisitions, has been relentless. But a good deal of hypersonics know-how has been cribbed and delivered in plain sight, largely
driven by what political scientists and intelligence officers describe
as the CCP's Xi-mandated civil-military fusion: the use of academics, businessmen, and tech professionals to steal technology for the
benefit of the country's military force. The goal in all these operations
remains the same: to target critical defense technologies, often
developed using billions of dollars of US funds, and steal them to advance China's military capabilities and erode US and Western air and
sea dominance. Chinese dominance in space is the newest domain in
which the country seeks to overtake the United States and its allies.
As military experts underscore, it's the ultimate high ground. Establishing domination in this theater could provide China a decisive
advantage in the event of any future kinetic conflict with the United
States. Imagine Pearl Harbor, but a surprise attack not on ships but
rather satellites. In such a scenario, American forces would be ren-
dered effectively blind before any amphibious invasion of Tawain.
What you can't see, you can't shoot.

For years, hypersonic missiles, defined as ballistic devices moving
up to five and twenty-five times the speed of sound, have transfixed
the imaginations of military strategists as a next-generation warfare tool. The tactical advantages are obvious; a delivery system that

moves at extremely high speeds and can change course—as opposed to the predictable parabola patterns of most missiles—to hit its targets presents extraordinary deterrence problems for rival armies. How, for example, do you catch up with or intercept a missile that outpaces your own defense capabilities? Meanwhile, the extreme long-range capabilities of hypersonic missiles allows for them to be fired from Earth and then reenter the atmosphere from what has generally been a relatively less monitored military frontier, space.

Understandably concerned about such a extraterrestrial attack scenario, the Department of Defense has invested significantly in hypersonic detection technology. One firm in particular, HRL Laboratories, a Boeing and GE joint venture[6] based in Malibu, California, has been building "space-based missile warning and tracking, space-based surveillance, and airborne infrared countermeasures systems." Such sensors could be used to detect nuclear missile launches and track both ballistic and hypersonic missiles. In January 2023, HRL hired Chenguang Gong, an electrical engineer, to work as an application-specific integrated circuit (ASIC) manager responsible for tracking the design, development, and performance of readout integrated circuits used in the company's infrared sensors, a vital component for detecting and tracking missiles and other objects.[7]

After three months at HRL, Gong, who had been born in China and become a naturalized US citizen in 2011, announced that he was quitting the company, presenting his managers with a rarely heard "It's not you, it's me" rationale for doing so. He claimed that "he felt he was not doing a good job and [HRL] should hire someone better," an FBI agent later testified.[8]

HRL security immediately began evaluating Gong's computer and network history, eventually discovering that he had downloaded over three thousand company files onto personal storage drives only two weeks before submitting his resignation (the two-week window from when employees leave a firm is often the likeliest time frame for activity by insider threats). The company alerted the FBI, and Special Agent Igor Neyman began investigating. Many of the files were clearly marked as HRL property and designated as "Export Controlled" and "Proprietary Information." As if that wasn't clear enough, some files stated even more explicitly that they contained "technical data within the definition of the International Traffic in Arms Regulations and are subject to the export control laws of the U.S. Government." Other documents bore wording further warning that transmission "by any means to a foreign person, whether in the U.S. or abroad, without an export license or other approval from the U.S. Department of State, is prohibited."

According to court papers, Chenguang Gong didn't seem to care much about IP protection at large. His past employment record certainly made that clear. Prior to joining HRL, he had worked with several tech companies, and an FBI forensic analysis of his email communications indicated that he had been stealing documents—many also marked as proprietary—from his previous employers and used such stolen information to apply to several tech companies and CCP-sponsored talent programs from 2013 to 2020. In a proposal sent to the 38th Research Institute of China Electronics Technology Group Corporation, a high-tech research institute in Beijing, for instance, Gong allegedly offered to make high-performance analog-to-digital converters similar to those produced by his American employer. He noted that the global market for those products "is basically monopolized by several companies in the United States" and that the export of those items from the United States requires a "government export license." In 2019, subsidized by talent program organizers, following a familiar modus operandi of the Chinese intelligence playbook, Gong traveled to China twice to participate in conferences. In 2020, he also reportedly pitched to his perspective Chinese partners manufacturing "low light/night vision" image sensors for use in military night vision goggles and civilian applications and provided clips of a sensor developed by Fairchild Imaging,[9] his employer from 2015 to 2019. Apparently HRL had missed these red flags in their pre-employment background screenings and paid the price for not doing so.

During interviews with the FBI, Gong lied repeatedly about his actions, according to Special Agent Neyman, and frequently changed his story. At that point, he had already accepted a job at HRL's primary competitor, a career move that made his file copying even more suspect. He started work on May 1, 2024, but ten days later, after learning that Gong had transferred files onto personal storage devices, the new company terminated him. On February 7, 2024, just days before Gong's planned trip to China, he was indicted for theft of trade secrets.[10] Meanwhile, according to Neyman, the whereabouts of two of the three storage devices Gong allegedly used to transfer the files on the sensitive schematics for tracking hypersonic missiles, and therefore enabling the means to defend against them by American forces, remain unknown. One can only presume where they most likely ended up.

Remember Los Alamos

The Los Alamos National Laboratory, located thirty-five miles northwest of Santa Fe, New Mexico, is funded and administered by the Department of Energy's National Nuclear Security Administration. Launched in secret in 1943 as the classified Manhattan Project site to develop the atomic bomb, it's the top government-funded research facility in the United States. With a mandate to address national security challenges through the development of cutting-edge science and technology, the Los Alamos Laboratory houses ten research facilities, a classified research library, and a workforce of about eighteen thousand people.

In 2024, the laboratory wore its heart on its sleeve, or at least its website, broadcasting its System Technology Modernization mission to align with the nuclear deterrence objectives of the United States. In the list of ten initiatives, hypersonic research clocked in at number nine. The lab declared its intent to conduct payload and systems integration with hypersonic platforms and invest in hypersonic flight analysis and platform design. It also specified working with Texas A&M University's University Consortium for Applied Hypersonics.[11]

Los Alamos Laboratory didn't have the best track record at keeping vital national security secrets secure. It had previously been at the center of a state secrets theft case involving Wen Ho Lee, who was suspected of delivering nuclear warhead plans to the PLA. (Lee, who repeatedly denied any wrongdoing, ultimately pled guilty to mishandling restricted data in exchange for the dropping of fifty-nine other counts against him.) Analysts suspect this espionage likely played a key role in China advancing its nuclear weapons program. Washington was, at the time, rightly outraged and duly launched an investigation into how such a critical breach could have occurred. Any lessons learned or recommendations on strengthening security protocols for employees at the lab with access to sensitive information weren't, apparently, adopted.

Indeed, Lee's theft of nuclear warhead secrets wasn't the only presumed material security breach. Incredibly, Dr. Chen Shiyi, a leading scientist supporting the PLA's efforts to research and develop hypersonic weapons, served as the deputy director of the Center for Nonlinear Studies at Los Alamos in the 1990s as an Oppenheimer Fellow. Chen, a world-renowned expert in fluid dynamics and turbulence, returned to China in 2001 and was rewarded with a coveted appointment: director of the State Key Laboratory for Turbulence and Complex Systems at Peking University. There he directed a government-funded lab that helped develop the PRC's hypersonic glide vehicle by, among other things, building the first hypersonic wind tunnel in China. It is not difficult to connect the dots on Chen's role in the PRC's hypersonics program and his previous role in Los Alamos. One could reasonably surmise that the knowledge Chen gained there played a key role in enabling the PRC's eventual eclipse of the United States in hypersonic R&D.

Chen wasn't done just yet. In January 2015, Chen was named president of the Southern University of Science and Technology (SUST) in Shenzhen, where he has fixated on recruiting former Los Alamos staff. During his first seven years at SUST, fifteen scientists from Los Alamos joined the school, including four permanent staffers, ten postdoctoral researchers, and a visiting scholar. Intrigued by a report that the influx from the US-funded program had been dubbed the "Los Alamos Club" within Chinese circles, Strider Technologies, the American security and intelligence firm with headquarters in Utah, conducted a deep dive into the aggressive Chinese recruiting campaign focused on the lab's staff.

Strider found that Chen, who has not been formally accused of any wrongdoing, had prioritized the hiring of Zhao Yusheng, an eighteen-year Los Alamos veteran who had led a joint DOE/DOD research project to use high-pressure materials to improve the designs of warheads capable of penetrating deep into the earth. In addition to receiving $19.8 million in US government grants for sensitive research,[12] he'd been given DOE clearance to receive top secret restricted data and national security information.

Another Los Alamos veteran, Shan Xiaowen, reunited in Shenzhen with Chen at SUST. At Los Alamos, the duo had collaborated on studies of computational fluid dynamics to determine how particles move around vehicles, an essential component of aerospace design. Later at SUST, Shan was named chair of the Department of Mechanics and Aerospace Engineering and then put in charge of the school's Tech Intelligent Aviation R&D Center in 2019.

The extent of the brain drain from New Mexico across the Pacific as found by Strider's investigation was staggering. As of 2022, 162 scientists who once worked at Los Alamos in some official capacity had returned to work in China, according to Strider's report. Again, while none of this selected group has been formally charged with violating US law, circumstantial evidence suggests deeply concerning ties to the CCP. At least seventeen Los Alamos alumni, including thirteen permanent staff members at the American research center, were accepted into the CCP-sanctioned Thousand Talents Program, the 2008 IP acquisition initiative to recruit leading scientists, academics, and entrepreneurs from around the world to "share" their expertise in China. Overseen by the CCP Central Committee Organization Department,[13] the Thousand Talents Program (TTP) was the signature program, literally ten times the size of the Chinese Academy of Sciences' Hundred Talents program launched in 1994, to lure foreign scientists to China for a minimum of six months of paid research. The TTP launched with a bang, unveiling separate programs for youths (targeting future academics), overseas high-level experts (academics), innovative talents (for academics and commercial talents), and entrepreneurs (commercial talents only). The program's doctrinal origins could have been pulled from Sun Tzu's *The Art of War*, which advised Chinese rulers to recruit "living spies" who can travel back and forth among the enemy's camp.

While on the surface the TTP, along with dozens of similar state-run talent programs in the PRC, are publicly described as initiatives to promote academic collaboration, their ultimate mission is to operate as fronts for technology espionage operations. Under the guise of education and sharing, these programs target experts in specific technologies and provide funding, lab, and even corporate support in exchange for IP transfer guided by Made in China 2025 as the master collection plan.

In 2019, the Thousand Talents Program was rebranded. It was probably a wise move. In the eleven years since it had been launched, the program had generated one negative story after another, as its "talents" had been caught participating in various acts of espionage, trade theft, and fraud schemes. Rename, obfuscate, and continue with the attack. It's a classic ploy of the CCP and modus operandi for the MSS. The mission of the TTP wasn't changed in any material way. It was simply rebranded and assigned to the Ministry of Science and Technology, folded in with dozens of less prominent but equally cash-happy recruitment schemes, including BRI Educational, Culture, and Health Intellect Recruitment Program; the National Major S&T Special Talent Recruitment Program; the Overseas Famous Teachers Plan; and the Key Educational Intellect Recruitment Plan, to name a few.[14]

While many of the "experts" targeted by the TTP have connections to China via birth or family, the IP-focused organization does not discriminate. Dr. Charles Lieber, the former chair of the Department of Chemistry and Chemical Biology at Harvard University, signed a contract with the Thousand Talents Program from 2012 to 2017, according to a Department of Justice indictment.[15] He was paid handsomely; his three-year deal provided a salary of $50,000 per month, living expenses of up to 1,000,000 Chinese yuan (approximately $158,000 at the time), and $1.5 million to establish a research lab at the Wuhan University of Technology (WUT). Lieber was never prosecuted for handing over technology or engaging in an explicit act of espionage. Instead, his alleged crime centered around making false statements to DOJ investigators about his involvement with the talent group.[16] Lieber is considered one of the leading experts on nanotechnology and would eventually end up back in China heading up another university research center there. Similarly, Dr. James Patrick Lewis pled guilty to defrauding West Virginia University after signing his Thousand Talents Program deal. Lured by a talent program offer of a $143,000 living subsidy, an $86,000 annual salary, and a $573,000 research grant, he requested time off from his university job to care for his newborn child but instead spent the time secretly working in China.[17]

There are other kinds of talent programs; some recruit from the West, and others, such as the China Scholarship Council (CSC), send Chinese students into academic programs abroad. In 2024, the Department of Defense noted that the CSC "compels scholarship recipients to acquire advanced technologies, some of which have military applications" and awards funding to active-duty PLA members. "Some CSC-funded students have openly stated their intent to use collected technologies and proprietary knowledge to benefit PRC institutions.[18] America's open university and research communities have been ruthlessly exploited by the CCP to reap the benefits of Western academic collaboration to fuel and advance its own scientific progress. China's extensive poaching of researchers at America's preeminent government and military research lab working on hypersonic-related technologies underscores this point like few others.

Security Undersight

L. J. Eads, a former US Air Force intelligence officer and signals analyst with a background in programming, spent years studying satellite- and missile-related telemetry—the art of tracking and analyzing the signals of ground, air, and space weapon systems. Since leaving the service, he has focused on tracking US-funded science and technology collaborations that have yielded or contributed to academic papers that have ties to PLA-supported institutions. He now manages the Sino-American Hypersonic Vehicle Research Collaborations Tracker, which catalogs articles written by and with Chinese researchers with ties to both US academia and the

PLA. For intelligence operatives who have no idea how the PLA leap-frogged over the United States in hypersonic weapons development, Eads's tracker suggests that lax American university policies and the US government's failure to enforce its own laws about technology transfer are complicit.

In 2011, Congress passed the Wolf Amendment, proposed by Rep-resentative Frank Wolf (R–Virginia), which prevents NASA research from benefiting China's space program. Wolf didn't appear to be mo-tivated primarily by preventing the transfer of leading US technology to China; he was more interested in using the legislation as leverage to force Beijing to improve its horrific record on human rights and re-ligious freedom.[19] The thought of NASA sharing any form of sensitive research with Soviet Russia during the Cold War would have seemed beyond absurd. But most in Washington hadn't yet come to see the CCP in the same light.

Whatever the motivation, the amendment passed, and its most recent iteration prevents using government funds for NASA, the White House Office of Science and Technology Policy (OSTP), or the National Space Council to collaborate with, host, or coordinate bi-laterally with China or Chinese-owned companies—unless the FBI certifies that there is no risk of information sharing and that none of the Chinese officials involved have been determined by the United States to have direct involvement with violations of human rights.

This policy has been controversial in certain scientific quarters, particularly among think tank idealists who advocate that the U.S. and China unite to conquer space together in an efficient, mutually beneficial outcome. This utopian fantasy, however, ignores decades of China's one-way policy of technology acquisition. Underscoring that one-way vision, the Ministry of Science and Technology's offshoot, the Institute of Scientific and Technical Information of China (ISTIC) has begun instituting its own proprietary Digital Object Identifier (DOI) system. The "Chinese DOI" eschews the internationally accepted DOI system used by the global science community to track and locate research documents.[20] Why go to such lengths to create a separate entity? "They want to keep a lot of their flow of information between their own institutes, enterprises, universities, their military—more private within their own DOI system," Eads explained.[21]

The Wolf Amendment *should* in fact be controversial—but for very different reasons. It's a paper tiger. Its language forbids the establishment of bilateral partnerships between NASA recipients and Chinese institutions. But it says nothing about *multilateral* partnerships. This provides a work-around, Eads explained, if a NASA grantee has a bilateral partner that in turn collaborates with an institution that has a relationship with a Chinese university. In such cases there is nothing to stop the Chinese third party from gaining access to all the research results and disseminating them further.

The scale and depth of NASA's research is not trivial. Its 2025 budget awards $279 million for research into advanced air vehicles, more than a quarter of its aeronautics research funding.[22] It also recently handed a $10 million grant to Wichita State University's National Institute for Aviation Research (NIAR) to develop advanced materials for hypersonic applications. This is particularly concerning, says Eads, given the school's apparent history of skirting the Wolf Amendment's intent. According to Eads, one principal administrator at Wichita State University has directed several NASA grants totaling over $8 million for collaboration efforts with institutions in the PRC, including at least two suspect 2024 collaborations.[23] The first, with CNPC Engineering Technology R&D Company Limited of Beijing, studied the performance characteristics to improve predictive degradation modeling of various products.[24] Why is that potentially problematic? "The development of granular aerogels for sound absorption could inform the design of hypersonic systems by improving shockwave and vibration management," Eads explained. Less sound means harder to detect, and harder to detect means greater lethality. Given the extent of the PLA's collaboration with virtually all universities in China, the chances seem high, if not inevitable, that this "shared" research could easily end up in the hands of Chinese military researchers developing the country's emerging weapons technologies.

The other potentially problematic grant involved research with WanDong Medical, part of the Chinese home appliance company

Midea Group, on high-tech hybrid sound absorbers with "potential applications" that include "soundproofing packages for aircraft."[25]

Until President Trump issued National Security Presidential Memorandum 33, requiring agencies conducting US government–supported research and development to strengthen their security measures against foreign government interference and exploitation,[26] the United States had no research security policy in place, Eads said, adding, "This is kind of mind-boggling, but agencies like IARPA [Intelligence Advanced Research Projects Activity] and DARPA funded basic research for the US intelligence and defense community, and traditionally, the only security around that research has been focused on export control. DARPA might be directly funding or co-funding Chinese research on a physics study. But as long as we don't give them some US government IP that's under export control, the project will be fine."[27] Such seemingly obvious controls and security measures are no doubt welcomed by those intent on protecting America's vital research. But a lot of damage has already been done.

Eads, who is the director of research intelligence at Parallax Advanced Research, a national security advisory firm, attributes America's previous fast-and-loose attitudes to political policy. "It seems pretty obvious that knowledge and research information we produce could fuel an adversary's military. But for some time, maybe before China's buildup, we were trying to become really good friends with China, hoping they could become more democratic like the United States and become close allies. So a lot of political aspects impacted where we're at today."[28] It was an epic miscalculation by Washington about the threat posed by collaborating in sensitive research with a foreign partner, and one that would endanger American national security for decades to come.

A Pentagon Paper

In December 2024, the Department of Defense issued its annual report to Congress on the PRC's military capabilities. It did not mince words around the significance of China's rapid advancement in hypersonics: "The PRC has the world's leading hypersonic missile arsenal and has dramatically advanced its development of conventional and nuclear-armed hypersonic missile technologies during the past 20 years."[29] It is worth noting that no mention is made of who helped it make those advances. The complicity of America's own research institutions, whether intentionally or unintentionally, in helping the CCP achieve this remarkable feat was glaringly left absent in the report.

Star Wars 2.0?

One of the most powerful and successful weapons systems in US history was perhaps one that was never built.

When President Ronald Reagan announced the Strategic Defense Initiative (SDI) on March 23, 1983, he was believed by many to effectively begin a new form of arms race with our Cold War rivals in the USSR. The idea was considered either widely ambitious or wildly fictitious, depending on whom you asked—critics derided it as a sci-fi fantasy, calling it "Star Wars," while others maintained that it was critical to ensuring the United States could defend itself against a Soviet nuclear strike. The idea was that the United States would launch space-based X-ray lasers to blast Soviet nukes out of the air.[30] One metaphor at the time was that the lasers would constitute in effect a protective dome around America.

The program achieved several things. In the short term, it inspired talks of détente. Several years later, after the United States had spent tens of billions of dollars researching the project, the Soviet Union collapsed. The full story behind that collapse involved, among other explanatory causes, crop failure, a successful covert operation between the CIA and French intelligence to blow up the trans-Siberian pipeline, and a collaborative credit embargo to force the Kremlin into financial default.[31] But it remains an article of faith that the SDI particularly shook Soviet leadership to its core. It prompted a technological and financial arms race that the USSR's rickety economic realities simply could not sustain. Ten years after its announcement and four years after the collapse of the Berlin Wall, President Bill Clinton officially scrapped the initiative.

The advent of hypersonic technology and missiles has once again prompted the perceived need for missile defense systems. The ability of such missiles to enter space and then reenter the earth's atmosphere sparks serious questions about their ability to threaten America's deterrence capabilities—and the homeland itself. While mutually assured destruction (MAD) seems a relic of the Cold War, its theoretical underpinnings remain as relevant today as it was then, especially as China grows the stocks and capabilities of its own nuclear arsenal. Hypersonics, for all intents and purposes, appear at the center of a new arms race between great powers.

The implications of this race have already started to become manifest. One week after taking office on January 20, 2025, President Donald Trump signed an executive order to create a new space-based missile defense shield called the Golden Dome—a shout-out to Israel's similarly designed Iron Dome defense system. The document setting out the creation of the Golden Dome makes clear what it's primarily trying to defend against: "attack by ballistic, hypersonic, and cruise missiles . . . the most catastrophic threat facing the United States."[32] No doubt the sensitive missile detection sensor technology pilfered from the California-based HRL as described earlier would be relevant to such a defensive system.

Indeed, China's utilization of illicit research to advance its hypersonic program underscores the very real, and very serious, implications of the Great Heist. Stolen notes or research reports from some lab aren't trivial matters; they have the ability to, at their tail end, reshape the very balance of global power and threaten the very ability of America to deter nuclear powers. Hypersonic missiles are already shaping the outcomes of battles in Ukraine and the Middle East— both in Iran and Israel. But it's important to remember that the kinetic impact of such weapons is, ultimately, made material by ones and zeros, digital code and files contained on laptops and generated by the best brains in the world. In twenty-first century warfare, such information, like never before, *is* power. And for America to retain its mantle as the world's preeminent military superpower, baffled exasperations such as "we have no idea how they did this" about how rivals have rapidly advanced their lethal capabilities must never be allowed to happen again.

While critical to determining the outcome of battles, what the Chinese understand perhaps better than anyone is that military power remains one aspect of how wars or conflicts are won. Economic warfare can prove just as important, and Wall Street, largely unaware of the threat before it, would soon become the next frontier of Beijing's relentless espionage campaign.

CHAPTER 12

Financial Instruments of Destruction

Venture Capital and Private Equity

IN THE winter of 2015, in the Canadian winter wonderland two hours north of Vancouver that is Whistler Mountain, Peter Celinski lost sight of his two kids zipping down a ski run. They disappeared into trees, out of sight and out of earshot, forcing their concerned dad to follow suit. This particular instance of parental terror had an upside. As Celinski, a novice skier, struggled to reach the bottom of the run—where he did, in fact, reunite with his kids—he had an epiphany: Given that there had been so many digital and communications breakthroughs, there had to be a simple way for people to talk to each other while enjoying the great outdoors.[1]

Returning to a snow-free civilization—in this case, the San Francisco Bay area—Celinski surveyed the communications device market, looking at walkie-talkies, cell phones, and portable radios. What he found, ultimately, was a gap in the market. There was no lightweight, hands-free, wireless solution designed for active users—cyclists, runners, climbers, or, yes, skiers.

An Australian techie with a PhD in neural networking, Celinski had identified a market need with a wide array of commercial and even governmental user applications. Having previously worked for audio and telecommunication firms helped provide him the chops to innovate and create what he envisioned as the "GoPro of walkie-talkies," a simple, use-anywhere "group voice chat" device.

Celinski assembled a small team, named the device Milo, which also doubled as the name of the start-up company. Celinski sought $100,000 on Kickstarter to build sets of miniaturized lapel directional microphones linked together in a mesh network. The response was astounding; he raised $2.5 million, the fifth largest tech campaign in the site's history.[2]

With seventeen thousand orders on Kickstarter, the Milo team sought more investment. There was plenty of interest, but the easiest money came from an unexpected source, Shenzhen Capital Group, a large venture capital (VC) company owned by the Shenzhen municipal government and the second most active VC investment firm in China.[3]

The group wanted to invest $1 million. It asked for nothing in return, according to a source familiar with the company. No board seat. No management rights. No advisory role. Nothing. Once Milo approved the deal, the money showed up within a matter of days. No apparent strings were attached.

Two years later, as Milo was going into production, members of British Intelligence came calling. They thought Milo's mesh network system, which didn't rely on a cellular network, had national security applications for potential surveillance team communications. It would be difficult to hack by adversaries. As intriguing as that relationship was, profitability for Milo would begin with the sale of seventy thousand units or more, not an order in the dozens, which was what British Intelligence expressed interest in (or at least could afford). Unlike the CCP-run China, the United Kingdom doesn't have dozens of government-backed VC firms that the British Security Service (MI5) or the Secret Intelligence Service (MI6) could turn to. Nor were they empowered or funded to invest in start-ups or act as a private VC firm themselves, regardless of the critical nature of the technological capability they were after.

A new idea surfaced. In-Q-Tel, the not-for-profit VC firm funded by Congress to develop sophisticated software, infrastructure, and material sciences for US security and intelligence organizations, might be a perfect fit for Milo's ingenious technology. In-Q-Tel was intrigued by Milo's capabilities and decided to invest in the technology with an eye toward developing it further for inhospitable environments and determining if the communications from the devices could be encrypted to the required standards for military or intelligence operations. Milo's team was thrilled by the possibility of working with In-Q-Tel and opening up entirely new business opportunities. It appeared to be a perfect match for both parties.

But as soon as In-Q-Tel discussions began—more than two years after Shenzhen Capital's investment—the phone started ringing off the hook. Suddenly, the silent VC backer wanted access to the sensitive research-and-development records.

Shenzhen Capital Group's timing was beyond curious; it was downright suspicious. According to a consultant brought in to help facilitate the In-Q-Tel relationship, it was clear that nefarious actors with ties to the VC firm had already gained illicit access to Milo's internal communications.

One possible option for the firm was to chart a course to exit Shenzhen Capital Group and remove it from the cap table altogether by buying its share out. But that proved to be easier said than done. Another was to restructure Milo in a manner that would dilute the Chinese investment. That was problematic because even with a dilution Shenzhen would still be an investor in Milo and remain an inside threat.

Ultimately, a security sweep resulted in a profound disappointment for Milo's leadership team. "It's too late, fellas," the consultant concluded. "They're already in your system and reading your internal communications, which is how they learned about national security opportunities."

The dilemma was painfully obvious. A fox-in-the-henhouse scenario had emerged; by accepting an investment from a firm with funding ties to the CCP, Milo had unwittingly set in motion a possible security vulnerability. Thereafter, any contract, whether it be for the US or British governments, would be untenable. Not only were future security capabilities for Western governments impacted, but the company's bottom line also inevitably suffered as a result. Both American public and private sector interests took a hit.

Infiltration by Cash Infusion

The story of Milo, which was named one of 2022's best inventions by *Time*, is instructive because it provides a window into how and why the CCP and MSS have aggressively entered American capital markets to turbocharge their technological development.

One central element of spycraft involves creating a "cover" for agents and sources who obtain intelligence. If an operation goes wrong, a good cover can allow operatives to paint a picture of "plausible deniability"; in other words, credentials that, for example, prove that they are academic researchers, not intelligence operators. An effective cover also unlocks access to persons or information that would otherwise be difficult if not impossible to access.

The CCP's tech investment strategy—to target real people with real money (but secretly working for the CCP)—has proven to be an effective use of such covers. The open nature of Western capital markets provides a natural built-in alibi for such Chinese operatives; they are cloaked in capital that can open doors like nothing else. Embedding in VCs and investment vehicles is a cost-effective, and legitimate, cover for CCP actors to engage with the sprawling tech ecosystems across America and the breakthrough (often dual-use) technologies and IP they are developing.

One such example is the state-owned China Investment Corporation (CIC), founded in 2007, which manages approximately $1 trillion in assets and frequently invests in private companies and start-ups that typically face limited scrutiny by regulators—especially when compared to defense majors like Lockheed Martin or Raytheon. The CIC's investments offer an aboveboard pipeline for acquisition that aligns with the CCP's strategic goals of improving and onshoring China's technology capabilities while expanding its industrial capacity (as outlined, naturally, in Made in China 2025). With such commercial cover, the potential accusation that the CIC is illicitly targeting investments to obtain coveted technology can be easily brushed aside. The Chinese firm can insist that it is simply playing by the rules of the free market, making informed speculative bets to grow its capital and generate returns for investors.

The decision to weaponize investment in the tech sector is a logical extension of the CCP-sponsored Thousand Talents Program, which sought to access the creators of high-value intellectual property at US universities and research laboratories. Such talent recruitment was an excellent strategy, since gaining access to human sources is usually the most effective tool in the intelligence-gathering playbook. But access to companies with digital networks housing their most sensitive IP can oftentimes provide even faster, safer pathways for technology acquisition.

Those targets often include innovative, cash-thirsty American start-ups—companies working on cutting-edge next-generation technology, be it in telecommunications, like Milo, drug therapies, robotics, or AI. Accessing these companies is not, strictly speaking, a covert MSS operation; rather, it is a conscious state-level exploitation of capitalism that, at least initially, plays by the rules of the Western financial system's game.

In the 1990s the CCP allowed investment trust companies to raise foreign cash by selling shares of vast portfolios. At the same time, CCP General Secretary Jiang Zemin began espousing a new vision for growth called Going Out, which called for Chinese enterprises to expand and invest overseas. His policy gradually metastasized within the CCP's domestic and global frameworks. The vast majority of Chinese foreign investment was controlled by state-owned enterprises (SOEs); still, by 2005, more than seven thousand Chinese enterprises—doubtless many with ties to SOEs—had invested in 160 countries and regions. Much of this investment was focused on the developing world, especially Africa, where China had quickly come to see the continent's strategic value particularly in resources like rare earth minerals.[4]

In 2007, China established the China Investment Corporation

(CIC), its sovereign wealth fund, debuting with an initial capitalization of $200 billion. Nearly half the pool, $90 billion, was for overseas investment.[5] Deng Xiaoping may have been the CCP visionary behind technology acquisition, but Jiang determined that Going Out was the most efficient and rapid means of gathering advanced technology and armed the CIC with the funds to launder both legal and illicit acquisitions.

The fund got right to work. By the end of 2010, according to China's Ministry of Commerce, more than thirteen thousand Chinese investing entities had established sixteen thousand overseas enterprises in 178 countries and regions. In 2010, Chinese enterprises cut 188 mergers and acquisition deals totaling $38 billion, frequently targeting European firms. Nanjing Automobile purchased MG Rover, Geely Global bought Volvo, and PetroChina brokered a joint venture with Great Britain's Ineos, then the fourth largest chemicals company in the world.

Starting in 2011, however, investment began to shift its crosshairs toward the United States. When Made in China 2025 debuted four years later, it codified many policy moves that were already in play. The decisive document called for supporting "enterprises that carry out mergers and acquisitions (M&A), equity investment and venture capital investment overseas." It also advocated boosting "qualified enterprises that issue stocks and bonds overseas and encourage various forms of technical cooperation with overseas enterprises."[6]

For the SOEs, as well as private ventures, identifying the most promising venues for resource exploration in the twenty-first century was not rocket science; it was more like simple arithmetic, or for a CCP apparatchik, like running a query on Baidu's search engine. The most fertile investment arena on the planet was Silicon Valley. There, giant VC institutions such as Sequoia Capital, Kleiner Perkins, and Andreessen Horowitz amassed and deployed billions of dollars to "seed" start-up enterprises across America with cash with the hope of reaping huge payouts, lucrative acquisitions, or, in the worst cases, loss-leading write-offs. The CCP's SOEs simply had to do three things to ensure access to innovative IP was all but guaranteed: scour the start-up terrain to find relevant tech, make the investments, and avoid the Committee on Foreign Investment in the United States (CFIUS) while doing so.

The numbers tell the story: In 2011, Chinese investments in US tech companies totaled $0.3 billion. By the end of 2015, the year Xi unveiled Made in China 2025 as a ten-year plan, that number was already $9.9 billion. That same year, Chinese investors backed 188 US tech start-ups, another record.[7]

Coincidentally—or, more likely, predictably—2015 was the year Shan Xiangshuang, the mustachioed billionaire founder and chairman of the "government-approved" private equity and fund-managing CSC Group, launched Hone Capital in the United States. Under Shan, who had begun his career as a CCP member, CSC allocated $115 million for the fund and instructed Veronica Wu, his Beijing-born, US-educated strategist and newly appointed Hone managing partner, to invest in hundreds of high-quality early-stage start-ups as fast as possible. In a matter of months, Hone became a powerful investment force, if not one of the top seed investors, in the American start-up landscape.

It did so by surveying the VC sector and executing brilliant takeovers. Wu, who'd previously worked on Apple, Motorola, and Tesla's Chinese ventures, initially struggled to answer an existential question: "How do we access the top deals so that we can build that network of trust?" A friend, and consultant in the industry, mentioned a possible solution to tapping into the pipeline of the most intriguing early-stage targets: AngelList, a website that had begun as a hybrid job board/social network for start-ups and had morphed into an all-things-early-stage investment portal. Wu's friend suggested the site "might be an interesting hack into the VC scene."[8]

Wu was blown away. "The platform provided access to a unique network of super connected people," she said. "We also saw the huge potential of the data that AngelList had. There's not a lot of visibility into early seed deals, and it's difficult to get information about them. I saw it as a gold mine of data that we could dig into." It wouldn't be the first, or last, time China effectively used open-source intelligence (OSINT) as part of the Great Heist.

Hone cut a reported $80 million deal to become AngelList's largest institutional shareholder, and CSC's website in turn bragged about opening the "Silicon Valley express."[9] Over the next three years, CSC reportedly committed $400 million to Hone for start-up investments and real estate deals, resulting in deals with 360 companies. This included partial ownership of the payments platform Stripe, the driverless-car maker Cruise, and Boom, the Colorado-based maker of supersonic passenger planes. At one point, ten Hone-funded companies were privately valued at $1 billion or more, including two that went public.[10]

After hitting a peak investment of $20 billion in VC ventures in 2018, China's mania for American start-ups cooled slightly. In 2020, VC firms participated in 247 rounds of funding for start-ups, including 54 deals in financial and business services and 52 for firms in the health, pharmaceuticals, and biotech space. For fast-rising juggernaut Hone Capital, things began to devolve with surprising speed. Starting in 2019, with CSC experiencing fiscal troubles in China, Hone began selling off some stakes and transferring others to another CSC company. Soon, Hone dismissed Veronica Wu and CFO Purvi Gandhi from the company and in 2020 socked them with a suit alleging that they had been engaged in fiduciary mismanagement and fraud regarding a Hone subsidiary called Upshot.[11] The two former executives, who have not been charged with a crime and declined to comment due to ongoing litigation, have spent the past five years battling Hone in court. In 2024, it appeared that the bad blood had spilled over into the realm of national security concerns. The FBI had begun an investigation to see "whether Hone Capital accessed information about the technology, finances or clients of start-ups for the benefit of its Beijing-based owner or Chinese authorities," according to a *Financial Times* report.[12] As is typically the case in the shadowy world of espionage, the evidence connecting the VC investments and the ultimate acquisition of its related IP by actors directly within the PRC remains circumstantial—but ominous nonetheless.

Of obvious concern was Hone's connection to Boom, the American company based in Denver developing a supersonic liner, which has government contracts with the US Air Force and NASA. Had

Hone's $10 million investment created an opening for IP acquisition? Boom executives have dismissed the idea, the *Financial Times* reported. But court papers raise a credible albeit sinister specter, with Wu alleging that Hone's management had incentivized investment in technologies with "critical intellectual property" and that she had been fired in 2020 for reporting "violations of laws and regulations and she refused to take part in the same."[13]

Interestingly, Wu openly discussed the perils and pitfalls of welcoming Chinese investment into the Western financial ecosystem in a 2017 interview posted on CSC's site. She suggested that some such deals would have likely unintended consequences: "Founders should be careful not to accept Chinese money before they understand the trade-offs. Chinese investors tend to want to own a big part of the company, to be on the board, and to have a say in the company. And it might not be good for a company to give up that kind of power, because it could dramatically affect the direction of the company, for good or bad. It's smart to insist on keeping your freedom."[14] Give her points for honesty. Masked behind relatively benign platitudes, the embedded warning for foreign firms was there: Conduct business with Chinese entities at your own risk.

The news of possible Hone misdeeds did not surprise anyone at the US National Counterintelligence and Security Center (NCSC). In late July 2024, the NCSC issued a two-page bulletin warning that foreign adversaries were investing in start-ups to obtain critical data, technology, and intellectual property that might threaten national security. The alert specifically called out the Chinese government for directing the investment in and acquisition of US companies by China-based firms "to support PRC state plans." It specified that "VC investment from China has focused on U.S. emerging technology sectors like Artificial Intelligence and other PRC government priorities." The alert also relayed reports of China-based VC firms' targeting and paying "employees of U.S. startups to acquire technology, then fund competitors in China who try to monetize the stolen technology."[15] The NCSC report may go some way toward explaining why, in January 2024, the Department of Defense (DOD) added IDG Capital, a China-based VC/private equity firm, to its roster of

"Chinese military companies" operating directly or indirectly in the United States. The government warning was meant to make clear to US private sector entities about just whom they were working with.[16] As noted earlier, the investment arena is the perfect cover for PRC-aligned actors to obtain both legal and illegal technology IP. A monetary investment—or just the potential of a monetary investment—operates as a key to open access to sensitive information. It opens doors to IPO prospectuses and pitch decks that are often hard to come by. Such "cover for status," in spy parlance, creates a "legitimate" forum for further discussion, exploration, and requests, because *any* investor (naturally) wants to understand what they are investing in.

When a Chinese firm invests in a US tech start-up, it *might* be a purely profit-seeking investment. But if that firm has ties to state-backed funding, CCP bigwigs, or a state-owned enterprise, it can be reasonably assumed that the Chinese government will eventually get its hands on the information derived from the tech start-ups. If enough intelligence of value is gathered, the investors might not even need to make any actual financial investment. If they learn the names and email addresses of the start-up's tech team in early stages of due diligence, for instance, they can keep their money and use that information to target key employees. Or they can hire hackers to phish their way into the start-up's network to steal it electronically. Because so much of the tech start-up world exists in the shadows and so many start-ups are cash strapped, guarding against such tactics can prove extremely difficult.

Hone Capital, sticking to the CCP playbook of constant denial of any wrongdoing, is one of hundreds of Chinese investment funds that are amassing vital technology. Plowing capital into a company does not entitle investors to access its trade secrets. You can't buy stock in Apple and demand access to future iPhone specs. But, as apparently happened in the case of Milo, Chinese investment funds can pony up enough cash to gain at least some access to start-ups. And that puts them in a better position to later acquire more sensitive IP using that initial access to the firm's business plans.

While Hone aims to cast a wide net in the hopes of future gains—in effect a *spray-and-pray* investment method—others, such as Hou An Innovation Fund, are more clearly aligned with specific tech acquisition goals of the CCP. Formed in 2017 with backing from CIC, the CCP-driven Silk Road Fund, and the Shenzhen government-owned Shum Yip Group,[17] Hou An also attracted investments by private institutions, including Hopu Investment Management Company. It then approached the Japanese behemoth SoftBank about creating a new division of Arm, the British software and semiconductor firm that SoftBank had acquired in 2016.[18]

The deal for Arm China, which gave Chinese investors 51 percent ownership, was replete with national security issues from the very get-go given the nature of Arm's product. The company manufactures Advanced RISC Machine processors—robust, sophisticated semiconductor chips that underpin cell phones and other mobile technologies, as well as the architecture for chip design. The company's market share was sizeable. In 2022, 29.2 billion chips based on Arm architecture were used in more than 95 percent of smartphones, 63 percent of Internet of Things devices, and 24 percent of cars.[19] This means that Arm plans and components are integrated with the major players in the microprocessor sector, providing tech for Nvidia graphics processing units (GPUs), automotive systems, and aerospace applications. Perhaps most critically, Arm GPUs and chip architecture can be utilized in the industrial automation of chip manufacturing. As of 2023, Arm was "still the leader in supplying technology to Chinese firms developing processor chips," according to a microchip industry analyst.[20]

Arm China's semiconductor-manufacturing equipment aligns perfectly with the goals of Made in China 2025. To achieve "the transformation and upgrading of the manufacturing industry," the strategy calls for China to develop its own ability to design, build, and export products free from any reliance on foreign firms. Such strategic autonomy, Xi surely surmised, will allow China to survive any attempts by the United States to "decouple" from its economy or retaliate with a barrage of economic sanctions like it did against Russia in 2022 following its invasion of Ukraine should Beijing undertake a similar action against Taiwan.

The United States now bans the use of American-owned technologies in China that enable the production of semiconductor-manufacturing equipment or semiconductor microchips to "train frontier AI models that have the most significant potential for advanced warfare applications."[21] Those applications include a slew of frightening, futuristic-sounding weapons that loom in the not-too-distant future, including unmanned intelligent combat systems, enhanced battlefield hardware with advanced decision-making capabilities, automatic target recognition, precision guidance systems for hypersonic missiles, and high-speed orchestrated cyberattacks. The US ban aims to prevent the production of sophisticated microchips with high performance density—the amount of computing power packed into a given area of a microchip—or those built for data centers from reaching China's military-industrial complex.

The Arm/SoftBank joint venture created numerous headaches for SoftBank as it set about trying to spin Arm into a separate IPO. Regulators objected to the existence of the joint venture, and SoftBank sought to win back control, something the CCP could not afford to let happen.

"China does not want to lose Arm at this juncture," said a Chinese official tied to Arm China. "The chip war between the US and China continues to escalate and Arm is a must-have ally for China's chip industry."[22] The PLA clearly understood what was at stake over the fate of who owned such companies and their IP.

OVER THE past twenty years, the CCP's non-traditional intelligence activities in financial markets have picked up speed, penetrating companies to collect valuable privileged data, much of it to expand government goals and fuel modernization of the PLA. Ironically, that expansion and modernization have been underwritten by capital infusions from another source: American investors.

There is an inescapable circular irony that should be self-evident to anyone examining the CCP's use of capital markets in its IP theft campaign. As documented earlier, American politicians and businessmen sought to help "open" China to investment because they were in search of profits and because many believed—despite the evidence of Tiananmen Square—that increased trade would promote democratic change in the PRC. Then, over decades, a cause-and-effect reaction occurred: China became the manufacturing hub of the entire world and the destination of billions of dollars of capital, which funded China's rise and compelled American financial institutions to pour more money (and technology) into Chinese companies, further propelling the CCP forward in its goal to outpace American military and economic power.

So America's pursuit of profits—of capital—has been weaponized against our own national interests. It's a powerful lure. In 2005, Neil Shen, a Chinese-born trader with a Yale MBA and buffed résumé, got the backing of two Sequoia Capital partners to launch Sequoia China. Launched in 1972, Sequoia Capital had scored huge returns on early-stage investments in Apple, Atari, and Google, to name just a few. But by any metric, the new division's numbers were impressive. Shen's division produced huge wins with a diverse portfolio, with funds yielding as much as 37% in annualized returns. But over the years, some of Sequoia China's bets were placed on companies that some critics said operated in gray areas and out-and-out red zones. It reportedly helped raise $700 million for 4Paradigm, a Chinese company building AI for PLA battlefield programs; invested in dozens of Chinese semiconductor firms, and invested in DJI, a Chinese drone maker used by CCP for surveillance of China's Uyghur Muslim population. In 2014, it bought a chunk of ByteDance, the company that owns the social media giant TikTok, and evidently alerted the home office, which also plunked down money on the firm. Since then, TikTok's vast reach on American cell phones, its perceived algorithmic power, and its data collection abilities have made it "a potential threat vector," according to John F. Plumb, a top Defense Department cyberthreat adviser.[23]

In 2023, perhaps aware of geopolitical trade winds and its holdings' potential for bad optics, Sequoia Capital spun off its China wing. HongShan Capital Group (HSG), the new entity, is still run by Neil Shen, but his attention may be diluted by his position on

ByteDance's board.[24] The separation was well timed; Sequoia China had caught the attention of the House Select Committee on the Strategic Competition Between the United States and the Chinese Communist Party, a bipartisan group formed in 2023 to study CCP threats and defend against its assaults on America. In October 2023 the committee sent a letter to two Sequoia Capital executives requesting additional details behind their "troubling investments." It noted that "for more than a decade, Sequoia Capital China's significant U.S. dollar investments in PRC entities have included certain investments that contributed to the CCP's human rights abuses, the PRC's military modernization, and its overall efforts to undermine U.S. technological leadership."[25] Washington was finally catching on to the threat posed by CCP activities in this new domain of economic competition.

Sequoia is not the only investment house to concern the Select Committee on the CCP. The committee issued an explosive report in 2024 laying out the billions of dollars of funding by US financial institutions to Chinese firms blacklisted or on watch lists for ties to China's military or CCP human rights abuses. Chief among the financial enablers flagged were two industry leading powerhouses: Morgan Stanley Capital International (MSCI), the world's foremost index provider, and BlackRock, the world's largest asset manager.

Asserting that MSCI's China indexes channel $3.7 billion into Chinese firms working against American interests and security, and that BlackRock had invested a minimum of $1.9 billion in similarly dubious companies, the committee wrote, "Index providers and asset managers both make decisions that result in the funding of PRC companies that support the People's Liberation Army (PLA) and the CCP's human rights abuses."[26] In the investment calculus of many Wall Street analysts, financial returns apparently trumped any patriotic sentiments or geopolitical concerns.

That apparently being the case, both companies claimed that they had "limited discretion to independently exclude specific problematic entities," according to the committee report. This lack of flexibility remains a mystery. There are no laws that we know of compelling companies to select and promote specific companies. In fact, the brokerage firm Charles Schwab reports that index listings change all the time. But apparently that flexibility doesn't apply to America's two biggest China funds. Perhaps these companies' hands are in fact tied by contracts or other agreements the public knows nothing about. BlackRock deny any wrongdoing. "With all investments in China and markets around the world, BlackRock complies with all applicable U.S. government laws. We will continue engaging with the Select Committee directly on the issues raised." MSCI did not issue a statement beyond saying it was studying the matter.[27] However, in 2024 the company's board of directors supported rejecting a shareholder's request for a report on whether listed index companies supplied goods or services to the Chinese military, calling it "unnecessary because our indexes are intended to measure market performance, are not investments or investment recommendations, are fully transparent to users of the indexes, and do not directly or indirectly fund the Chinese military."[28]

The concerns of the Select Committee on the CCP, as laid out in its report, appeared not to be assuaged by such public pronouncements on Wall Street: "It is time for Congress to pass legislation to prevent Americans' hard-earned savings and retirement dollars from funding a foreign adversary's military advancements and human rights abuses," it declared.[29] Given escalating tensions in the Taiwan Strait and China's blistering modernization of its military, which has no doubt been funded in at least some measure by American capital invested in the core technologies it now utilizes, such action by Washington can't come soon enough.

———

AS NOTED earlier in the chapter, in conducting its new form of economic espionage in the form of financial investments, the CCP has sought to avoid perhaps its greatest obstacle: the Committee on Foreign Investment in the United States (CFIUS), an interagency committee that exists to review foreign investments in US businesses as well as real estate purchases by foreigners near airports, harbors, military installations, and other government facilities. In other words, the committee has one primary function: to determine if a transaction will impair US national security and to try to stop it from happening if it will.

The stories we've looked at in this chapter are just a partial and illustrative demonstration of the CCP assaults on the financial and venture capital worlds taking place. Some, such as that of Milo, seem like above-board subterfuge, where an infiltration took place and no one knew it was happening. Some involve a mix of both subtle strategy and brute force, such as that of Hone's cornering of a market tool that identifies the most lucrative VC investment opportunities in Silicon Valley. Others, such as that of Arm China, are backed by sovereign capital, while yet others are enabled by a more old-fashioned American motive: a thirst for profit above all else. CFIUS, as far as we know, did not examine any of those deals. (And admittedly, the Arm deal was not in its jurisdiction.) But CFIUS exists for a very good reason, looming as a possible powerful alternative to the WTO's toothless reign and an antidote to China's malfeasance and American corporate cluelessness. While CFIUS is starting to step up to a greater degree in the face of China's unrelenting espionage campaign, it needs to act faster and bolder. The SEC should also move to begin delisting Chinese companies that pose serious security and investor protection risks. Quite simply, most Americans with 401(k)s or pensions don't want to invest in CCP-linked firms, in essence providing the capital for a geopolitical foe intent on defeating them. Beijing's unprecedented theft at scale of the personal health care data on nearly every American would drive this point home.

CHAPTER 13

The Health Care Assault

THE CREW used various weapons: programs and attacks with names out of a William Gibson cyberpunk novel or a *Matrix* movie—hacker exploits with names such as *Mudcarp, Bronze Mohawk,* and *Feverdream.* Other monikers were slightly less blaring but sounded even more sinister: GreenCrash, Hellsing, Kryptonite Panda, Leviathan, Periscope. Those were the crew's virtual crowbars, their tools of stealthy infiltration and exfiltration, that allowed them to get into computer systems and get out again without being caught. They'd been at it a long time and done a lot of damage—so much that in 2021, the FBI dubbed the group APT40, as in advanced persistent threat, and began plastering members' pictures on the Bureau's most wanted bulletins.[1] The Department of Justice indicted them on economic espionage and other charges.[2]

One of the APT40 team actors named by the FBI was Zhu Yunmin, a founding member. In the summer of 2009, he packed his bags and hauled them 1,600 miles south from Beijing to work in the Haikou office of the Hainan State Security Department (HSSD). When he got to the sunny, tropical port city southwest of Hong Kong, he met his fellow intelligence officer Ding Xiaoyang. They evidently shared a passion for computers and a boss with big plans for them.

Zhu wasted no time in gathering intelligence. A messy-haired desk jockey, he hunted for open-source documents regarding leadership and funding for the US Centers for Disease Control and Prevention, according to the indictment. By early October, just months after arriving at his intelligence post in Haikou, he began tracking the US State Department's Biosecurity Engagement Program. It was interesting, challenging work, like solving a jigsaw puzzle. He searched the internet, harvesting names and email addresses of scientists, experts, government officials, and websites, and divided them into various categories for future use.

To further support his work, Zhu appeared to get the go-ahead from his MSS supervisors to recruit potential hires and told a friend that he was on the lookout for talented hackers capable of launching network infiltration who were interested in a salary and benefits. Eventually the outfit would post employment opportunities that offered monthly salaries between $1,200 and $3,000 and bonuses as high as $15,000. Not bad gigs for young Chinese techies. They also hired linguists to help them translate documents and write spoofing emails.[3]

After Zhu had been at his job a year, HSSD created a bogus company, the FBI found, Hainan Xiandun Technology Development Company, with an address at Hainan University, and identified a professor there to act as the entity's "manager." Zhu became a company man for a company that didn't actually exist, teaming up with Ding, who was the front operation's official boss on paper.

Ding cut a more impressive, youthful figure than the disheveled Zhu did. A photo of Ding, winner of the MSS Young Leaders award, shows him wearing a tuxedo and bow tie, looking more like a high school student at prom than a James Bond–type asset. The dynamic duo, Zhu and Ding, were joined by another MSS operative, Cheng Qingmin (Manager Cheng). According to the indictment, the fake company was rounded out by Wu Shurong, a baby-faced computer whiz who lived up to his profession's devious image by having three hacker handles: goodperson, haor3n, and Shi Lei.

The team at Hainan Xiandun allegedly registered numerous domains to host impersonating websites and conduct phishing operations to obtain the passwords and ID data of employees at targeted organizations. Those domains also served as callback sites designed to receive and store forwarded information from malicious attacks. Using malware code from the MSS, the group launched cyberattacks and synced its domains to receive "beacon" alerts sent by the intrusive software. Those forwarded messages informed the hackers when new computers were compromised.

The Hainan Xiandun group had data, it had targets, and now it had the back-end infrastructure in place. Starting in 2012, the hacker quartet roamed the globe, conducting covert snatch-and-grab IP operations, all with the ultimate goal of fueling the growth of the PRC's state-mandated interests.

In the United States, their early targets included labs at research facilities in California and Florida, from which they stole data relating to vaccine research on the Ebola virus. The group also gathered intelligence on MERS, HIV/AIDS, and Marburg viruses. It raided a company making proprietary genetic-sequencing technology and attacked the National Institutes of Health (NIH) in Bethesda, Maryland, the world's largest public funder of biomedical research.

The group relied largely on spear-phishing attacks, the FBI determined. They sent emails to employees at a targeted enterprise and often built look-alike bogus company websites to create an aura of legitimacy and convince recipients that the communications were totally legitimate. When a duped employee clicked a link in a Hainan Xiandun–spawned email, malware was instantly downloaded to their computers, providing access to their files and an entry point to probe supposedly secure networks.

The indicted hackers, who remain at large, were sophisticated and sneaky. They hid their tracks with state-of-the-art tricks, burying the spyware in misnamed documents placed deep in nooks and crannies of computer file systems. Successful operations were replicated for other targets. Over six years, the MSS lead team broadened its focus from medical research to target entities working in the aerospace/aviation, maritime, and defense industries. It also took aim at universities and government ministries in several foreign nations. Such cyberoperations would prove one of the most critical, and ultimately impactful, avenues for executing China's Great Heist against America.

A National Infection

The breadth of targets, and the industries involved, for such cyberattacks was surprising. The work of APT40 was part of a long-standing MSS interest in health care IP, data, and other related targets abroad. In 2020, two other hackers, who had similarly been outsourced to a Chinese state agency, were caught probing three pharmaceutical companies, including Moderna, to steal IP related to covid vaccine research.[4] The computer bandits, Li Xiaoyu and Dong Jiazhi, who remain wanted by the FBI, were working under the supervision of an MSS officer tied to the Guangdong State Security Department, according to a DOJ indictment charging them with stealing hundreds of millions of dollars' worth of IP. In addition to the pharmaceutical companies, the team stole data from two separate medical device companies in the United States as well as several engineering and technology firms. Any and all data were welcomed by Li and Dong, who also snatched the personal identifying information (PII) of millions of students and teachers from a large educational software company.[5]

Typically not associated with more traditional espionage targets, health data and related PII are critical to the MSS's strategy to fulfill President Xi's Made in China 2025 technology wish list. On January 29, 2015, Anthem, one of the nation's largest health insurance companies, reported a massive data heist. Investigators concluded that the names, member health identification numbers, dates of birth, Social Security numbers, addresses, telephone numbers, email addresses, employment information, and income data of 78 million customers had been exfiltrated—that is, stolen—by PRC hackers. The company claims that no specific health data were obtained, which is reassuring—until one considers the implications of the initial data heist. The stolen information likely provides everything needed to access individual health records at a later date. If you have a name and corresponding Social Security number and can query a relevant electronic health records database, the correlated personal data will be there for the taking.

Disturbed by China's targeting of such sensitive personal information about Americans, in February 2021, the Intelligence Community's NCSC issued an alert with a title that pulled no punches: "China's Collection of Genomic and Other Healthcare Data from America: Risks to Privacy and U.S. Economic and National Security." For a subject that might understandably breed hysteria—is there anything more personal than your genetic and medical information?—the document began in the dry intonation and language of any government report. But it soon shifted gears: "While no one begrudges a nation conducting research to improve medical treatments, the PRC's mass collection of DNA at home has helped it carry out human rights abuses against domestic minority groups and support state surveillance. The PRC's collection of health care data from America poses equally serious risks, not only to the privacy of Americans, but also to the economic and national security of the U.S."[6] Health care data was an unlikely vector of great power competition, but China had once again changed the rules of the game.

The NCSC document makes a compelling case that the acquisition of such data, the "bonding agent" of our digital world, and relevantly applied information technology such as AI can be weaponized as tools of power and control by hostile governments. Genetic information can be used to make predictions about its owners. It can indicate "whether you are prone to addiction or high-risk for cancer," for instance.

The NCSC alert also underscored the target-driven nature of the MSS's covert collection focus: "The combination of stolen PII, personal health information, and large genomic data sets collected from abroad affords the PRC vast opportunities to precisely target individuals in foreign governments, private industries, or other sectors for potential surveillance, manipulation, or extortion." If a Chinese case officer was looking for a new source to recruit, in other words, it could use data on the target's health and any related vulnerabilities to craft an effective recruitment pitch, perhaps underscoring how the extra money gained from stealing information on their behalf could help go toward paying skyrocketing medical bills.

Beyond flagging the mere black arts of employing health data for espionage, the NCSC alert also cited a 2020 government report on Beijing human rights abuses, which included China's use of genetic data to surveil and control minority populations in Xinjiang. How could such data be abused in the United States, where the CCP has no legal jurisdiction? The NCSC offered scenarios similar to those outlined above, noting that PRC hackers had also stolen Equifax's financial records of 145 million people: "Data associated with an embarrassing addiction or mental illness could be leveraged for blackmail. Combine this information with stolen credit data indicating bankruptcy or major debt and the tools for exerting leverage increase. Such data sets could help the PRC not only recruit individuals abroad, but also act as potential leverage against foreign dissidents."

In executing the Great Heist, exfiltration of terabytes of proprietary data was a means to an end for the CCP.

And it is willing to do anything to get it.

TikTok Anxiety Syndrome

At first blush, it might seem odd to mention the immensely popular, China-owned social media platform TikTok in a chapter about espionage in the health care sector.

TikTok is many things. It's seen by many as a fun, easy-to-use broadcaster of videos, a messaging app, and no doubt a powerful sales and marketing tool. But above all, it's an incredible tool for data collection, dissemination, and, when desired, manipulation. This is no mistake: Users provide data; TikTok analyzes it, and then uses it to suggest more content, which users respond to, thereby creating a never-ending feedback loop of user engagement.

The average TikTok fan provides reams of information: likes; dislikes; lists of friends, obsessions, anxieties; personal stories; and countless photos and videos documenting their life, the places they go, the people they see. Just watching a video feed provides information; do you watch and like a clip, or do you swipe it away? Either action creates data. TikTok feeds all this information (and who knows what else) into its algorithms to program and broadcast relevant content—and revenue-generating ads—to each user's feed. On the surface, putting aside the issue of how addictive the interface and community are, TikTok seems to be a user-friendly, benign platform, similar to other social media platforms. Several expert examinations have argued that the app is really no different, at least data collection-wise, from its competitors.[7]

So why has this site, beloved by young people in particular, become a political punching bag in the United States? For three reasons: First, the more data an intelligence outfit has, especially in a world in which AI relies on machine learning models with processing power that can analyze and assess that data, the more accurate and refined the targeting will be. Second, data about an individual—even seemingly innocent data—can potentially be dangerous to the health and welfare of that individual. And that, in turn, might threaten a nation's collective health and welfare. While the issue remains a hot topic in Washington, with some rightfully raising concerns about the dangers to freedom of speech enshrined in the First Amendment by the government blocking an app, even if foreign-owned, one cannot casually dismiss the very real dangers of allowing the Chinese Community Party unfettered access to the nearly infinite terabytes of personal data from broad swaths of American citizens.

It may be hard to draw the precise connection between hugely popular media influencers and a threat to American national security. Imagine, however, that a teenage girl creates a secret account. She uses a fake name and never films her face, confident that she will remain anonymous. One day she uploads a post saying that her dad has been having problems at work. Or that he's lost a fortune on gambling on FanDuel. Or that he engages in other potentially sinister activity. Wanting to share the drama, she also includes the hashtags of her favorite web personalities, which helps the post generate views. With that resulting spike, the disturbing content is flagged by TikTok—or MSS—as containing potentially controversial and intelligence-worthy information. Imagine that TikTok's surveillance system then automatically retrieves the registration data that reveals the teen's true identity and IP address, which the MSS can readily obtain. That information is run through AI and locates a senior engineer at Lockheed Martin who uses the same public IP address. It's the girl's father—and he works on America's designs for advanced missile systems. Thus a dramatic anonymous post on the rather silly social media site has exposed potentially embarrassing or possibly even criminal behavior about an employee who has access to vital military plans that the MSS wants. In this scenario, TikTok is a perfect data provider for targeting and exploiting the potential vulnerabilities that can enable a successful recruitment of a clandestine source by Chinese case officers.

While, as of early 2025, there was no known public evidence that the PRC had used TikTok data for such targeting, no reasonable person in the West should be under any illusions that it won't or has not done so already. As demonstrated throughout this book, when it comes to espionage and the theft of IP and data, the PRC is creative, relentless, and unconstrained by international laws and norms.

To an authoritarian regime with totalitarian elements like the CCP, data collection is an obsession. Stolen data directly contributes to China's strategic collection objectives. In Beijing's eyes, the more data the better, no matter how or where it's obtained. Most notably, it's the critical fuel for China's AI large language models. In 2021, the CCP forced Apple, an American company that prided itself on protecting the data of its users, to transfer the data of all its Chinese users to state-owned servers in Guiyang, China, according to *The New York Times*. "Chinese state employees physically manage the computers," the paper reported. "Apple abandoned the encryption technology it used elsewhere after China would not allow it. And the digital keys that unlock information on those computers are stored in the data centers they're meant to secure."[8]

An Apple statement dismissed the paper's charges. "We have never compromised the security of our users or their data in China or anywhere we operate. Many of the assertions in this report are based on incomplete, outdated and inaccurate information," the Silicon Valley–based company responded.[9]

Given that Apple makes nearly every component of its products in

China and that the Chinese market accounts for about 20 percent of its sales, Apple CEO Tim Cook evidently had little room to maneuver. China is not afraid to retaliate against private companies, and the very threat of such action can give it tremendous leverage to get its way. Cook, like many foreign CEOs caught in the crosshairs of the CCP, apparently capitulated to the Party's demands regarding the data access[10] just as it did when the CCP demanded that the company remove an app that allowed pro-democracy protestors to track police movements in Hong Kong.[11] The tech giant, for the record, insists that by taking such actions it was merely abiding "by the laws in all of the countries where we operate, including China, and our teams must remove apps that fail to comply with them."[12] The clash between idealistic aspirations and the cold harsh market realities of dealing with the PRC's regime continues to prove a constant source of tension for American companies seeking to capitalize on the world's most lucrative consumer market.

After more than twenty years of relentless, illegal, and hostile data acquisition, after the promises of President Xi to President Obama to stop data and IP theft have proven utterly worthless, the idea that TikTok's vast troves of personal data—often *intensely* personal data—will be safe from MSS access defies credulity. Beyond just collecting the data, TikTok has the algorithmic capabilities to sift, sort, and match it with other relevant data points from other sources. Imagine, for instance, if its proprietary data points analyzing users for signs of mental health issues, sexual preferences, drug and alcohol use, or money problems were extracted and combined with an AI engine to sort users into categories for potential blackmail. The data could then be used as blackmail to force the users to provide technology plans or network passwords to such plans. Protecting American freedoms, one could perhaps argue, sometimes requires taking the extraordinary steps to restrict the freedoms of totalitarian regimes operating in our markets.

It's not just the private sector that needs to make sense of large volumes of data. To enable successful HUMINT operations, so do spy agencies. In the CIA, targeting officers identify the people, relationships, and organizations who have access to the information about the most critical issues facing the United States. Driven by the priorities of policymakers, this includes foreign intelligence requirements about military plans, government initiatives, and strategic alliances around the world. Other intelligence is focused on opportunities to disrupt terrorist attacks, illegal arms trade, drug networks, cyberthreats, and counterintelligence measures. All Western intelligence agencies function in a similar manner: first finding the right collection targets to focus on, then working on the means of how to best steal from them.

The targeting officers at the MSS take a similar approach. But they are more obsessed with important tasks that, generally speaking, Western intelligence services typically don't focus on: profiling individuals to facilitate the theft of commercial technology, including IP, and data. American spies do not, for example, send agents or hackers to Stockholm to capture Swedish Spotify listener data in order to target and lure young engineers at Ericsson to a spear-phishing site offering music by their favorite artists. Our government, and by extension our national intelligence apparatus, isn't interested in acquiring Ericsson's telecom networking plans to increase the market share of an American competitor like AT&T or to advance a five-year government plan. The CCP, which reportedly is the ultimate owner of Huawei, is.

If that last scenario about Spotify sounded plausible, that's because it is. The MSS, however, has found an easy way to obtain such information: TikTok already knows its users' favorite artists.

CHAPTER 14

The Elements of Infiltration

The American Chemical Sector

THE CCP doesn't just want our data; it wants our formulas.

In the high-stakes world of global espionage, microchips may grab the headlines, but it's the invisible alchemy of chemistry that can also give rise to similarly valuable technological revolutions. Coatings, compounds, and proprietary materials—these are the quiet titans behind smartphones, satellites, missiles, and medicine. And when a single chemical formula can create a billion-dollar market advantage or a game-changing military edge, theft becomes not just tempting but strategic. For the CCP, trade secrets buried in beakers and production lines are just as valuable as any top secret schematic. And increasingly, it's willing to deploy everything from corporate partnerships to cyberattacks in order to steal them.

Welcome to the shadow war for the molecules that move the modern world. Access to these patented creations can translate into enormous commercial opportunities, leading to equally enormous profits. They also bolster the unforeseen (and seen) military and geopolitical advantages that come with technological superiority and innovation. A chemical formula that reflects heat might, for instance, lead to revolutionary manufacturing and performance developments in everything from weapons to engines to aerospace technology and beyond. As the PRC extends its claim as the manufacturing center of the world and the CCP continues to achieve the ambitious goals of Xi Jinping's "national rejuvenation" through Made in China 2025, schemes to steal critical technology, chemistry, and manufacturing processes have accelerated. Naturally this has come with the blessing, funding, and coordination of established state-owned companies and CCP programs in and outside of the MSS.

Unsurprisingly, then, the expensive chemical processes developed on American soil and paid for by American dollars have been targeted and raided. Three attempted heists of extremely valuable chemicals underscore the strategic value put on this sector by China and the extent to which it's willing to go after them. The cases further highlight the CCP's fundamental attitude to bypassing fair competition and market realities by using freelancers, government funding, and corporate power to conduct nothing less than high-tech larceny. The return on investment is, of course, huge. Unless things go wrong.

A Transparent Operation

Diamonds, it turns out, are, theoretically, an engineer's best friend. Adam Khan, the Illinois-based electrical engineer and former CEO of Akhan Semiconductor, fell under the glittering spell of nano-diamonds, microscopic diamond particles, while a student at the University of Illinois Chicago campus. Wowed by the mechanical, optical, and heat distributive powers of these crystalline carbon fragments, which are one millionth of a millimeter in size, he eventually came up with a novel method of coating various materials such as glass and plastic with a patina of nanodiamonds.

Khan's patented formula, which he eventually dubbed Miraj Diamond Glass, had instant and obvious applications. First and foremost, the coating had astounding protective properties. In the age of smartphones and omnipresent transparent screens, the coating process was a magic bullet, able to help manufacturers create nearly unbreakable and unscratchable smartphone screens. By 2016, Akhan had raised about $15 million in funding via a formal first seed round and two convertible note rounds—a sum that was more than doubled in 2022, with a late-stage funding round.[1]

By 2016, Akhan's head of operations, Carl Shurboff, was sending sample screens to major cell phone manufacturers to solicit business, including Samsung and Huawei. Within two years, Khan was in contact with the top ten global original equipment manufacturers. In August 2016, a California-based Huawei engineer began emailing Akhan, revealing that the telecom giant was "actively looking for new technologies for our innovative product in this fast pace [sic] consumer electronics industry," according to a *Bloomberg Businessweek* report.[2]

By February 2017, a signed agreement was in place for Akhan to ship two samples of Miraj screens to Huawei's San Diego office, which Huawei was supposed to return within sixty days undamaged. Akhan also sent Huawei a notice that US export laws, including provisions of the International Traffic in Arms Regulations (ITAR), applied to Miraj—a classification rooted in the fact that microdiamond coatings have several potential military applications, including in laser weapons and mitigating heat dispersal for missiles.

Huawei blew off the return deadline. Shurboff's subsequent emails demanding the immediate return of the coating sample were ignored. Months later, though, in August, the sample finally arrived. When Shurboff opened the package, he got a shock: the Miraj sample was scratched and broken into numerous pieces. As Shurboff tried to piece the original together, like a 3D puzzle, it became clear that a number of shards were missing. As he surveyed the wreckage, his heart sank. "I thought, *Great, this multibillion-dollar company is coming after our technology. What are we going to do now?*"[3]

According to Khan, two subsequent conversations with Huawei's representative, including one that was recorded, confirmed that the sample package that had been returned to Illinois had been shipped from China, not California.[4] As for what Huawei had done with the samples—aside from apparently breaking export laws—was anyone's guess. The company's infamous past fueled Khan's concerns. He suspected that the company might have tried to reverse engineer Miraj's secrets, "perhaps how we came about constructing this diamond matrix, the techniques that we used to implement this, and then perhaps taking it a step further." He also worried about Huawei's exploring some of the defense applications of the materials.

Akhan contacted the FBI, which shipped the broken sample to its lab in Quantico. Subsequent gemological analysis concluded that at some point Huawei had blasted it with a 100-kilowatt laser, according to a report in *Bloomberg Businessweek*. A device that strong could be easily classified as a weapon, the FBI said.

As the FBI listened in, Khan and Shurboff spoke to their Huawei contact, probing for more details and gaining further confirmation that the glass had been sent to China. The Huawei representative maintained that her company was interested in contracting business with Akhan and offered to set up a meeting with a senior Huawei executive at the upcoming Consumer Electronics Show in Las Vegas. The Akhan executives agreed to meet. They also agreed to wear recording wires for the FBI. A sting was on. Or was it?

The prearranged meeting in a Las Vegas conference room did not happen because the Huawei rep failed to show up. Instead, the two men met in a food court with a senior supply manager from Huawei's Santa Clara office. The executive from China couldn't make it, supposedly because executives were no longer flying to the United States in the wake of the arrest of Huawei's CFO in Canada. But the supply manager stressed that Huawei wanted to continue to do business with Akhan.

Ironically, the sting ended up putting Akhan into an awkward spot. That afternoon, Shurboff bumped into reps for another potential client, the smartphone maker RED, who reportedly became suspicious that Akhan might be double-dealing or trying to start a bidding war. Days later, in a move to assure prospective clients that everything was above board, the company went public about Huawei, issuing a press release noting that it had "recently cooperated with a U.S. federal investigation into what appears to be a theft of its intellectual property by Huawei Technologies Co., Ltd."[5]

Fittingly for a tale involving diamond technology, going public about Huawei's apparent IP violations refracted in several directions for Akhan Semiconductor. "We heard from a number of other companies that had gone through similar experiences with Huawei," Khan recalled. "We also had several folks reach out to us to offer to litigate against Huawei under a contingency basis. But really, because they hadn't actually put out a product, it was hard to assess what damage had been done."[6]

The company waited, monitoring Huawei's filing. "We saw some additional trademark and patent filings around, quote, unquote, *Huawei glass*, diamond glass, but nothing material came from it," Khan explained in an interview. "So we continued on developing the technology for consumer electronics. We had worked with a top OEM to bring it to pre-market with that OEM, sort of waiting for the other shoe to drop." Meanwhile, Akhan's communication with the FBI and Department of Justice ebbed; other than Huawei's allegedly having violated the 2016 Defend Trade Secrets Act by shipping the coated screen to China, there wasn't much of a case.

Then the American company began to experience IT issues. There was a denial-of-service (DOS) attack on the company's website. Khan hired Dark Wolf Solutions to improve the company's cybersecurity and run penetration tests. Its people determined that Akhan was being targeted by Structured Query Language (SQL) injection attacks. Experts found tool kits used by Chinese hackers and an exploit developed for a Chinese application. Despite Herculean efforts, they could not pinpoint the ultimate source of the attack.[7]

The company was also besieged by job applicants, many of whom were Chinese citizens with ties to government-owned tech firms or Chinese universities closely associated with the PLA. Like the DOS and SQL penetration attacks, hiring became another point of attack the company had to manage.

Khan revealed that in 2023—after another major round of funding raised $20 million and agreements were put in place with a major OEM and the Department of Defense—he left the company. The founder says he cannot comment on the events that led to his departure. In his wake, however, the company evidently floundered and eventually shuttered. Khan said he couldn't comment on who owned the coveted IP left behind in its wake. When asked what lessons he drew from the Huawei saga, his words suggested that perhaps there is a deeper story. "The global reach, the sophistication of the apparatus within state-owned enterprises in China, their proximity to academia, to venture capital, to other capital sources was quite astounding. That was an eye-opener for me for how deep their influence really penetrates." Nanodiamonds wouldn't be the only chemical formula China's multipronged intelligence apparatus would try to steal. Others would include some of the most iconic American brands in the world.

Secrets in a Can

As highly guarded industrial secrets go—not to mention pop culture mystique—it's hard to top Coca-Cola's legendary billion-dollar recipe. The official corporate story is that after Dr. John S. Pemberton invented the fizzy elixir in 1886, the formula was kept a close, unwritten secret. In 1919, Ernest Woodruff and a group of investors purchased the company with a loan that used the secret formula as collateral. Woodruff asked for the formula to be written down and placed the sacred recipe in a New York bank vault. Once the loan was repaid, the formula was transferred to an Atlanta bank, where it remained for more than eighty-six years, until it reached its current home in The Vault at World of Coca-Cola. There, amid tourist-friendly bottle cap and taste exhibits, the details lie locked away in plain sight.[8]

Coca-Cola and other food manufacturers harbor other secrets worth guarding. One little-known but vastly important one involves something called BPA-free coating. For years, Coca-Cola and other producers of comestibles used a chemical called bisphenol-A (BPA) to line their cans to minimize flavor loss and prevent container corrosion. On the heels of reports suggesting that BPA might have harmful effects, Coca-Cola, along with other companies, began searching for BPA-free alternatives.

In December 2012, Xiaorong You, then a forty-eight-year-old woman who went by the name Shannon You, was hired by Coca-Cola as its principal engineer for global research. You had been born in China but had come to the United States to obtain a master's degree from Kent State University and a PhD in polymer science and engineering from Lehigh University. She had become an American citizen in 1999 and moved to Delaware with her husband and child, taking a job as a senior chemist for DuPont. Then she got a job as a materials engineer at Honeywell Life Safety, where she worked for three years before moving to Atlanta.[9] You's new job at Coca-Cola was a chemist's dream, one that gave her access to the sophisticated, cutting-edge—and *secret*—information of a number of chemical companies, including AkzoNobel, BASF, Dow Chemical, Toyochem, and Sherwin-Williams, developing BPA-free technologies.

Coatings are everywhere in the world, from mani-pedis to airplane fuselages and from computer keyboards to car paint jobs. There is an entire vocabulary for industrial coatings: polyurethane, epoxy, alkyd, and acrylic, to name a few. Coca-Cola didn't manufacture the lining used in its cans of soda; it purchased coated cans from a third-party supply company. But as the leading beverage manufacturer in America, it had the market power to dictate what coatings its soda cans would use, meaning that for several years You had a rare front-row seat to the development of the state-of-the-art coatings that Coca-Cola was evaluating. For nearly five years, she had access to the chemical formulas that could, in a sense, feed the world.

In the summer of 2017, Coca-Cola announced a big restructuring plan, laying off 1,200 employees. You was among the casualties and was given a sixty-day notice before termination. But she'd been already quietly working on a plan B, an exit strategy to make the most of her access to top secret formulas: the incredibly thin films that lined aluminum beverage cans, preventing their sugary contents from eating away at the metal. With her Aunt Fan acting as a go-between in China, according to reports, she'd spent March negotiating with Liu Xiangchen, the general manager of the Weihai Jinhong Group, to steal the non-bisphenol-A formulas and sell them to the chemical company, which would then spin off a second company in China to manufacture products using the stolen American trade secret information. As part of the deal, Xiangchen's company would sponsor You's application for the Thousand Talents Program, in order to arrange payments as compensation. In addition, the company had her apply to another CCP-funded program run by the government for

Shandong Province, called Yishi-Yiyi.[10] That was the plan, which also included eventually putting You on staff and making her part owner of the new company. Now, with the end of her employment at Coca-Cola approaching, it was time to start her heist.

She began trying to copy files. But as a departing employee, her ability to copy and paste or drag and drop files onto external drives was blocked—and her attempts were registered by the company's IT system.[11] Growing desperate to capture those trade secrets before her final day at work, You began pulling up documents on her screen and photographing them with her cell phone camera. It was slow, painstaking work. Then, just before she was processed out of the company, she learned of a vulnerability in the Coca-Cola security system: She could upload the BPA-free documents to her Google Drive account. And that was what she did. Then she signed a slew of documents stating that she had not taken any proprietary information from the company, and in return for her complete lack of honesty was given a hefty severance check of $33,912.[12]

The chemist was out of work barely long enough to file for unemployment benefits, soon joining the Eastman Chemical Company in Kingsport, Tennessee. But about two weeks into her new gig, she traveled to China, spending four days in September likely as part of her Thousand Talents Program application, orchestrated with Liu Xiangchen's help.

Over the next nine months, You, Liu, and their go-between communicated frequently. They had a lot to discuss: the equity split of their new company, approaching an Italian company to back a joint venture, the progress of the Thousand Talents Program application and the Yishi-Yiyi award program, the importance of hiding You's involvement in the conspiracy while she remained in the United States, and paying You for the work she had already done in furtherance of the conspiracy, among other topics.

Meanwhile, You had come under scrutiny from her managers at Eastman, who were unhappy with her job performance. After one meeting in June, she had a major meltdown, demanding to see senior company executives until she was asked to leave the building. That night, she logged on to Eastman's system and began transferring files, evidently unaware that her behavior was now the subject of close monitoring by the company. The next day she was confronted by security and IT staff, who demanded access to her laptop and hard drive—and accompanied her to her home to retrieve the devices.

There on the hard drive, clearly named and plain as day, were Eastman files and the proprietary documents You had stolen while at Coca-Cola. The company alerted the FBI and handed the hardware over to federal agents.

Eastman naturally fired You, who quickly landed a new job as a principal engineer for XG Sciences in East Lansing, Michigan. Remarkably, she didn't break stride with her tech theft plans. Between August and September 2018, she flew to China twice and met with executives from Metlac, an Italian chemical company that she was wooing for a joint venture. When she returned to the United States, customs agents seized her computer. Obtaining a warrant, the FBI found confidential information belonging to Eastman and the other chemical companies. It also obtained warrants to access her Gmail and Yahoo! email accounts.

In February 2019, the FBI arrested You in a barely furnished apartment in East Lansing containing a single folding chair, a folding table, and a mattress on the floor. Surveying the furnishing and aware that You had $200,000 in checking and savings accounts in the United States and at least $70,000 spread over several bank accounts in China, prosecutors concluded that she was an imminent flight risk, even with her husband in Boston and a daughter in Northern California. Liu Xiangchen, who remains in China, was also indicted, while the go-between Aunt Fan, coconspirator number one, according to court papers, was not charged.

You fought her detention and waged an aggressive defense at her trial, claiming anti-Chinese bias. But none of that could erase her shoddy tradecraft and her crass actions and attempts to cash in on the CCP's talent programs to bring an entirely new business to China—one that relied on $170 million of research and development costs to American companies. On May 9, 2022, she was sentenced to fourteen years in prison for scheming to steal trade secrets, engaging in economic espionage, and committing fraud. The judge ordered her to pay a $200,000 fine.

You appealed the verdict and challenged the fine. The judge in the case, J. Ronnie Greer, examined the alleged R&D losses and concluded in a well-reasoned 12,000-word decision that they were understated, putting the loss at $30 million.[13] He affirmed You's conviction at a resentencing hearing, refusing to alter his initial sentence. You's letter supposedly expressing regret for her actions left Judge Greer outraged. Noting that a copy of the secrets she had stolen had never been recovered, he ripped into the convict: "You put citizens of the United States in jeopardy in favor of a communist enemy with which we are at economic war." Then he sent her to prison, saying, "You have never accepted responsibility."[14]

A Whiter Shade Assailed

Red, of course, is Chinese people's color of choice. For centuries, its various shades, from crimson to vermillion, have saturated Chinese society, serving as the color of celebration, prosperity, and good luck. Ming Dynasty leaders wore red robes, brides wear red wedding dresses, and the walls of the Forbidden City are painted red. Despite the CCP's selectively censorious relationship to its past—the Cultural Revolution's "Four Olds" campaign once aimed to obliterate old customs, old cultures, old habits, and old ideas—red has survived. It's emblazoned on the national flag and serves at the backdrop at CCP-controlled political rallies and press events.

So it would have been understandable if Walter Lian-Heen Liew, a Singapore-born ethnic Chinese California-based businessman, was surprised when his contacts in the CCP gave him a mission: to steal a formula for white paint. No doubt his confusion abated when he learned that the coveted formula generated about $2.2 billion annually for the American chemicals giant DuPont.

The color in question was titanium dioxide (TiO_2), a white pigment that has come to be regarded as the dye that creates the aesthetic ideal of white. As such, TiO_2 has nearly limitless commercial applications, providing the preferred foundation of white paint, plastics, and paper.

But titanium dioxide is hard to make in an efficient, economical manner. DuPont came up with a novel process that involves stripping the pigment out of ore, which is mixed with coal and chlorine in a ceramic oven known as a chlorinator. This mixture is heated to over 1,800 degrees Fahrenheit. The resulting lavalike substance is then put into an oxidizer, where as the name suggests, it melds with oxygen, forming a fine white powder. As a bonus, DuPont's TiO_2 chloride route process produces titanium tetrachloride ($TiCl_4$), a material with aerospace and military uses, including making smoke screens. DuPont is not the only company that manufactures TiO_2. But its proprietary method yields a product that has made it the global leader—a position that the CCP wanted to usurp.

Walter Liew was a naturalized US citizen. But he was also a longtime CCP stalwart. In 1991, government officials had praised him for being a "patriotic overseas Chinese." At that same meeting, he later recounted, he had met one of the CCP's most powerful leaders, Luo Gan, then the secretary general of the State Council. Luo had given him "directives so that I would better understand China and continue to make contributions to her," Liew later wrote in a letter.[15] Luo's involvement was a remarkable example of even the highest levels of Chinese Communist Party leadership being directly involved in orchestrating industrial espionage.

One of Luo's instructions involved obtaining the secrets behind DuPont's state-of-the-art TiO_2 manufacturing process. Liew took the assignment to heart. To quote a future nemesis, Assistant US Attorney Peter B. Axelrod, the ambitious CCP acolyte "began a 20-year course of conduct of lying, cheating, and stealing."[16] China was prepared to play the long game.

Liew was the right man for the job. He had an engineering degree, the relentless tenacity of an extreme entrepreneur, and a gift for connecting with CCP government-backed initiatives. After building an acrylic resin paint additive plant in China in the mid-1990s, he set his sights on TiO_2.

After researching the space for years, he began targeting former DuPont employees who could help him recreate the TiO_2 process. In late 1997, he located a former DuPont engineer, Tim Spitler, who was living in Reno, and drove there to see him, beginning a relationship that would span fifteen years. Liew sent Spitler gift baskets each Christmas and paid for the funeral of Spitler's daughter, who committed suicide in 2006. Spitler, for his part, drew sketches of DuPont parts and gave Liew DuPont documents, including a blueprint for a TiO2 plant in Delaware. Liew paid him $15,000 for those plans, according to a Bloomberg report, but they were worth much more. Not only did those documents provide a road map for a TiO2 start-up; he could use them to convince backers, bankers, and prospective partners in China that he had the keys to a lucrative new product line.

That same year, Liew reportedly found a second source, Robert J. Maegerle, a former DuPont mechanical engineer. Ttitanium dioxide production was his specialty. According to court papers, Maegerle faxed Liew confidential data relating to DuPont's TiO2 plant in Taiwan and then later provided photos of the company's facilities and more proprietary information about processing TiO2.[17] With two former insiders on his team, Liew increased his efforts to find backing in China. He went to the very top, sending a letter to the chairman of the Pangang Group Steel Plate Company, the state-sponsored steel giant. The letter, later produced by prosecutors, basically admitted that his company had illegally obtained DuPont's nontransferable technology, writing, "After many years of follow-up research and application, my company has possession and mastery of the complete DuPont way of titanium white by chlorination."

The pitch worked. Between 2006 and 2011, various Pangang subsidiaries paid Liew's Oakland company, USA Performance Technology, $27 million, according to court records.[18] As plans proceeded for Pangang's entry into TiO2 production, DuPont received a heads-up from an Australian consultant who had seen Liew's plans. Intent on impressing his masters in the PRC, Liew had referenced DuPont's success in the plans acquired by the Australian consultant. Not long after, a second tip arrived in the form of an anonymous letter, charging that Liew and an employee had sold China "embezzled Titanium Technology from a US Company."[19] DuPont contacted its lawyers and the FBI.

In July 2011, federal agents searched Liew's home and offices in

California. While examining the purse of Liew's wife, Christina, an agent found a key to a safe deposit box at the Bank of East Asia in Oakland. When the agent asked Christina about the key, Liew, speaking in Chinese, instructed Christina to stay silent. Christina feigned ignorance about the trinket.[20]

Soon after that exchange, Christina left the house with her purse and key and headed to the Bank of East Asia, unaware that she was being tailed by federal surveillants. She removed a swath of documents and drove to a motel, where she was joined by Pangang Group executives. The FBI raided the motel and recovered records linking the executives from Pangang Group to the Chinese government. The FBI and DOJ then began the process of charging and prosecuting Liew and his spy network.

In early 2012, Tze Chao, a DuPont employee for twenty-six years, confessed to having provided trade secrets on the production of TiO_2 while consulting for the Pangang Group. In his plea agreement, Chao, a seventy-seven-year-old Delaware resident, admitted that he had "learned that the PRC government had placed a priority on developing chloride-process TiO_2 technology in a short period of time and wished to acquire this technology from western companies."[21]

On July 10, 2014, Walter Lian-Heen Liew and his company, USA Performance Technology, were both sentenced. Liew was sentenced to serve fifteen years in prison, forfeit $27.8 million in illegal profits, and pay $511,487.82 in restitution and a $2,000 special assessment. Later that year, his associate Robert J. Maegerle was sentenced to serve thirty months in prison and pay $367,679 in restitution and a $400 special assessment. Liew's wife was sentenced to three years' probation after pleading guilty to evidence tampering.[22] Tim Spitler, the former DuPont employee who had furnished the factory blueprints to Liew, committed suicide in 2012.

In the initial charges against Liew, the Pangang Group and three of its wholly owned subsidiaries were named as co-defendants. The companies resisted the summons but were then hit with a 2016 superseding indictment on charges of conspiracy to violate the Economic Espionage Act of 1996. Then the Pangang Group did something shocking: It moved to dismiss the charges on the grounds that it was entitled to sovereign immunity under the Foreign Sovereign Immunities Act (FSIA) of 1976. In doing so, it tacitly admitted that it didn't matter if the charges were true or not; Pangang was a PRC-owned company and was therefore immune to prosecution.[23]

While the CCP seems to regard the claims of sovereign immunity as a real-life "get out of jail free" card that underwrites its ripping off US companies, its motions to dismiss the charges were denied, based in part on the fact that three subsidiaries, by their status as satellite companies, are not wholly owned by China. As it stands, this case, which threatens to prove the CCP's direct ties to state-supported IP theft, still awaits trial.

It wouldn't be the first time a Chinese firm had its sovereign claim rejected. One dogged American businessman spent a decade figuring out how to counter that defense and win back $80 million from companies tied to the CCP's largest state-owned enterprises, Aviation Industry Corporation of China.

CHAPTER 15

Energy

Gale Force Theft

ONE MORNING in Baoding, China, a hundred miles southwest of Beijing, dozens of men in matching coveralls marched silently onto the factory floor of HT Blade, a high-tech wind turbine blade manufacturer. They weren't employees, nor were they contractors. They didn't speak to anyone as they entered. They simply fanned out across the building, gripping thick nylon lifting straps, searching for their prize: a proprietary rotor blade mold made of steel, aluminum, and fiberglass half a football field in length.

They found it.

With eerie coordination and the silent approval of a government "official," and likely CCP member, who had escorted them in, the intruders surrounded the massive mold. They broke into two teams, one on each side, hoisted it up, and walked it out the door and across the street, right into a rival factory owned by Guodian United Power Technology Corporation, a state-backed competitor with far more political clout than market share. Employees at HT Blade stood frozen by their incapacity to challenge the CCP. Their most valuable asset was being physically walked out the front door in broad daylight, in full view of management, without their making a single effort to stop it. Because in China, when the CCP gives the order, there is no stopping it.

Patrick Jenevein, a Texas-based entrepreneur and cofounder of HT Blade, wasn't there to witness the event. But he's played the hard-to-imagine scene over in his head more times than he can count. For him, it wasn't just the brazen theft of a high-tech manufacturing form that was important, it was the perfect metaphor for doing business in the PRC: One moment you're building a billion-dollar company; the next, you learn you've been legally looted by your own government-backed business partner.

Not that the heist of turbine forms was a total surprise to Jenevein, a charming, razor-sharp, loquacious Texan polymath and businessman. He'd been filing lawsuits against his former business partner, AVIC, and had well-earned trust issues as a result.

This was a relatively new development in his life. Jenevein, a history major at Davidson College who had wound up building wind farms and natural gas power plants in the American Southwest and Midwest, had been collaborating on projects in China for a long time. And during certain parts of his journey, he had truly believed that his work adhered to the Jenevein family motto that had been instilled in him as a young boy: Do well by doing good.

That was all set to change. In 1995, Jenevein was approached by Dr. Yih-Min Jan, a physicist from the University of Houston. Recently retired from the Los Angeles–based petroleum company ARCO, Jan was working for the China National Petroleum Corporation (CNPC) to improve oil extraction using microbes to reduce the weight of hydrocarbon composites. Jan had noticed lots of gas leakage in China's oil industry, something Jenevein's companies specialized in capturing. After developing an unofficial mutual admiration society, the two men took off to the oil fields of western China to explore opportunities there. While their plans to start a gas-capture power plant didn't work out, they founded the company Tang Energy Group and established a joint venture to build a series of other power plants in western China, using wind turbines to generate electricity. For Jenevein, the initiatives were gratifying. He was pleased to be engaged in profitable business that might also help the local economy. He was indeed doing well by doing good.

Gradually, however, he would discover that his power plant offered hidden riches—and future losses—he hadn't foreseen. In China, he learned, anything to do with combustion turbines—also called jet engines—has to involve Aviation Industry Corporation of China (AVIC). So he met with AVIC officials and began a long relationship with them. Along the way, he discovered that doing business in China means dealing with something more unpredictable than the invisible forces of the free market; it means dealing with the invisible forces of the CCP. Several power plants into Tang's work, the CCP announced that it would set the prices for the energy generated by them. The CCP didn't care about Tang's investments or its need to make a profit. Jenevein and Jan, however, did. And so, Tang arranged for AVIC to buy out its shares.

Large wind turbines were very appealing to AVIC. The massive growth of wind farms would create important economic growth and ecological advantages. But long turbine blades had other potential uses, including military ones. The forms, composite materials, and airfoils—the highly calibrated cross-sectional shape of the blades— could be adapted for use with drones or propellers. Tang and AVIC united to start HT Blade, a 75%/25% joint venture, with AVIC holding the controlling interest.

HT Blade made wind turbine rotor blades, the extremely long, aerodynamic appendages of the modern windmill. The blades, made of sophisticated composite materials, such as fiberglass, carbon fiber, and polymer foam, are shaped by the composite being poured into carefully sculpted molds. The high-quality product was an instant success. By 2004, the company was distributing profits, and Tang, wanting to ensure profits for its investors, sold a portion of its holdings.[1] By 2010, it was the second largest independent blade manufacturer in the world, behind only LM Glasfiber, Jenevein said. The company was so profitable that discussions began with the venture capital firm Kleiner Perkins, which projected a $1.8 billion IPO for the company, meaning that Tang stood to make $450 million from its 25 percent share of the company.

Jenevein and Jan came up with a new idea to ensure global success: HT Blade needed to sell its blades worldwide to buyers with wind turbine generators. To capture that market, the partners decided, they would form their own company to build wind farms. When they informed executives at AVIC about their plans, the company immediately offered to partner with them. The Tang duo turned them down, explaining that the PRC-based company could not benefit from tax credits and stressing that they were forming the new company to help grow HT Blade. Then AVIC offered them $600 million for a 20 percent share. It was an offer the partners couldn't refuse. "We said, 'OK, we'll find a way to let you buy 20%,'" Jenevein recalled.[2]

The new company was called Soaring Wind Energy. In April 2009, Tang and AVIC signed an agreement specifying, among other things, that an AVIC subsidiary would provide $300 million to develop wind power projects, $200 million to purchase equipment from Chinese SOEs, and $100 million for additional expenses.

It seemed, perhaps, too good to be true. And maybe it was; Jenevein was well aware that the whims and power of the CCP added a wild-card element to any business dealings in the PRC.

So he insisted the agreement specify that any disputes would be heard in a US court, specifically in Dallas, Texas. It would prove to be an act of prudent foresight.

Government-Sanctioned Industrial Larceny

Then strange things started happening. The comrades at AVIC insisted on lending HT Blade money. But the company was already profitable. It didn't need money. A cash infusion would create balance sheet problems that could be weaponized to create ownership problems, almost like an enforced loan-sharking operation. "They said, 'HT Blade needs to borrow this money,'" Jenevein recalled. "We said, 'No, it shouldn't.' And they said, 'Yes, it does. And by the way, HT Blade is going to secure the loan with company collateral.'"

Mystified, Jenevein asked, "What collateral?"

"And they said, 'IP and other assets.' So they went after our position by creating debt with collateral that they could then foreclose

upon when they created a situation where the borrower AVIC controlled could not repay the debt." The CCP's lawfare machine, a
critical prong in China's whole-of-society approach to IP theft, was
spinning into gear.

As discussions about an IPO progressed, Jenevein attended a
board meeting of HT Blade and went out to a board dinner where
alcohol was freely flowing. At one point, he was discussing the like-
lihood of approval to take the company public, and one tipsy fellow
board member said something astounding: "We're not going to get
the last approval, because the foreigners are going to make too much
money."

Jenevein couldn't believe his ears. His plugged-in colleague was
saying that those in charge—AVIC and the CCP—would lose face if
the Western company made a large profit. He was both stunned and
honored by that admission, which showed that the board member either viewed him as part of the team or was too drunk to realize what
he was saying. Wanting to be sure he understood, he asked, "Who's
the foreigner? Isn't that me?"

The colleague laughed. "Oh, yeah. It's you. Sorry."

Not long after that drunken confession, HT Blade's IPO plans
were shelved. Then the powers that be at the State-owned Assets
Supervision and Administration Commission of the State Council
decided to eliminate HT Blade altogether. It took a company valued
at $1.8 billion and divided up its assets, gifting cash assets to Baoding
Huiyang Aviation Propeller China and all marketing and contracts
to Chinese firms Sinoma International Engineering Company and
Zhongfu.

Like a water-deprived tree in a drought, HT Blade withered away.
The forms that had been stolen in broad daylight were nothing com-
pared to that unilateral asset redistribution. From all appearances,
Tang was party to a brazen $450 million robbery, blessed by the State
Council.

It was a harbinger of things to come for Soaring Wind Energy.
Jenevein's 2024 book, *Dancing with the Dragon: Cautionary Tales
of the New China from an Old China Hand*, his fascinating account of his misadventures in China, offers astute analysis of the

CCP's realpolitik industrial and legal strategies that can turn even the most profitable foreign venture in the country into a minefield. He also provided a short version of his own joint venture's demise: "Along the way, AVIC hired our general manager, diverted financing, and even stole a wind farm from us." Jenevein admitted that the last point should be rather embarrassing for just how brazen it was. But he explained that AVIC hadn't just approached SWE's management; it had also contacted one of the lawyers SWE was working with, a guy named Steve DeWolf, who was an experienced litigator for wind farm companies.

"After AVIC got to DeWolf, he flipped contracts from our Soaring Wind Energy joint venture to Ascendant Renewable Energy, which was an outfit AVIC set up based in Lubbock, Texas, to be able to develop wind farms around the world."[3]

AVIC was trying to export the CCP's "catch, raise, and kill" philosophy. Partnering with Tang, it gained access to the company's best practices, critical contacts, and potential wind farms. Ascendant Renewable Energy Corporation was going to pirate the business acumen of Tang Energy and, with AVIC's deep pockets, take over the market and destroy SWE. As outlined in Made in China 2025, Beijing was intent on dominating this green technology of the future.

Extreme Lawfare

The clause in the joint venture's initial agreement—the one requiring that all legal disputes would be settled in the United States—was now Tang Energy's only recourse. "There's a famous quote in Texas," the Dallas-raised Jenevein drawled. "Lawsuits aren't pink teas. They're battles. This case definitely wasn't pink tea."

Jenevein isn't an engineer, but he builds power stations and turbine blades. He's not a lawyer, either. But he's a quick study. He and his attorneys had a hunch that AVIC's lawyers would claim that the company was an entity of the PRC government, making it a sovereign entity, which would shield it from any legal or financial claims under the Foreign Sovereign Immunities Act (FSIA) of 1976.

To dismantle that defense and reach into the PRC's financial reserves, Tang prosecuted and won under an "alter ego" theory of law. AVIC tried to hide behind a corporate veil. With its alter ego strategy, Tang and SWE lawyers would pierce that so-called veil. They aimed to use documents, emails, and public records to establish that AVIC headquarters in Beijing had initiated principal-agent relationships, directing all its subsidiaries to violate the various agreements with SWE. They would tie AVIC's financial liability to its headquarters for its subordinates' activity in Texas.

The first shots were fired when Tang, relying on the joint venture agreement, called for dispute resolution. Later, with SWE and the four other investors, it charged AVIC headquarters and its subsidiaries, including AVIC International USA (aka Catic USA) and Ascendant Renewable Energy Corporation, with violating its non-compete agreement. AVIC subordinates responded by bringing two lawsuits, first by AVIC International USA in August 2014 and then by Ascendant Renewable Energy Corporation. To right that wrong, Jenevein's team requested that the AVIC group be held liable for damages resulting from the breach and stripped of ownership of SWE.

The International Centre for Dispute Resolution, the international division of the American Arbitration Association, handed down its award on December 21, 2015, affirming the alter ego theory and noting "The evidence overwhelmingly shows that AVIC HQ, AVIC International, AVIC IRE, AVIC TED, and Ascendant operated as one entity with respect to [several agreements]. AVIC HQ exercised such complete control over the other entity Respondents in this case the AVIC Respondents operate as one entity."[4]

In twenty-one subsequent blistering paragraphs the arbitrators named names of senior AVIC executives—an embarrassment in a nation where a sniff of bad publicity can result in grave consequences. The loss of face, as the expression goes, was ensured by two other determinations in the report: AVIC International USA was stripped of its ownership of SWE and ordered to pay $62.9 million for breach of the SWE agreement.

AVIC, as Jenevein's team expected, asserted its immunity under the Foreign Sovereign Immunities Act. The US District Court for the Northern District of Texas eventually confirmed the arbitration award, and AVIC challenged the ruling in the Fifth Circuit Court of Appeals with two separate filings. Again, Tang Energy won both decisions. In early 2020, AVIC lawyers were running out of options and petitioned the Supreme Court. Their request was denied. As Jenevein put it, "The Supreme Court said, 'We don't even have a dissenting opinion to work from. We're not going to hear your case.'"

For Jenevein, that non-decision by the highest court in the land was a huge win. AVIC had no standing to appeal. Not only that, but on October 5, 2020, AVIC International USA filed for bankruptcy. It was time to start settlement talks. Jenevein had several goals he wanted to achieve. He had spent nearly a decade of his life battling with AVIC in the legal arena. In the previous decade, he'd been vital to building a billion-dollar business with it, only to have his value stolen. He wanted justice; the AVIC International USA bankruptcy allowed the company to plead poverty, putting a damper on collecting the full award, which exceeded $85 million. But a deal was struck to settle for $24 million.

Equally important to Jenevein was some kind of accountability. The ruthlessness of AVIC was, of course, part and parcel of the CCP's culture, which views conducting business as essentially an act of war. But executives had made the decisions and carried them out. Tang Energy had been targeted multiple times. He wanted senior AVIC executives to sign the agreement. While none of the signees admitted to wrongdoing, Jenevein believed their signatures would amount to a loss of face and reputational damages. Au Zhen, identified as AVIC's chief auditor; Bai Xiaogang, identified as China Aviation Industry General Aircraft's chairman of the board; and Jiao Yan, identified as AVIC International Holding Corporation's general counsel, among others, signed the settlement. The CEO of the bankrupt AVIC International USA signed a declaration in support of the "Confidential Global Settlement Agreement and General Release of Claims." The "confidential" settlement would be filed in California bankruptcy court, however, where anyone could access it and see that the CCP-owned AVIC Corporation had admitted to violating corporate agreements and misappropriating funds—a clear-cut loss of face. Perhaps a small but nonetheless gratifying win for Jenevein.

In the PRC, people in high places who make mistakes often suddenly disappear, often winding up in prison. Jiang Jiemin, the former head of the China National Petroleum Corporation, vanished until he was sentenced to sixteen years in prison on bribery charges; more recently, Foreign Minister Qin Gang disappeared in June 2023, while a former defense minister, General Li Shangfu, mysteriously departed in August 2024. "I don't know what happened to Jiang," said Jenevein. "I know that some of the people we worked with at AVIC have disappeared. We even helped the head of AVIC, Chairman Lin, disappear. In 2015 Tang sent him a letter saying, 'Dear Chairman Lin, we're sure that you'll be shocked to know that there's corruption in your organization.'"

Jenevein may have been swindled out of his business but at least he didn't end up in a cold prison cell in Beijing.

Jenevein, who now runs the Pointe Bello strategic intelligence firm, where he continues trying to do well by doing good, still has his sense of humor intact, but finds it hard to put a value on his experiences taking on the CCP.

"If you just look at the cost versus recovery, we came out ahead. If you look at spending a decade of your life, of some of the finest years of your career, well, I'm trying to yield a return on that today. Part of that is doing things like this, trying to help people understand what the Communist Party is up to. I fear that we're in the most dangerous time in my life, and that includes the Cuban Missile Crisis."

Those who know China best are often those trying to ring the alarm bells the loudest.

Power Drains

Patrick Jenevein isn't alone. Wind turbines are a big business. While he was building and battling AVIC and its subsidiaries, AMSC, a Massachusetts-based company formerly known as American Superconductor, was wooed, raided, and stripped of trade secrets that cost the company $550 million, caused its valuation to plummet, and forced the company to cut nearly seven hundred jobs.[5]

Sometime in 2010 Sinovel Wind Group Company, China's leading state-owned wind turbine manufacturer, approached AMSC. The two companies had worked together since 2005, with AMSC providing electrical components and engineering support services for several Sinovel turbines.[6] But now the Chinese manufacturer was after something else: the American company's software to regulate the flow of electricity from wind turbines to the electrical grid. A deal was cut: Sinovel would pay AMSC $800 million for goods and services to use in Sinovel turbines.

AMSC didn't receive all the money promised. Instead, Sinovel acquired the technology it wanted when company executives allegedly convinced Dejan Karabasevic, the head of AMSC's automation engineering department in Klagenfurt, Austria, to leave the company for a job with the Chinese firm. On March 7, 2011, Karabasevic logged in to the AMSC computer system in Wisconsin and secretly downloaded source code to his computer in Klagenfurt. With that code, Sinovel no longer needed to pay AMSC to enable it to retrofit old turbines with new software.[7]

Karabasevic's actions were exposed very quickly. Six months after his download, he pleaded guilty in an Austrian court and was sentenced to twelve months in prison and two years' probation and ordered to pay €200,000 in damages.[8]

In the United States, charges were also filed in 2013 against Su Liying, the deputy director of Sinovel's Research and Development Department; Zhao Haichun, a technology manager for Sinovel; Dejan Karabasevic; and the company Sinovel more broadly. While the three men reside in countries with no extradition treaties (China and Serbia) and have not been arrested, Sinovel was found guilty in a 2018 jury trial on all charges it faced, including conspiracy, trade secret theft, and wire fraud. A $1.5 million fine was levied—a small sum compared to the company's $57.5 million settlement.[9]

But wind turbines aren't the only US energy sector targeted by the PRC. Data may be the oil of the twenty-first century, but electricity is still required to collect, store, mine, and analyze that data. Consequently, other US companies have been targeted across a wide range of energy-related technologies, ranging from attacks on battery technology, which we discussed earlier, to solar panels, petroleum, and nuclear power.

In 2014, the Department of Justice unleashed its first-ever trade secret charges against a foreign government—unsurprisingly, China—indicting five officers in Unit 61398, a cyber-espionage team within the third division of the PLA. The officers targeted Westinghouse's nuclear reactor plants and US subsidiaries of the German company SolarWorld, among others. The Westinghouse heist occurred in 2010, three years after the company announced plans, together with several different PRC entities, including the State Nuclear Power Technology Corporation (SNPTC), to build a total of four AP1000 reactors in Sanmen and Haiyang. During that time, one military hacker stole confidential specifications for pipes, pipe supports, and pipe routing within the AP1000 plant buildings. Ironically, the hacker also stole internal Westinghouse emails that discussed strategies for collaborating with a PRC partner that might eventually become a competitor—which was undoubtedly why the PLA was trying to steal Westinghouse's secrets.[10]

The attack on SolarWorld, a manufacturer of solar panels and turnkey solar power systems, was less about acquiring technology and more about eliminating competition. In 2012, PLA hackers ransacked the computer systems in the company's offices in California and Oregon, copying thousands of emails and documents containing proprietary financial, inventory, production, distribution, and marketing materials. That raid coincided with PRC solar firms' flooding the market with inexpensive products. The theft of SolarWorld's internal numbers, projections, and plans was executed to give Chinese competitors an unfair market advantage, helping them undercut the German company's prices, determine where inventory should be shipped, and even locate new sales channels. The WTO terms agreed to by China back in 2000 to conduct fair business practices now seemed like ancient history.

Not surprisingly, several cases of stolen tech and IP involved companies in Houston. One of the Texas city's many nicknames, "The Energy Capital of the World," goes a long way to explaining why. At least two Chinese energy companies and their proxies were busted there for stealing from petro-industrial companies. The PRC firm Jason Energy Technologies Company (JET) and its American subsidiary, Jason Oil and Gas Equipment (JOG) USA, used the insider threat playbook to target Houston's Forum Energy Technologies, the maker of Duracoil, advanced coiled tubing used in oil well operations, according to a 2020 indictment. JOG bribed a Forum employee to pass along proprietary documents, pictures, and data related to manufacturing Duracoil. It also flew the employee to China to help its plant manager implement Forum's methods, resulting in a "new" product, ReliaCoil, which is currently for sale on the Jason Energy website. According to the Department of Justice, which filed charges, the employee pled guilty to conspiracy to commit trade secret theft.[11] Forum filed a civil suit against JOG, which was resolved through mediation in June 2022.[12]

North Houston hosts the manufacturing plant of Trelleborg Marine Systems North America, a Swedish company that is one of the leading manufacturers of syntactic foam. The special foam is a strong, lightweight, extremely buoyant material made of tiny hollow spheres suspended in an epoxy resin, used for deep-sea oil and gas drilling. It also has military applications,[13] which is why a PLA unit tasked with ensuring China's maritime dominance decided to loot the company's closely guarded trade secrets.

China's Ministry of Industry and Information Technology (MIIT) contributed to a $3.1 million campaign to fund a raid on Trelleborg's Houston office, according to a 2016 criminal indictment. Shan Shi, a China-born naturalized US citizen, spearheaded the operation. Shi was a graduate of Harbin Engineering University, a school administered by an MIIT offshoot that has strong ties to the PLA and China's navy, and was a senior technical adviser for the China Shipbuilding Industry Corporation. After signing an agreement with Taizhou CBM–Future New Materials S&T Company (CBM), to develop the manufacture of syntactic foam, he decided the fastest way to jumpstart that development was to steal Trelleborg's trade secrets. He set up a competing firm, CBM International (CBMI), in China and hired at least four current and former employees of Trelleborg to steal company documents, plans, and manufacturing details over a five-year period.[14] Shan helped set up a plant in China to compete with Trelleborg. He was subsequently busted after attempting to sell his stolen process in the United States, sentenced to sixteen months in prison for conspiracy to sell trade secrets, and ordered to forfeit over $330,000.[15]

On July 22, 2020, the US government ordered China to close its consulate in Houston, charging that the sixty-person office was primarily an operational center for diplomats (and intelligence officers) to aid economic espionage and the theft of scientific research materials. A Beijing spokesman for China's Ministry of Foreign Affairs urged the United States to immediately reverse the decision, and the Chinese Embassy in Washington, DC, issued a terse response: "The U.S. accusations are groundless fabrications."[16] To companies like Trelleborg, which bore the costs of China's acts of theft, the reasons behind taking such actions were very much grounded.

IN EARLY 2025, China escalated its Great Heist up a notch. Cybersecurity analysts and Western security officials discovered that Chinese-made solar inverters, the vital connectivity from solar tech to the electricity grids, installed across hundreds of American towns and cities, contained unauthorized communication modules. Not just any modules, but ones capable of sending and receiving data via covert channels. Not malware. Hardware. Embedded deep within the circuitry of the machinery. These weren't isolated flaws, either. They were features, purposefully and deliberately engineered and distributed across the heart of the US energy grid under the banner of so-called green progress.

To the untrained eye, a solar inverter is rather harmless: a gray box, humming quietly on the side of a building. In the eyes of Beijing, however, it was the opportunity to develop another vector to spy on the United States to gain critical data.

Such spyware, however, can do more than just collect information. It can also deliver kinetic effects. If needed, the modules in question could be remotely activated to manipulate energy flows, sabotage frequency regulation, or black out strategic nodes at a moment's notice. The end result? Already fragile American energy grids shut down, blackouts, and ensuing social and economic chaos. In fact, one such incident already occurred in the fall of 2024 when China disabled solar panel inverters in the United States.

In other words, China isn't just exporting solar panels and other green technology like wind turbines; it's in effect exporting covert sabotage capabilities under the guise of green energy. And, so far, America has taken the bait—chasing climate goals without doing its due diligence on the wiring under the hood that powers its way of life.

This is a new and more ominous face of the Great Heist. Not just the theft of designs, trade secrets, or hardware schematics—but the insertion of what are in effect booby traps into the very infrastructure of America's modern life. A solar panel that powers your home today may, in the wrong hands, become a kill switch that helps take down the grid tomorrow. What stories like this make clear is that we are entering a new era of great power competition, supercharged by rapidly evolving technological advancements, where true sovereignty depends on not just knowing who wrote your firmware but also in having absolute fidelity over the supply chain of critical infrastructure. The final question isn't just *what* China will try to control—it's how long America will keep pretending it isn't already happening.

CHAPTER 16

The Seeds of Agri-Espionage

IT BEGAN with a shadowy silhouette kneeling in the dirt.

On a cloudless May morning in 2011, at a farm in Tama County, Iowa, a field manager for a leading US seed company noticed something odd. Crouched in a test cornfield was a thin man, Asian, dressed in business casual clothes, brushing his hands through the soil. Nearby, a car idled with another man inside. Visitors were rare in that part of Iowa; strangers poking around in test fields early in the morning even rarer.

The field manager approached the stranger. "What are you doing?" he asked.

The man stood up, flushed and nervous. He stammered that he worked at the University of Iowa and was showing the field to a guest from China. They were attending a conference. The story didn't add up. But when the farmer answered his cellphone for a call unrelated to what he was encountering at the field, the man darted to the car and sped off, swerving into a ditch in his hurry to get away.[1]

The field manager wrote down the license plate number. He didn't know exactly what was growing in the field he was standing in. A local farmer had leased the land to seed firm Pioneer and was managing their crops. But he knew it was important; the company's future depended on breeding new crops. As it turned out, it was one of Pioneer's most anticipated hybrid corn seed products, a trade secret worth millions of dollars. And the man in the field would come under FBI surveillance for orchestrating one of the most ambitious acts of agricultural espionage in American history. Agriculture—the ability to feed nations—had become the new frontier in the shadow war for intellectual property between China and America.

The Salt of the Earth

On June 1, 2016, another individual in the agricultural sector with ties to China, Jiunn-Ren Chen, abruptly resigned from his job at the Climate Corporation, a Monsanto subsidiary. He told his employer that he was moving to Taiwan to be with his family. What he didn't disclose was that months earlier, he had approached Sinochem Group's China National Seed Group Company, a state-owned Monsanto rival, or that he had just accepted a job offer there.

Having given notice, Chen got very busy, according to a civil lawsuit later filed by Monsanto. He downloaded fifty-two files filled with company trade secrets. Beginning a week earlier, he had uploaded several scrubbing software programs with names such as Disk Drill and CleanMyMac in an effort to stop IT experts from tracking his activity on his company computers, according to a forfeiture filing. Then he purchased one-way tickets to China, and he and his family bolted from America the next day. Two months after his departure, he sold his St. Louis home—via his attorney—for a $111,516.68 profit. The US government later moved to seize the funds.[2]

Chen has never been charged with a crime. But his actions alerted Monsanto's security team. About a year after Chen's departure, another employee named Haitao Xiang gave his two-week notice. He said he was resigning to join an agricultural remote-sensing start-up owned by his former thesis adviser. It sounded plausible if you ignored the warning signs to the contrary.

A few days after Xiang's May 25, 2017, resignation, Anne Luther, a senior investigator for Monsanto's Global Security Team, met with Jaret Depke, a special agent at the FBI St. Louis office. Luther shared several concerns with Depke about the sudden resignation of the senior research application engineer. She told the agent that the security team had reason to believe that Xiang, during his first year with Monsanto as an engineer, had misrepresented himself as a University of Illinois student in an attempt to acquire information from SpecTIR, a privately owned company specializing in hyperspectral imaging technology.[3] Now, the Monsanto security team suspected him of being an insider threat after his nearly nine years of working with strategically important trade secrets.

By the time of his departure, Xiang had pivoted careerwise, trading his gig at Monsanto to become an advanced imaging scientist for the same subsidiary that Chen had worked for, the Climate Corporation. The smaller company, originally founded by two Google employees, sold an agriculture management web platform called Climate Field-View to farmers. Its most popular app, later called Nutrient Optimizer, was a program that told farmers how much nitrogen to add to their fields. Xiang's work was essential to delivering accurate assessments; he managed the remote sensing functionality that estimated soil properties using satellite imagery. But he was also a cog in an expensive R&D wheel. According to the company, Nutrient Optimizer had emerged from years of research costing hundreds of millions of dollars—research that Xiang had access to.[4]

At Luther's prompting, Depke spoke with other Monsanto insiders, who shared a long list of Xiang's suspicious activity, including Google searches using phrases indicating that Xiang was worried about being prosecuted for sending documents to an outside entity: "as evidence to accuse me," "company information to the third party," and "can use it to [sic] against me in the future."

On June 8, a day before Xiang's exit interview at work, Depke contacted US Customs and Border Protection Officer Art Beck, who ran a check on Xiang and discovered that he had purchased a one-way ticket from Chicago to Shanghai. He was scheduled to depart—without his wife and child—on June 10.

The timing of Xiang's departure and new job, combined with his computer searches and his access to trade secrets, was the kind of evidence that justified executing a search warrant. But obtaining a search warrant would take time, as Depke and Beck knew. Fortunately, Beck offered a fast alternative, one that exists only for customs officials: the "border search exception," which allows customs agents to seize personal property at the US border without a warrant. Beck alerted agents at Chicago O'Hare International Airport to keep an eye out for Xiang and inspect his electronic devices.[5]

Xiang completed his exit interview, growing visibly nervous. The next day he drove to O'Hare, passed airport security, and just as he was boarding his flight, CBP officers stopped him. In the ensuing search of his luggage, the agents seized six objects, including his cell phone, laptop computer, a SD card, and a SIM card; then they sent Xiang on his way.

Xiang was doubtlessly relieved to get on the plane. Although his ticket was to Shanghai, on June 12, he was due to start a job two hundred miles away at the Institute of Soil Science, Chinese Academy of Sciences, in Nanjing.

The new gig had been two years in the making. In 2015, Xiang had applied to the Chinese Academy of Sciences' Hundred Talents Program, one of the many variants of the Thousand Talents Program, and had flown to Nanjing for an interview the following year. In the end, he was awarded funds to run an agricultural research lab. As so often happens with Chinese scientists who return with valuable IP from abroad, more money showed up, enabling him to launch his own start-up. China dangles the potential rewards, and organic intelligence collectors materialize.

Xiang's devices arrived at the FBI's St. Louis office, and forensic images—copies of the content stored in the devices—were made. Depke located a set of files on Xiang's seized SD card marked with language identifying them as containing trade secrets or proprietary information. He shared the files with Monsanto's security team and got the evidence he needed to pursue full warrants: confirmation that Xiang had stolen trade secrets and attempted to leave the country with them. One of the files on Xiang's SD card was a ninety-six-page document on Nutrient Optimizer. Records showed that he had downloaded it from the company's file system to his company laptop back in February 2016.

The FBI obtained additional warrants to access Xiang's private email and web accounts. It also harvested his communications on Monsanto's email servers, including his pitch to the Hundred Talents Program.

For the next two years, the FBI monitored Xiang's comings and goings as he frequently traveled between Nanjing and St. Louis, where his wife and daughter still lived. St. Louis prosecutors had not had a corporate espionage case since President Clinton had signed the Economic Espionage Act in 1996, and they took their time fleshing out the case. Given that Xiang knew what files were on his seized devices—and that those files showed that he had willfully and repeatedly violated his legal obligations to the Climate Corporation—his decision to return repeatedly to the United States suggests that he was either naive or simply deluded.

On November 18, 2019, two FBI agents arrived at Xiang's St. Louis house, aware that he had booked a flight back to China that was scheduled to depart the following day. As his wife and daughter were at home, the agents invited him to chat over coffee. Then, after asking him a few questions, they arrested him and led him away in handcuffs.[6]

Two years later, Xiang pled guilty to one count of conspiracy to commit economic espionage, stating, among other things, that he "knew or intended that the offense would benefit a foreign government, foreign instrumentality, or foreign agent." He was sentenced to twenty-nine months in prison followed by three years of supervised release and a $150,000 fine.

After the penalty was handed down on April 7, 2022, the Department of Justice issued a press release that tried to capture the extent of damage done by Xiang and its implications. "The defendant took advantage of living and working in the United States to steal a valuable trade secret for the benefit of PRC entities," said Assistant Attorney General Kenneth A. Polite Jr. of the DOJ's Criminal Division. "This type of theft threatens employers large and small in every state, and it imperils our economic competitiveness as a nation. Individuals entrusted with valuable trade secrets should be on notice that if they abuse that trust—especially for the benefit of foreign nations—we will hold them accountable."[7]

The Xiang arrest was essentially an open-and-shut case, so airtight that the defendant copped a plea deal. Yet the wheels of justice at US law enforcement agencies churned for five years to achieve this result, five years to convict a spy who was obviously guilty. How many other hundreds of IP thefts were committed during that time? Xiang's prosecution underscored the impotency that has proven typical of America's fight against essentially an undeclared espionage war against it by Beijing. If deterrence of IP theft is a national security goal, the lack of speed to arrive at justice and the resulting prison sentence in the Xiang case must be seen as a limited success and a strategic failure. Such sentences will strike fear into the heart of no one—not desperate immigrants, not patriotic PRC citizens, not craven profiteers, and certainly not the MSS agents tasked with IP collection in support of Xi's imperial vision.

Stalking Seeds

The targeting of Monsanto and other Western agribusiness leaders is the direct result of another existential crisis that, in a sense, has nothing to do with the West. It's a humanitarian crisis that looms as a perpetual threat to the CCP. With the PRC's population exceeding 1.4 billion people, the regime must feed roughly 20 percent of the global population. But the country's borders contain less than 10 percent of the world's arable land and 6 percent of the world's water resources. Those numbers add up to a constant national food insecurity challenge.

This is not a new development. Unfortunately, famine has plagued China for centuries, if not millennia. During the final hundred years of the Qing Dynasty (1644–1911), the last imperial government, repeated famines left tens of millions of people dead. The Great Famine, the largest known famine in human history, occurred between the spring of 1958 and 1962, the result of a perfect storm of ineffective governance and planning driven by Mao's Great Leap Forward "reforms." Mao's centralized planning encouraged supervisors to file inflated reports of overproduction of foodstuffs so that the great Communist leader's reforms would be viewed as a success. This gross mismanagement, combined with massive floods in northern China and two years of drought, led to the deaths of an estimated 30 million people.[8]

The CCP has banned books about the Great Famine, and references to the monumental catastrophe are taboo. When the Great Famine is mentioned at all, it's cloaked in euphemisms, such as "the Three Years of Natural Disasters."[9]

Given its stark past and its present daunting environmental realities, it's no wonder that President Xi included agriculture in the Made in China 2025 agenda, calling for accelerated "development of high-end agricultural equipment" and "related breeding, farming, planting, management, harvesting, transportation, and storage."[10] No one wants to see a nation's people starve, least of all that nation's ostensible president for life.

This imperative made China's engagement with the international agricultural community critical. In 1999, it joined the 1991 Convention of the International Union for the Protection of New Varieties of Plants.[11] It is worth noting that in 2022, Rouse, the global intellectual property consultancy reported that China "has not yet agreed to the 1991 Act of the UPOV Convention." The Swiss-based UPOV is an agricultural equivalent of the WTO. It was formed in 1961 to provide a "system of plant variety protection, with the aim of encouraging the development of new varieties of plants, for the benefit of society."[12] The convention governs the ownership and use of newly developed plants and crops through established "Breeder's Rights." The theft of novel breeder "material" is a direct violation of UPOV rules. So is the importation or sale of qualified plants without approval.[13] Unfortunately, as with the WTO, the UPOV's effectiveness is severely constrained due to its weak enforcement tools. Once again, China reaped the benefits of a trade system it had no intention of fairly complying with. A little more than a decade after agreeing to the terms of the UPOV, that would become evidently clear in the American Midwest.

THE MYSTERIOUS man in the field in Iowa was named Mo Hailong, aka Robert Mo. He was a Chinese citizen and legal resident of the United States. He had come to America with his wife, Li Ping, to pursue a PhD in thermodynamics at the University of Kansas. After completing the degree in 2003, he took a job in Miami. But with a growing family—the couple had a girl and a boy—he struggled to find a research job that would cover the bills.

In 2006, Mo signed on to become the director of international business of the Beijing Dabeinong Technology Group Company (DBN). He owed the job, in large part, to a strong family connection. His sister, Mo Yun, was married to Shao Genhuo, the CCP-plugged-in billionaire chairman of the board of DBN, which owned the Beijing Kings Nower Seed Science & Technology Company. She arranged for her brother to join the company. His job, at least officially, was to obtain commercially available and other hybrid and inbred corn seed lines for possible use by DBN for breeding, planting, and/or producing corn seed in China.

Unofficially, as he eventually learned, his job requirements were different. DBN didn't want just common seeds that were already on the market; it wanted what might be termed "high-tech seeds," the proprietary, genetically modified kernels developed by sophisticated agricultural companies to produce corn yields that are disease resistant, pest resistant, and drought resistant. The value of such seeds was obvious, even to a newcomer like Mo. Such robust corn would offer huge cost savings to commercial farmers, enabling them to raise crops that would need less pest control and chemical treatments, not to mention less water. It would also help mitigate the most crippling threat to food security, crop failure.

But there was a catch: Those seeds were off limits. Agricultural leaders such as Monsanto and Pioneer regarded them as trade secrets, scientifically concocted biotechnology potentially worth hundreds of millions of dollars. The test fields were in effect laboratories. The male and female stalks of corn were precisely monitored, inbred from generations of crafted seeds. The company used those master seeds to make its own vast harvests, collecting the kernels to fuel sales in the commercial seed market.

In discussions with his boss, Li Shaoming, the CEO of Beijing Kings Nower Seed Science & Technology Company, it soon became clear what was expected of him. According to a book on the case, *The Scientist and the Spy*, Dr. Li devised a simple plan to obtain high-tech seeds: Steal them from American companies.[14]

A few months after his initial encounter in the Pioneer test field, which company officials later revealed contained highly anticipated inbred corn seed products that had been years in the making,[15] Mo again toured Iowa cornfields, this time with two other men. Once again, they attracted attention, appearing at an unmarked Monsanto test field near Bondurant, Iowa, in August—harvest season. Police arrived, and a deputy took the names of the three trespassers: Mo, Wang Lei, and Li Shaoming, the vice chairman and CEO of Kings Nower Seed, respectively. Mo provided a slightly more accurate description of their behavior, stating that his two associates were from China. They had flown into Chicago and were "driving across the Midwest 'looking at crops.'" He expressed surprise at the encounter with law enforcement, claiming that in China, the farmers welcome the assistance of others, even if of strangers.[16] A spurious explanation indeed.

With two clear and present red flags raised, the FBI began investigating Mo and a steadily growing cast of characters associated with Kings Nower Seed. That month, they tracked Mo mailing 341 pounds of "corn samples" from Des Moines, Iowa, to his home in Boca Raton, Florida. It was the first of many suspect shipments.

Two years of intense investigation and surveillance ensued. The FBI followed Mo through Iowa and Illinois on trips that lasted several days at a time. Agents documented him purchasing multiple bags of Pioneer Hi-Bred corn and failing to sign the required "growing agreement" that binds the buyer to adhere to usage terms. It also tracked him buying bags of Monsanto's DeKalb corn seed and transporting them first to storage facilities and then to a farm in Monee, Illinois, a property he had found and purchased, assigning ownership to Kings Nower Seed. Whenever Mo or his cronies returned a rental car, the FBI would search it, sometimes finding and confiscating corn kernels.

Mo was joined in those exploits by two fellow employees from Kings Nower Seed, Ye Jian and Lin Young, both citizens of China. At one point the FBI taped a conversation between the two men, who were critical—and very clear—about the illegal tasks the company CEO had set for them:

Ye: You can forget about ever coming to the US again, assuming things go wrong. You can never come. Isn't that ruining an individual's future?

Lin: If it's just not being able to come to the US again . . .

Ye: That's no biggie.

Lin: That's no biggie. I don't think it's that simple. I actually studied law!

Ye: Oh yeah, you practiced law.

Lin: These are actually very serious offenses . . .

Ye: They could treat us as spies!

Lin: That is what we've been doing! What I am trying to say is, as for the charges, there could be several.

Ye: Yeah.

Lin: It's trespassing other people's private property, that's one; secondly, theft/larceny; and the third, violation of IP law. That's three charges.[17]

On September 30, 2012, after a yearlong investigation, agents listened in to a conversation as Mo drove with Li, Ye, and Wang Hongwei, a man who had flown in from Vermont. The men discussed plans to transport bags of corn out of the country, including those moved by Mo. They noted that previous deliveries had been sent and all had arrived at their intended destination. Mo also took pains to remind Ye to thoroughly clean their rental cars to avoid leaving any telltale traces of their crimes.

Then the men departed for the airport. Yi and Li were flying to China, and customs agents stopped both men to check their bags. Li had packed two bulk-sized microwave popcorn boxes that looked factory sealed. When agents opened the boxes, they found approximately a hundred small manila envelopes stowed beneath two actual microwave packages of popcorn. Each envelope contained kernels and had a number—2155, 2403, 20362—written on it. Investigators suspected that the numbers had been used both to obscure the origin of each seed and, when matched to a decoding key, to identify its origin. In other words, tradecraft.

In addition to envelopes, Li's other bag contained approximately thirteen brown grocery bags bearing handwritten numbers. Each of these bags contained additional envelopes with corn kernels inside.

As for Ye, his bag contained thirty Subway napkins wrapped around individual kernels of corn, all carefully secreted in the clothes in his bag.

Wang, meanwhile, boarded a domestic flight to Burlington, Vermont, and the FBI prepared a team to conduct surveillance and alerted the Customs and Border Patrol if Hongwei attempted to do the obvious: cross into Canada.

Leaving Patrick Leahy Burlington International Airport in a rental car, Wang suddenly went into Jason Bourne mode. He made a series of sudden turns to detect and evade a trail. Pulling a quick maneuver and veering into a mall parking lot, he succeeded in doing just that. It was a smooth move.

But a smoother move would have involved changing cars, which he failed to do. When he pulled into the Highgate Springs port crossing that evening, the customs agents were waiting. After finally stopping him, they found forty-four paper grocery bags hidden in the vehicle and in his luggage, again annotated with mysterious numbers. Each bag held about twenty manila envelopes containing varying amounts of corn kernels. The search also turned up a notebook containing numerous GPS coordinates accompanied by handwritten notes in Mandarin Chinese. He also had a digital camera containing hundreds of pictures of various cornfields and what appeared to be production facilities of corn seed manufacturers.

During questioning, he claimed to have been in Vermont for days. When he was shown evidence of his Chicago flight, he came clean about traveling to Chicago. He also said he had purchased the corn from an individual in Chicago named Mo Hailong. Eventually, he was sent on his way, minus his corn kernels.

A year later, Mo Hailong was indicted along with five co-conspirators, Li Shaoming, Wang Lei, Wang Hongwei, Ye Jian, and Lin Yong. Only he was arrested; the others lived in China or Canada and allegations against them remain unproven. The charges, however, were that the men had stolen inbred lines of seed that can take up to five to eight years of research and a minimum of $30 million to $40 million to develop. On July 2, 2014, the DOJ announced a superseding indictment and the arrest of Mo's sister, Mo Yun. Yun ran DBN's research project management and was the wife of DBN founder and chairman of the board Dr. Shao Genhuo. Prosecutors said she had been a key part of the conspiracy to steal the high-tech seeds.

Yun caught a break when the judge hearing the case ruled that instant messages, pivotal evidence in the prosecutors' case, couldn't be used in the trial. The suspect was released from electronic monitoring and given back her passport.[18] Her brother was not quite as lucky. He copped a plea in late 2016 and was sentenced to three years in prison and three years of supervised release. He was also ordered to pay Monsanto and Pioneer $212,500 in restitution, as well as forfeit farms near Monee, Illinois, and Redfield, Iowa, to the US government.[19]

In 2021, the CCP instituted what seemed like a workaround regarding seed theft and IP protection. It introduced amendments to China's Seed Law containing clauses promoting the legal rights and interests of owners of new plant varieties. (It also kept intact the rights of individual farmers to use any seeds they have.)[20] By putting those laws on the books, the CCP might be seen as encouraging agricultural R&D and signaling its intent to play by international laws. But the presence of a law in China does not mean that it will be executed. Article 35 of the Chinese Constitution states Citizens of the People's Republic of China shall enjoy freedom of speech, the press, assembly, association, procession, and demonstration. Article 36 promises "freedom of religious belief."[21] The lofty words and claimed aspirations promoted on paper by the CCP are laughable and stand in stark contrast to the behavior associated with an authoritarian regime with growing totalitarian tendencies. The PRC laws claiming to protect agricultural IP will be disregarded in practice. The larger question is indeed how the new edict plays against the ultimate law of the land. For nearly eighty years, rule of Party, not rule of law, has prevailed in the PRC. The law is whatever the almighty Xi and the CCP say it is, and Xi is intent on achieving his goal of national rejuvenation through Made in China 2025.

Agri-espionage is not about harvesting this year's yield; it's about developing tomorrow's seeds. It's about creating seeds with drought resistance, pest immunity, and nitrogen efficiency that can sustain nations. These traits are worth billions of dollars—and, for a country with 1.4 billion mouths to feed, existential.

In June 2025, news broke of a potential sinister twist on agri-espionage indicating, like the booby-trapped solar power inverters, another ominous escalation of the Great Heist by Beijing. According to an affidavit from FBI Agent Edward Nieh, a Chinese researcher at the University of Michigan named Yunqing Jian and her boyfriend Zunyong Liu conspired to smuggle samples of *Fusarium graminearum*, a fungus that causes blight, into the United States. Among the worrying allegations in Nieh's report: Jian was in the country on CCP government funding, she had signed a statement confirming her membership in the CCP and her dedication to it, and Liu's phone contained an article titled "2018 Plant-Pathogen Warfare under Changing Climate Conditions," which cited *Fusarium graminearum* as an example of a type of destructive disease and pathogen for crops.

To make matters worse, the duo repeatedly lied to US authorities.[22] These worrisome allegations raised the possibility of a reverse agri-operation with horrifying implications. Was CCP member Jian here to unleash a crippling strand of fungus against American crops?

This recent event underscores why agriculture, which many may perhaps initially consider as relatively benign and low tech, is so important to Beijing. The IP of companies like Monsanto and Pioneer is, as it relates to America's core national interests, just as valuable as that of Lockheed Martin or Intel. It doesn't matter how advanced your fifth-generation stealth fighters are if you can't feed your people.

A proprietary seed line is no different from a satellite blueprint; it just grows in soil.

As the cases of Mo Hailong, Jiunn-Ren Chen, and Haitao Xiang show, China's hunger is not just for grain; it is for controlling the DNA of the world's food supply.

CHAPTER 17

Inside the Situation Room

Stopping the Great Heist

As former intelligence officers, one of whom served and advised two presidents, we are frequently asked questions about the proper, measured, effective responses to stop the Great Heist. Everyone wants to know what policies and practices need to change. Simply put, how can we combat the Great Heist?

The short answer is that it must come from the top and be a national initiative. The following two chapters, set in the two places in America where we must begin to affect and effect change—the White House Situation Room and the corporate boardroom—are fictional and not based on any real-life characters. We hope they are instructive—not to mention more engaging than listing off bullet points.

CROFT DECIDED to get there early. It was his meeting. Yesterday, the president had summoned him to the Oval Office to tell him the news: "Director Davis is still in the ICU. You're driving tomorrow, leading us all into the future. Do not crash."

It was supposed to have been Davis's show. Three months ago, the president had asked the director of national intelligence for a plan, and the grind had started immediately. Croft, the national intelligence principal deputy director, had been churning out eighteen-hour days. He divided his never-ending workdays into two parts. First, he dealt with the operational nuts and bolts of handling budgets and personnel. Then, prepping for the director's project, he held meetings, asked questions, and made requests.

The US government has eighteen different intelligence agencies across a wide swath of national security missions. There was a lot to aggregate. So Croft spent the evening hours in his office, seeking light in the literal and metaphorical darkness, poring over intelligence assessments, reports, and strategic pitches. He sorted through the puzzle pieces, hoping that they'd yield eureka moments, flagging the most impressive work to share with his boss.

But now Director Davis was recovering from emergency surgery: colon blockage. Croft knew that there would be jokes about this, national security doves saying that they had always known that the guy was "full of it." Not that anyone would say that to Croft. Everyone knew he was in lockstep with his boss.

The agenda had been set. Initially, Director Davis discussed listing it as "Subject Classified," but not providing a more descriptive meeting subject was a rarity for National Security Council meetings chaired by the president. "I want to get everyone's undivided attention," he told Croft. "'Subject Classified' will build anticipation and the kind of attention the topic deserves."

Then he called it the China Broken Windows Project, a name borrowed from New York City's successful strategy to reduce crime by eliminating any signs of disorder. The idea was that the United States needed to police everything, everywhere, all the time to finally stop the PRC's espionage and theft campaigns, an undeclared war by the CCP to overtake the United States economically, militarily, and geopolitically.

The two men and others—strategy emissaries from the Department of Homeland Security, the CIA, FBI, the Department of the Treasury, and other stakeholders—engaged in game theory exercises to examine the potential outcomes of dozens and dozens of strategic and policy actions. If they had more time, they might run computer simulations, too. The goal was to be holistic. They considered actions not just from Beijing's perspective but for their potential impact on Main Street and Wall Street and among friends and allies of the United States around the globe. Eventually, the enormity of the task hit home, and the director concluded that the name didn't quite fit. Vandalism and cosmetic solutions weren't the problem; a vast undeclared war was. And that war was being funded and weaponized by the CCP to raid and rob American corporate and research institutions and erode the United States' geopolitical power via elaborate espionage campaigns. That was why today's agenda now had the broadest possible name: Stopping the Great Heist.

Croft picked up his agenda folder, plastered with the highest classification markings, and made sure it was all there: the introduction he'd written with Director Davis, the mission statement, the lineup. He had one hour to lay it all out, and he prayed that the president would sign off on it. He heard the director's voice in his head: "This isn't just politics. This is about our collective economic well-being and our ability to sustain our nation. Otherwise, the nastiest double bind in the history of national security crises is going to rip us to shreds."

"It's more like a quadruple bind, Director."

"In 3D, Croft. No! Not just 3D! It's *six*-dimensional chess."

Croft took the stairs to the ground floor of the West Wing. The Situation Room was the centerpiece of a 5,500-square-foot warren of rooms devoted to national security and perhaps the most digitally secure real estate in the world.

In addition to the Situation Room—Croft knew some people liked to call it Whizzer, short for White House Situation Room, but he wasn't one of them; this wasn't fun and games—there was a watch center manned 24/7 by civilians and military officers, filled with giant monitors and secure communications, and two additional conference rooms. In 2023, the floor had been given a $50 million makeover that hadn't been just about new mahogany paneling and inlaid stonework; it had included see-through glass walls that could darken with the press of a button.[1] The real focus was on state-of-the-art high-tech communications equipment and security software. The rooms weren't just soundproofed, muted with acoustic baffling; they were "TEMPESTed," too. That was intel techspeak—"Telecommunications Electronics Materials Protected from Emanating Spurious Transmissions"—for "a frequency intercept free zone." Phones, computers, and audio speakers can give off radio-frequency (RF) signals and electromagnetic radiation that can be decoded. TEMPEST technology decayed and eroded those signals. Such technology prevented eavesdropping on meetings or any form of telecommunications including cell phone usage.

Not that you could use a cell phone down here. They were banned in the Situation Room. Croft went down the steps and into the reception area. He gave his name to a Secret Service agent, who checked an attendance sheet. Then he handed his cell phone to the agent, who placed it in a locker and gave Croft the access key. "Please follow me, Deputy Director Croft," he said. The last check-in task involved walking through a full-body scanner to ensure that no recording or transmitting equipment was taken into the room.

Croft stood alone, surveying the room. He looked at the two rows of empty chairs: the fourteen that encircled the long table and the ring of seats that lined the walls. He looked at the gleaming, polished wood of the table. There was a leather place mat at each seat, and just beyond each place mat was a triangular nameplate. The president would sit at the head of the table, of course, with the American flag and presidential seal behind him. But the rest of the National Security Council members also had assigned seats. He walked around the table, imaging the audience: veep Margaret Anne Wingfield to the left of the president of the United States, he affectionately referenced as POTUS; then the secretary of state and the NSC cabinet members.

He completed the circle and found his name. He was the second from the president's left, with the chief of staff between them.

He sat down, opened his folder, and pulled out the last page, one he and the director had drawn up just before the director's stomach pains had started. "Stopping the Great Heist" was emblazoned in 20-point bold type and stamped with a common West Wing reminder: Top Secret/SCI for "sensitive compartmented information." There was also a second stamp: EYES ONLY—RESTRICTED HANDLING. They had argued about the title: The Great Heist. Croft argued with the director about everything. Or rather analyzed. If the documents leaked, Xi and the entire CCP would think that they were being mocked, Croft had worried.

"It's how CCP bureaucrats know they are alive," the director had joked.

"That's my point, exactly, sir," Croft replied. "No point inflaming them."

"Leave it for now. Maybe I'll ask POTUS."

The title was still in place. He reviewed his list of talking points:

1. Crushing the can
2. Strategic decoupling
3. Supply chain initiatives
4. Market access—private sector public accountability
5. Global coalition
6. Investor and valuation reform
7. Security & enforcement tools: FBI, CFIUS, SEC
8. NatSec Law reset
9. Escalation planning
10. The undeclared war

He looked at his watch, an old, predigital Bulova. It had made it through security. Three minutes to go. The room would start filling up. He remembered the director having given him a reality check once when he had started getting into granular issues:

"Croft, we've got twenty-five minutes to present the intelligence-based recommendations for maximum impact and then convince the president to green-light the actions while getting all NSC cabinet members to have skin in the game. We can't get in the weeds."

———

AT 11:02, the president started the meeting and got right to the point:

"Three months ago, I asked Director Davis to prepare strategic recommendations to address the China threat. It was a big ask. I told him to talk to stakeholders and give me a 360-degree platform, a reset for America. They have stolen tens of billions of IP, technology, innovation, and know-how from America and the West and are now reaping trillions from the Great Heist. It must stop.

"Deputy Director Croft, who I'm told led much of the initiative and consulted with many of you, is here to present the analysis and findings."

Croft sat up in his chair.

"Thank you, Mr. President and National Security Council members. We wanted to start with an uncomfortable truth. Even prior to joining the World Trade Organization in 2001, the PRC had engaged in a dedicated campaign to steal every facet of value from America and the West. Now they deploy dedicated intelligence resources that outnumber our manpower by at least five to one; they steal military plans, critical software, valuable research, chemical formulas, and databases filled with personal identifying information. They raid the private sector and the public sector. And they have done so for decades with impunity, and it knows no bounds.

"Your predecessors, for many reasons, failed to heed the incontrovertible intelligence pointing to the PRC's aggressive plans to underwrite their great technological leap forward by stealing America's commercial secrets, and from the West more generally. Your predecessors, for the most part, kicked an incredibly destabilizing and dangerous can down the road. We are not going to dwell on the unfortunate political and commercial realities that allowed that to happen.

"Instead, we will present today essential steps to crush that can."

"Great. Convince me."

"I'll try, sir." Croft looked at his list. There was a digital version. He wondered if he should share it on the monitors. No. Not yet. Visual aids were great, but they were also potential distractions. Let everyone stay focused on his pitch. He cleared his throat. "Some understandably angry policy strategists have floated knee-jerk ideas about decoupling our economies."

"Give me a break," the president said. "We can't operate a hospital without China, never mind a Walmart or an army base."

"We all agree. However, we believe strategic, partial decoupling is essential for national security reasons and is an achievable goal vis-à-vis the PRC/CCP. Our domestic supply chain must be strengthened and protected so that we can use partial decoupling as a threat and a weapon. Let me add that the United States is the CCP's greatest source of revenue. Any commercial business that can flourish domestically and globally from within our borders will hurt the CCP revenue there. This theme and potential weapon is a centerpiece of our strategy."

POTUS leaned forward and pressed, "What are we decoupling and how?"

"Essential technologies, Mr. President. Your secretary of defense already has an operational list of no-go zones concerning cooperation with the PRC related to sensitive technologies. It's a point of departure but again achievable, everything from telecom equipment to port cranes to sensor manufacturing. We believe the list will grow with time and continued analysis. Mr. President, your Executive Branch's departments and agencies focused on national security must make strategic decoupling from China's supply chain a top priority. There is no more urgent matter in terms of immediate actions. Our analysts have found China-made products with preinstalled backdoor entry points in everything from drones to medical life support devices to shipping cranes at major ports."

"That's a big ask."

"I refer you to World War II, sir. Industry, government, and Rosie the Riveter all mobilized quickly."

"That's quite a point of reference."

"I know, sir. I'm not an economist, but I believe historians claim it led to great prosperity."

"World War II."

"Sorry, sir. But we need to return to the arsenal, to our democracy, so to speak."

"Carry on."

"Okay, so we make our own electric cars end to end, or cranes or tanker ships or petri dishes, what then?" It was the vice president. Croft had expected her to be hostile. Her husband was a Silicon Valley billionaire, a guy whom Director Davis and Croft agreed might not embrace their proposals and solutions.

"This is a complex initiative. We can build out domestically. But our clout becomes far greater if it is part of a global initiative. Everyone here knows about Beijing's Belt and Road Initiative, cutting loan-shark deals in the global South so they can seize infrastructure or help despots in Africa and Latin America and gain access to natural resources and buy political influence. That's all worrying. But Europe and the US control seventy percent of the world's capital. We need to leverage our relationships on the Continent. If the US and Europe don't buy from China, its economy will take a massive hit. There simply isn't enough cash in the markets to keep China's manufacturing capacity at even close to full employment. We need to strengthen and unite with market strategies and the flow of investment capital so that we support each other rather than the nation that has been ripping us off."

Louis Gonzalez, the marine turned economist turned banker turned Treasury secretary, leaned forward to speak.

"What is it, Louis?" the president asked.

"Two things: I'm concerned about constraints to capital movement, and I'd also like to note that Europe is just as addicted to cheap Chinese goods as we are."

Croft raised his hand to his forehead to salute his fellow veteran. "Thank you. I'll be getting to the movement of capital in a second. And the issue of cheap goods is vital. It's part of what got us here in the first place. So bear with me."

It was time to use the slides he had prepared. He signaled to the on duty NSC staffer to start using PowerPoint. "These are the annual numbers of US investment dollars being poured into China for the last twenty years."

"Where's the matching return on investment slide?" Gonzalez asked.

"The return on investment?" Croft asked. "You mean GM's five-billion-dollar write-down on its business in China? You mean all the American factories that have shuttered in the last four decades? You mean China's estimated control of eighty-three percent of the electric vehicle supply chain? Will any of the policymakers in this room explain to Secretary Gonzales where he might go to learn about the return on investment in China? Victor, help me out here."

"I got this, Croft." It was Victor Melville, the steely-nerved CIA director. "The ROI is this meeting, right here in this room. That's what that money has returned. Sure, BlackRock, other private equity, and the tech sector have profited. But look up at that chart. Pick a year. In 2021, when some might say our return on investment was covid, we had $1.18 trillion in US funds invested in Chinese securities![2] That money doesn't boomerang back to our shores. It ricochets back to CCP coffers. It builds state-owned factories, funds PLA security and defense spending, and makes CCP members rich. It has funded a war against us. That's what Croft is laying out, clear as day. That's part of the can we've been kicking. And it must stop. Right here, right now."

"Thank you, Director Melville," said Croft, suppressing a smile and making a mental note to send the man a bottle of Johnnie Walker Blue. "Secretary Gonzales, I am happy to meet with you or anyone else in this room to delve into these numbers further. As you can see, America has invested trillions of dollars in the PRC. But this slide represents only part of the dollar deluge we shower on China. It doesn't include the billions of dollars American and multinational firms invest in doing business there—building factories, closing on manufacturing agreements, launching joint ventures."

The president slammed his hand on the table. "Which gets us back to the supply chain, doesn't it?"

"Exactly right, Mr. President. It's all entwined, a brilliant, giant capital-catching web. This is why we advocate focused, strategic decoupling. But bear with me. Next slide, please."

An image of Earth appeared on the screen with the heading "Global Capital." As it spun around slowly, numbers popped up on each continent: North America: $136 trillion; Europe: $103 trillion; Asia-Pacific: $75 trillion; China: $74 trillion; India: $12 trillion; Latin America: $11 trillion; Africa: $5 trillion.

"This is a snapshot of the world's wealth. Add up the US and our allies in Europe and Asia, and, as I mentioned, you've got about seventy percent of the world's capital. Those are the markets China needs to sell to. You think they can feed their 1.4 billion people selling cheap electric cars in Africa?"

"That is a tough scale," agreed Tim Fried from Homeland Security.

"Let him speak!" the president said.

Croft kept his poker face, but it was a struggle. The president wanted more. He would give it to him. "The takeaway from these numbers and China's existential thirst for capital is to establish a global initiative capable of denying it market access and investment. It can and should start with us, because the CCP has been targeting us more than anyone. But it needs to be an international coalition. Think of it as a WTO with a spine.

"The economists we've consulted agree: Closing access to markets closes access to cash. But because of China's current control of the supply chain and shipping channels, we must strategically counter it. It took the PRC twenty years to truly dominate manufacturing. We don't have to match them widget for widget. We have to choose and own sectors. We've started by protecting and manufacturing chips and critical technology. But we need to aggressively expand in multiple directions. Covid, for example, demonstrated it would be wise, from a national security perspective, to manufacture more pharmaceutical drugs and health care technology domestically."

"So microchips and biotech and IV drips, is that what I'm hearing? That's going to solve the crisis?" It was the veep again. She sounded cynical.

"No, this is a 360-degree plan—to repel China from the war it's been waging for decades. Working with other nations to create alternative suppliers and limiting China's access to capital and to markets to sell its goods is absolutely central to countering the CCP. They've been quite open about what markets they plan to dominate. They have then committed to achieving that domination by stealing, or trying to steal, all competitive technology available—or, more accurately, unavailable. They have used strategic investments—money and talent—in America's private sector to acquire what they want to acquire. They are relentless and ubiquitous in their pursuit of America's commercial secrets. This has to stop. Theft is not part of the free market. Intellectual property arises out of huge investments and must yield fair compensation."

Croft realized that he was getting dangerously close to crossing the line from laying out an intelligence brief to being policy prescriptive. That could get him a yellow if not a red card in the NSC meeting. Time was running out. He flipped to the next slide. The image of the earth stopped rotating and froze with an outline of China's territory for all to see.

"How much of that $75 trillion was stolen from us and the West? How much was raised by selling counterfeit goods? Seized joint ventures? Stolen technology? I'd venture at least a third of that number over the last thirty years."

The president nodded and cleared his throat. "This is really interesting, and I have plenty more questions. But about the stolen tech, what about our corporations? What are they doing? Don't they have skin in the game?"

"You mean, what are they doing about the losses, Mr. President?"

"I mean it's their IP and data that are being stolen. That means the company's future is being stolen, too. Are you following that?"

"Yes, sir. Sorry, sir. They're now required to report any data hacks by law. That wasn't always the case. We, led by the FBI, advise them to invest in security resilience."

"Does anybody in this room think those are sufficient measures to protect the future of a publicly traded entity? Should every stockholder in America breathe easy knowing a board of directors and corporate America more generally have been warned about the CCP stealing their core business?"

The president looked around the room. The cabinet members were mostly poker-faced. One or two nodded with grins suggesting that they understood the president's point. He raised his head, making it clear that he was inspecting the outer rim of the room, where other council members and select advisers sat.

"That wasn't just a rhetorical question. Anyone got an answer?"

"Absolutely, sir." It was Joselyn Royce, the first woman director of the FBI. "I'm impressed, Mr. President, by your question. In fact, I believe you are stealing some of Croft's thunder."

"What does that mean?"

"It means you are exactly right: Stockholders should be *very* concerned. The fact is, the management of most companies doesn't give a hoot about China's hostile targeting and theft until it smacks them in the face. Our field agents go door to door, warning companies. We tell them, 'If you manufacture anything in China, they will steal your code, your technology, and even your staff.' And it doesn't matter if they are making kitchen gadgets or jet engines, the MSS is going to try to take it. And from all we've seen, they are virtually always successful in stealing any foreign corporate secrets that are moved into China. Isn't that right, Croft?"

Croft offered a tiny nod, urging her to continue.

"Honestly, Mr. President, we also tell them that whether they stay here or work with India, if they have something Beijing wants, look out, because they are coming for you—with either insider threats or outsider hacks. But corporate leaders don't always listen. They go into China anyway. And when we ask why, they look at us as if we're stupid. The answer is always some combination of 'Cheap labor,' 'That's where the supply chain is,' and 'We want to sell our stuff to a billion people.' Senior management is focused on next quarter's earnings to keep their jobs and get their bonuses. They minimize long-term planning. If the IP is stolen and a rival in Shanghai surfaces five years from now, that's going to be the next CEO's problem and the next board's nightmare."

The president stood up, ran his hand through his thick gray hair. Croft had heard about his nano-pacing, a tough act in a tight space. But POTUS, antsy and furious at what he was hearing, pushed his chair back to the wall and traversed the narrow width of the room.

"Croft, what's the strategy to make them accountable to national security and their stockholders? The business of America is business! But if we can't protect our business, there will be no more capital to throw around, and then we're all going out of business."

"You've steered this meeting exactly where we wanted to go, sir. So thank you. We need to use our tools; strengthen the oversight role of the Securities and Exchange Commission, give it teeth and expert staff. It should rival the FBI, and frankly, the Bureau needs to double its counterintelligence budget and personnel. The attorney general should also identify the domestic spy laws that need to be updated to take into account the very expansive and non-traditional nature of China's intelligence operations in the US. As for CFIUS—"

"CFIUS!" the president exploded.

"The Committee on Foreign Investment in the United States, sir."

"I know what it is. I'm not an idiot. Everybody complains about them."

Treasury Secretary Gonzalez began to cough violently. Croft wondered if the Heimlich maneuver had ever been performed in the Situation Room.

"Excuse me, Mr. President," Gonzalez said, catching his breath. "As the chair of the committee you just denigrated, I am literally shocked. If you have concerns, I hope you'll share them."

"Oh, jeez. Mr. Secretary," the president said, offering a sheepish smile and sitting down, "I'm truly sorry. It was just a joke. Or a semi-joke. Croft here has got me all amped up. I have a hunch he's going to share his concerns. Croft?"

"I will, sir. To be honest, CFIUS needs more resources and more time to do its job correctly."

"What do you mean?"

"Two companies spend months negotiating a big deal. It could be the acquisition of a tech firm that builds cooling systems, or it could be the sale of hundreds of square miles in Texas to a Chinese investment group. Of course, American interests are eager for a big sale. Naturally, Congress—your government at work—comes under all kinds of pressure from lobbyists and donors to speed a deal through. But anytime there's any China connection, it needs to be thoroughly vetted.

"CFIUS approved a giant purchase of land that just happened to be next to Laughlin Air Force Base. Now how smart was that?[3] What if the cooling company has tech to cool quantum computers or hypersonic transports? The buyers and sellers aren't going to admit that there are potential national security problems. That's why CFIUS needs more independent investigators and analysts to examine deals without external pressure. National security and intelligence agencies need a bigger voice on CFIUS. That structure was set up to promote foreign investment, not to stop it. But that was before anyone understood Beijing's undeclared war. We advocate a new process that includes punishing parties for failing to make disclosures about potential national security vulnerabilities. And even with these actions, China is going to use shell companies. We've already caught Huawei doing that. So we need to prepare for that."

"Tell me about the SEC."

"It's supposed to protect investors and ensure that companies are on the up and up. But as we've said, every company that has operations in the PRC has voluntarily and fundamentally exposed itself to CCP surveillance since every foreign company in China has a CCP representative on staff. As for joint ventures—that is a fool's game, too. American firms have had their holdings stripped by both the national and local governments. And while certain successful US companies have succeeded in grabbing market share with superior products, over time, Chinese firms have created comparable, cheaper rivals. We've seen it in the EV market and the automobile market more generally. We are seeing it with cell phones, green energy, and beyond. There's a national pride factor at work in China's commercial sector. Not only that, but the government offers billions in incentives to buy domestic EVs. The dream of American businesses selling products to a billion Chinese is just that: an unsustainable fantasy.

"Croft, I asked about the SEC."

"Sorry, sir. The director warned me about getting in the weeds. The point is, the SEC sets valuation guidelines. How can you count investment in China as a sound long-game move, given the government's 'catch, raise, kill' strategy being used by China, given its record of theft? Is owning a factory in Beijing good for balance sheets or a death knell?"

"You're saying devalue companies with PRC operations."

"It is something to consider. Also, the PRC still has currency restrictions. An American company may have $500 million sitting in Beijing, but it has to clear hurdles to remove it."

"So it's not liquid?"

"Not exactly, sir. Only theoretically. It needs all kinds of approvals, which means it can be stopped. And last I checked, you have to keep a reserve fund of fifty percent of all capital on hand."[1]

"That's a pretty big and sudden hit to put on our own companies—and everyone who invests in those companies: the pension funds, the 401(k)s and IRAs."

"We thought of it as a tool in your toolshed, sir."

"I mean, it would drag the stock market into a bear's den."

"Perhaps. Again, just raising the idea might be seen as a warning or threat to companies here. A corporate board might say, 'If our China earnings aren't part of our valuation, why should we invest there?' That's the logic. A disincentive."

"Ah. So this is a suite of strategic options and bargaining chips."

"Yes, Mr. President."

"Next time, frame it that way."

"Sorry, Mr. President.

"And this wouldn't destroy Wall Street?"

"No, sir. Not if we regulate it selectively. But honestly, sir, I defer to your secretary of the Treasury and your economic advisers on the impact of the threats of SEC actions."

"Regulate? Find another word, please." It was Mark Park, the NSC's most conservative figure. Croft had heard that the guy had problems with the Nuclear Regulatory Commission's name and mission.

"Indeed, I misspoke," Croft said. "I meant we could apply things sector by sector. And that brings me to one of the last points. We have a proposal that links specific critical industries and technologies ranked as threats to national security with a corresponding list of imports that need to be blacklisted."

"You mean like that gargantuan telecom hardening?" said the president. He sat down, wincing at the thought. "Where we are paying telecoms to get rid of Huawei?"

"Yes. But for other critical tech. There is no reason to purchase digital equipment that arrives embedded with hidden remote access. We've seen the exploits in drones, medical equipment, and who knows what else.

"Got it. Go on."

"Just a few more points, sir." The monitors surrounding the table lit up with another chart titled "Legal Reset." It displayed the average duration of espionage and illegal trade cases, from start to conviction, and the corresponding penalties.

"The agencies' directors are unanimous. One, we need a reset on national security and trade theft law. Two, we need a special acts law that lowers the bar and obstacles to a speedy trial. The sheer number of hacks and attacks is astonishing. We cannot continue to respond with legal peashooters, slow walking among high-speed campaigns. Any hope of deterrence requires faster trials or a low bar for arrests, incarceration, and the seizure of assets. Obviously, we need to protect due process, so we need to think this through carefully. Three—which in part elaborates on my second point—we need bigger penalties: seizure of corporate assets; billion-dollar penalties; twenty-year prison sentences. Bad actors need to understand that the risk will be far greater than the reward."

The president nodded. Croft had no read on whether he agreed or not.

"This last slide, sir, visualizes the interlocking, relational rationale behind these strategies."

The president read the slide heading: "'Crushing the Can,' huh? I like it. No more kicking the can crushed or otherwise down the road."

"This is how we end the Great Heist or, at a minimum, put a big dent in it. We initiate our own undeclared war effort, targeting supply chain initiatives coordinated with our allies to facilitate strategic decoupling from the PRC. We pair that with denying Beijing access to key US and Western markets. Western enterprises will be required to fill the gap, thereby encouraging domestic investment. If they want more incentives, the threat of valuation penalties on China-based assets should increase domestic investment, production, and growth. And that growth will be protected in part by new laws that expand prosecution, incarceration, and financial penalties.

"Of course, we have some work to do on escalation planning, preparing for Beijing's possible responses to any of these options."

"This a modest proposal, ain't it?" The president was smiling. "How in the world am I going to sell this?"

"It's a simple story, Mr. President. Just tell the truth. Yes, mistakes were made. Yes, the can was kicked down the road because nobody wanted to say what was really happening and the stock market loved the short-term profits. China has been fighting an undeclared war against America and the West. It has enriched itself, hurt our economy, and gained a military standing that no one saw coming. Built off of sound intelligence analysis, the administration has identified the first steps to stop the relentless attacks and protect our national interests. And make no mistake, as previous administrations have: Maintaining the status quo, as we have for decades, will end in disaster."

Croft closed his folder. Nobody said a word. Was this a normal reaction? Had he struck out or stunned them into a state of shock? He had no idea.

Then the president said, "Thank you, Deputy Director. Now is the time for the Security Council to live up to our name and protect America. The Great Heist must end, starting right now. We have already lost too much time. You will be hearing from my national security advisor on the next steps to make Croft's brief and the recommendations a reality." Again, no one spoke.

CHAPTER 18

Boardroom Blitz

RISHI GOT the call at 6:45 a.m. It was from his boss's boss, the CEO.

Right there, it was an awkward situation. Not the timing—he was up already and back from his run—but when the CEO of Overtal Industries International called, not Marty Gruber, the CIO, whom Rishi reported to, it was a bit troubling. Automatically, he started to worry.

Of course, anxiety was part of his job. "I'm the chief security officer," he liked to joke. "If I'm not worried, I'm not thinking."

But seriously, when he saw the name DOUGLAS FAIR, CEO, on his phone screen, his brain went into overdrive, wondering, Did something bad happen to Marty? Is something bad going to happen to Overtal? Or was this somehow related to Armacase Technologies, the story that had broken last night?

"Hello?" he said.

"Rishi, it's Douglas. Listen, Chairman Rochester called me at five thirty a.m. We are having an emergency board of directors meeting at four p.m. at Simons Gallagher. I need you there."

"Simons Gallagher the law firm?"

"Yes. It's a special board session. They've got some new secure facility there. Chairman Rochester set it up. Can you make it?"

"Yes, sir."

"Did you hear about Armacase? It's incredible. Completely decimated. Makes North Korea's attack on Sony Pictures look like a high school hackathon."

"Yes. Incredible," Rishi repeated. He could have added "predictable and awful," but he subscribed to letting the CEO have the last best word.

"Rochester—I mean *Chairman* Rochester—thinks we're next. That's why I'm calling. I know you report to Marty Gruber. But the chairman found out that the head of security reports to the head of information, and he blew a gasket."

"It's a fairly common structure."

"Not anymore, or not to him, apparently. He's bringing in an outside guy, a China expert, for the board to meet. So you are now our new acting CGSO—chief general security officer. Congratulations. We'll work out the compensation tomorrow and the scope of your responsibilities. Effective immediately, you report to me. I'll let Gruber know.

"But back to the China expert joining the board meeting: The key thing is whatever structure this guy comes in with, you speak the language more than Marty. He's all databases and taxonomy and other mind-numbing stuff, and maybe—on a good day—some two-factor authentication requirements."

"Does Marty know about this?"

"My next call, and as I noted, I will let him know about the immediate change in the chain of command."

"Who is the outside guy?"

"He runs an outfit called Omniveillance?"

"Oh, good: Ron Kendall."

"You know him?"

"A little. FBI, he's seen it all. An apostle of GSD."

"GSD?"

"Getting stuff done."

"Ah. See you at four."

Rishi disconnected and sent a text: "Ronnie, see you at 4. Take no prisoners. Your fan, Rishi."

THE ARMACASE story was all over the news, plastered on social media, and no doubt haunting the hearts and minds of the investment community in New York and the political class in Washington, DC. Markets in the Far East had closed with a big downturn as a result, and headline writers all blamed "the Armacase attack." Rishi thought that shorthand was a case of blaming the victim.

Not that the victim didn't deserve some or even a big part of the blame.

Armacase had spun off a subsidiary that made laser equipped drones, Zappatics, three years ago, hoping that one day it would be spun off and then go IPO. It had hired a Japanese firm, Trusistor, to design and manufacture transmitters, but it had failed to perform the required due diligence. A Jiangxi state capital fund owned the largest share of Trusistor. In a matter of months, Zappatics' IP had been copied and shipped off to Jiangxi, where a competing laser drone firm had blossomed.

After a forensic digital investigation, Zappatics leadership had decided to file a suit, and its CEO had called out Jiangxi's CCP leader in an op-ed in *The Wall Street Journal*.

That had been a strategic mistake. It had been a hop, skip, and jump for PRC hackers, employed or waved in by Trusistor, to infiltrate Zappatics and then Armacase. And there was zero doubt in Rishi's mind that the hacks had been executed within months of the initial agreement with Trusistor. It was ostensibly a best practice of the MSS.

The day after the op-ed ran, emails from the VP Sales to the CEO outlining indirect sales of rocket launchers to both sides of the civil wars in Sudan and the Democratic Republic of the Congo were leaked to the press. That same day, sealed records of two separate harassment cases involving the CEO and the chairman of the board were uploaded to Reddit. And AirDance Aeronautics, a subsidiary of AVIC, unveiled the SkyGun 888, a machine-gun drone that looked to everyone like the spitting image of Armacase's StealthShooter 2X.

The CEO had tried to circle the wagons, but a virus had locked the company's network. He had sent his CTO to Best Buy to purchase the outlet's entire stock of laptops. He had ordered limos to take his leadership team to meet with McArthur Watts & Shine's crisis management team.

At the market's close, Armacase's market valuation had fallen by 50 percent. Several European leaders expressed outrage over the weapons profiteering in Africa and declared their contracts with the company would undergo renewed scrutiny. And four more women had come forward with harassment charges.

The next morning, Armacase had issued a statement: The CEO was on indefinite leave.

No wonder an emergency board meeting had been called.

HAVING SERVED five years as chairman of the board of Overtal Industries International, Oscar Rochester prided himself on being a leader and a gifted strategic thinker. Rishi knew that because not only did he have a copy of Rochester's business memoir, *Aim Higher than the Bottom Line: Optimizing Corporate Leadership and Citizenship*, but he had even read several chapters of it, enough to cover his butt if he ever got caught in the elevator with the great man. So far, that had not happened. But now that he was ascending the company org chart, Rishi figured that might change.

The chairman, however, had not arrived when Rishi sat down at the massive conference table at Simons Gallagher and surveyed the room. The C-suite was there, aligned on one side of the table, along with Fisher, the senior counsel, and two of his team. Marty Gruber was missing in action, and Rishi felt a pang of guilt. But only a slight one; information security was important, and of course everyone in the C-suite knew that. But it was only one piece of comprehensive corporate resilience.

On the other side of the table were the board members. One of them looked vaguely familiar, and Rishi tried not to stare. Finally, he made the connection. The guy was a former national news anchorman, Jim Robards. What did he know about running a company? There at the far end of the table were two well-dressed women he'd never seen before, likely PR strategists, he thought. The most interesting things in the room, he decided, were the stylish acoustic panels that blanketed the walls and ceiling, and the gizmos with long antennae set up in each corner of the room. Were they oscillating jammers, pumping out disruptive electromagnetic waves? Secret white noise machines? Or some kind of bug detection? He had no idea.

At 3:55, Chairman Rochester walked in with Doug Fair and Ron Kendall, and the casual chatter immediately ceased as if someone had hit a switch. The three men sat down at the head of the table.

Rochester wasn't so much flanked by the much younger Fair and Kendall as he was outflanked. He looked tired and ancient, a far cry from the smiling portrait on his book cover. "Good afternoon," he said. "This is an emergency meeting of the board. As such, we will dispense with our normal rules of order after roll call. But for good order, board minutes will be taken. Markus?"

Markus was the board secretary, a gentleman notable for his bow tie and raspy voice. He read off a list of names, and the board members affirmed their presence. The number of board members far exceeded quorum requirements. While this was a previously un-scheduled board meeting, it was still an official board meeting. Now the chairman set out to explain why it had been called—in case there was any doubt.

"Thank you, Markus. And thank you all for coming on such short notice. The news in our business is not good. You have all seen the implosion at Armacase. I have, on my right, one of the leading corporate security experts in America, if not the leading expert. His name is Ron Kendall. He ran the counterintelligence division at the FBI for several years. He has a PhD in telecommunications engineering and a master's in public policy. I reached out to Ron some months ago to discuss a possible engagement. And I thought, given recent events, that there was no time like the present to bring him here to talk to us about security at Overtal and the threat emanating from bad actors."

Ron Kendall stood up. He had the vestiges of being a G-man: cropped haircut, physically trim for his age, handsome even if there was something slightly pugnacious about him, like the shade of his

$4,000 suit. It wasn't Bureau blue, that conservative official shade. It was lighter, more daring—an unspoken taunt to his past, a reminder he was faster and better than his peers.

"I talk better on my feet," he said. "Thank you, Mr. Chairman. First, a disclaimer. Or maybe more accurately, it's actually a claim. I don't want to be rude, I want to be honest, and I want to be helpful. So I'm going to speak the truth, as I see it. I've examined hundreds of corporate espionage cases and met with thousands of executives and business leaders. I meet with boards almost every day. And have done so for the last four years. That's not an exaggeration. What these leaders want to know is this: 'How can I protect my company and still make hefty profits?' Is that right, Chairman? Would you agree?"

"One hundred percent."

"It's a great question for people who have a legal, fiduciary responsibility and must answer to their shareholders. But the answer isn't great. The answer stinks. Especially if you do significant business in China.

"Let me ask you, Mr. Chairman, how much business do you do with China?"

"A considerable amount. We are opening a factory there as we speak."

"To take advantage of the battery supply chain for your devices?"

"Why yes. How did you—"

"I realize you have actual rocket scientists in your company, but because your firm manufactures mobile armaments that require energy sources, I do not have to be a rocket scientist to put two and two together."

Rishi smiled. This was pure Kendall. Rochester's mouth tightened.

"Remember, I'm not being rude! Just honest. You need to shut that operation down. I'm going to make a prediction: Twelve months after you open your factory, a PRC competitor in a nearby factory will be making the same product at a lower price. That nearby PRC factory may not even exist today, but it will within a year's time. If you don't believe me, let's bet five thousand dollars on it. Or ten thousand."

"Mr. Kendall," said the bow tie board secretary. "We, as a company, are entrusted to make decisions to ensure profitability. The factory in China reduces our costs in the extreme."

"That is great and true. But let's remember: Why are we all here today? Because Armacase, your competitor, is going down in flames, the subject of arson, cyber-bombing, and public incineration. It wasn't just a tech attack, it was a PR assault. And it started with IP theft, remember? It's a dumpster fire now."

"Yes. That appears—"

"Listen, I'm just reporting the facts. Armacase Technologies was warned by the Bureau, just like you guys were already warned about your factory."

"Is that true, Doug?" Rochester looked over at the CEO, who looked out at the table.

Fair shrugged. "Rishi, can you take this? By the way, Rishi Zuma is our newly promoted acting general security officer."

"Yes, I can answer the chairman," Rishi said, wondering if he should greet Kendall, too. He decided to play it safe. "What Ron—I mean, Mr. Kendall—said is correct. The Bureau has paid us social calls."

"Why wasn't I there?" Doug Fair asked.

"Doug," said Kendall, "this is a board meeting, but think of it as a court trial. Don't ask questions you don't know the answer to."

"It must have been a scheduling issue, sir," Rishi said. "I believe you were invited."

"Thank you, Rishi. Great to see you, by the way. Look, would it have mattered if Mr. Fair went to that meeting? I just told you to close your operation in Shenzhen or Guangdong or wherever your factory is, and immediately board members start talking about bottom lines, profits, and supply chains. This leads me to a question: Is the board the problem, is China the problem, or is the entire ecosystem the problem? Anyone want to answer? No? Rishi, don't let me down."

Rishi laughed. He remembered guys theorizing about Kendall's caffeine intake. "The answer is all three. But since we can't control China and we exist within the free market system with SEC rules—"

"THE ONLY PROBLEM WE CAN CONTROL IS THE BOARD!

Exactly! Do you guys love me yet? Don't answer. It's a rhetorical question."

Bow Tie raised his hand. "What do you advise a responsible board to do? How do we balance things?"

"You need to come to terms with identifying your company's crown jewels, which you must protect at all costs. Not all IP is created equal. Let me put it to you this way: What are you prepared to lose to the PRC, and what can you never see end up in their hands? Then the corollary question is: What are you going to do to protect the crown jewels?

"American companies are famous for innovation. It's a long-standing comparative advantage over virtually every other country on the planet. What can you do to keep that advantage? Explore joint venture opportunities with other like-minded firms, either domestically or outside the PRC. Avoid having your products rely on the Chinese supply chain. I know all of this is easy for me to say. But be a board that delivers on its fiduciary role and does not sidestep the problem. You're there to ensure that problems are solved. You hold the CEO responsible for executing on the board's directives! Form a China Threat Committee. Do you have the head of corporate security report to the CEO? Have you invested in email-scrubbing software and AI programs to identify solicitations and spear-phishing links? Does HR vet job candidates for possible connections to PLA-associated universities? Have you instituted a foreign travel disclosure policy? Do your contracts require complete confidentiality? Is your IP marked as proprietary and treated as the equivalent of the US government's top secret information? That's just a partial list of security best practices.

"The tone is set at the top. It's a cliché but it's true. The bigger point is, I'm talking about an enormous shift in the culture of the firm. You need a 'speak up' culture akin to 'See something, say something.' Every individual has a responsibility to enforce security.

"You are not in this war of security attrition alone. Standards are being set for cybersecurity. The Department of Defense requires its vendors and partners to obtain cybersecurity maturity model certification."

"We failed last year," Rishi offered. "But we should have it nailed now."

"Good! Almost nobody in the weapons world is up to snuff. Rishi can tell you what we saw at the Bureau every single day: one rip-off after another, stolen technology, stolen data. stolen know-how from deficient insider threat programs in corporate America. Clever schemes designed by China's Ministry of State Security spymasters that lead to employees' getting paid off by PRC state agencies to steal proprietary business plans and IP. Counteracting all that takes vigilance and smarts and *discipline.*

"Firms need to have their corporate security managed by 'the best and the brightest' within the company. Do not approach security as an afterthought or, worse yet, as an unwanted cost center. An effective, supportive board understands that security threats are real and ubiquitous and surface from unsuspecting points of entry. It also recognizes that quarterly profits are not the only measure of a successfully run company, and it creates a culture that supports that mindset."

Kendall paused for a moment to take a read of his audience.

"If you don't care, I guess I'm wasting all your time. But I think many of the people in this room should care about protecting your intellectual property and the security of your investments. If for no other reason, you owe it to the shareholder to care.

"For years, American companies were rabid to go to China and profit off all that cheap labor and a large potential consumer market. The nation benefited, too. Cheap labor meant lower-priced goods, which meant increased sales and huge profits. But it also meant getting ripped off by government-funded competitors in China. And rogue companies that the CCP allows to exist and even promotes because they both damage our position in the markets at home and abroad and support the PRC's modern-day Great Leap Forward.

"If Mr. Fair were to come here, as I have done, and say we need to prioritize our immediate and long-term security before our profits, what would you say?"

"Before today, I'd have questioned his sanity." It was the chairman. "But reading about Armacase gives me pause. A $40 billion company obliterated in about two days."

"Well, sir, that's the thing. It wasn't just two days, I can promise you that. The attacks were in process for months, if not years. They exfiltrated emails and documents and had them translated. The PRC amassed data on the firm. They schemed to co-own a Japanese tech firm to win a contract with an Armacase subsidiary, which unwittingly allowed the MSS to inject spies into the Armacase workforce. This kind of attack happens all the time. You won't see it in any Wall Street analyst reports, but the biggest industries in China are IP and data theft and piracy. And that's why I advocate that every board rethink its priorities with respect to the business threats posed by China." Kendall sat down. "I'm sure you must have questions, so fire away."

A hand shot up, silver bangles gleaming in the office light. "I'm Nicole Dreyfus from McArthur Watts & Shine's crisis management team. Thank you for coming and delivering such a dramatic presentation about dangers companies like Overtal Industries International face. I want to come back to what must be the elephant in the room for every business you meet with: How can companies remain competitive in a free market when they are prisoners to supply chains and investor demands for constant growth?"

"I don't have an MBA. I've been told, though, that great companies have retrenched. Some have made huge bets and taken on enormous debt. Apple was initially a flop. Amazon racked up billions in debt before its first profitable quarter. This is where I land in terms of an ideal state for a corporation in this environment: The boards and executive teams need to start with some ideal mix of vision, strategy, innovation, marketing, and execution, knowing that adversaries are out to get your corporate secrets. Live the values that often hang on the wall of the C-suite: honesty, transparency, customer first. And add security. I mentioned joint ventures before. Is it crazy to form a trade group that espouses domestic manufacturing to keep America safe? Consumers are addicted to cheap goods. But they are also addicted to American freedoms. Somehow the civic duty to make a profit and the civic duty to society need to be bridged. I don't know how you do that. But that's what strategy consultants are for."

"Don't get me started," said Doug Fair, "I know it's the CEO's lament, but these consultants—McDootle and Walter-House or whoever—have only two models: downsize or invest, choose one."

"Mr. Kendall is right, though," Nicole Dreyfus said. "We need strategy and branding. We need a plan. Or at least a plan for a plan."

"I recommend thinking short term versus long term," Kendall said. "Prioritize. Build security into all your modeling, or suffer the consequences."

"What about our new factory?" It was Bow Tie, who could not keep himself from asking a question, as though he were a board member. "According to you, we appear to be inadvertently building a monument to our own obsolescence."

"Yes, that's the risk. I don't know precisely what you're manufacturing, but there are defensive measures. I've heard of high-end firms retaining critical manufacturing or assembly in the US. They have key components or software installed here. Or they build the tricky tech here and ship it to China for assembly."

"This gets back to the centrality of the supply chain, cheap goods, and the company's crown jewels," said the chairman.

"Security, privacy, safety are selling points," Kendall countered. "Who knows, they might even induce tax credits in the future for promoting the national interest. If you can make a drug or sensor that doesn't come from the PRC, that reduces the threat of being compromised. Isn't there perceived value in that? What do your investor guys call it—alpha? Didn't Apple's claim about the iPhone supposedly being unhackable help it sell millions?"

"We're not a consumer goods company. Doug, you are being very quiet."

The CEO nodded. "This is sobering stuff. It's a lot to digest."

"I'm sure none of this is part of the core MBA curriculum," Kendall said. "We need new approaches by strategic thinkers and leaders, not just here but in Washington. And we all must be in sync in the face of PRC's vast market power. They are coming for your industry. They've issued five-year plans stating what's important for Xi Jinping. The PRC and CCP have made their collection priorities and requirements clear, what industries they want to control. They've targeted Boeing, Lockheed, and many more firms in America's defense-industrial complex. Look, you know this, they've busted into practically every telecom in the nation and globally.

"I'd be remiss not to highlight that you need a robust corporate security program at Overtal, including a robust domestic insider threat program. As we can see from what is happening to Armacase, their lax security program left it vulnerable right here at home. Were employees vetted? Was there cybertracking on their work devices? Was foreign travel reporting a requirement? Foreign contact reports? I could go on, but you get the picture. Again, a robust corporate security program is what is needed.

"After all, we're supposed to be better than Armacase? I'm sorry. They got more cash, more market share, more experience. How is that supposed to work?

"You're the guy with the seven-figure bonus. Figure it out. America needs you to be smarter and better. But really, you and every other board in the country need to wise up. Let me tell you something. Wait, is your general counsel here?"

"Yes. That's me, Tom—Thomas Calvino."

"Let me ask you, Tom: What if Armacase's board had a meeting just like this one a year ago and did nothing? And what if shareholders got the meeting minutes and hired a smart class action lawyer to sue for corporate malfeasance? Good case? Bad case?"

"Any case is a bad case, even frivolous ones. It depletes our resources. It's a form of warfare."

"Would you call that frivolous? The FBI warned them. A security expert warned them. And they ignored twenty years of documented international IP theft."

"It might be a problem."

"You guys have China-hack liability insurance?"

"I don't remember if it specifies China."

Kendall looked at his phone screen to check the time. "I'm sorry," he said. "I have another appointment. But before I go, I want to underscore one last thing. From my perspective, the best insurance is right in this room. The board can't control the markets. The board can't control PRC and the MSS subterfuge. It controls what Overtal does and needs to do, where it sources supplies, how it builds things. Your future depends on how well you can protect your products and infrastructure. Failure to do that is, in my perspective, malfeasance.

Again, I'm not trying to be rude. So dig your moats, build your castles, protect your IP, your people, your investors. Work with Washington to make corporate security a national security issue. Stand up and do your part.

"If you don't, this company and others will decline sooner than later. And the smart class action lawyers will be waiting."

Rishi thought of one more point. *Was it worth adding? Would Doug Fine forgive him? Probably. If security wasn't in ascendance at Overtal after today, he was in the wrong place.* "And Kendall," he interjected, "You forgot to add something. Those lawyers might call you to testify as an expert witness."

"Exactly."

Conclusion

CENTURIES AGO, as the Mediterranean sun descended behind the Palatine Hill, casting its warm golden hue over the most exclusive real estate on Earth, a naval commander named Gaius Duilius wandered through the bustling heart of ancient Rome.

Before him a rather strange procession materialized. Marching ahead of the triumphant commander on his path home was a personal torchbearer followed by a flutist and a band of chain-clad prisoners from Rome's most bitter rival: Carthage.

The traditional ceremony and procession rolled out for conquering Roman generals on such occasions dating back centuries was fitting. Rome, traditionally a land power more familiar with infantry tactics than sea battles, had just accomplished something astonishing.

In 260 BC, Gaius Duilius had led Roman forces to victory against Carthage at the Battle of Mylae, a naval confrontation off the northern Sicilian coast in what history would later term the First Punic War. Rome had long lived under the shadow of its great maritime rival, Carthage, whose ships ruled the Mediterranean trade routes, carrying with them vast riches from shore to shore. For generations, Carthage had maintained maritime superiority in the Mediterranean through a particularly well-guarded state secret: Its triremes, warships with three banks of oars, were marvels of technological precision and fearsome speed.

At the time, any challenge to Carthage's naval supremacy would have seemed unfathomable. How could such a naval superpower lose?

But one day, in an audacious stroke of fate seemingly crafted by the goddess Fortuna herself, a Carthaginian vessel ran aground near Roman shores. Eventually it would fall into the eager hands of Roman shipbuilders. Carefully dismantling the captured warship plank by plank, Rome's artisans learned the intricate construction methods of their rivals—measuring each timber, memorizing every seam. Like instructions from an ancient IKEA, the Carthaginians had used a numbered system of planks to allow for the rapid mass construction of ships. Now Carthage's closely guarded military secret was in Rome's possession. Its greatest military advantage, the end result undoubtedly of countless years of toil, would soon be turned against it by its most bitter rival.

In the shipyards of Ostia and Neapolis, armed with these new blueprints, Roman craftsmen set to work replicating the Carthaginian ship designs. And they improved them with a lethal innovation: the *corvus*, a spiked boarding bridge designed to grapple enemy ships and allow Roman soldiers—predominantly trained for land warfare—to storm aboard enemy decks. The sea would become like land. With stolen knowledge and crafty innovation, Rome rapidly transformed itself into a naval power capable of challenging—and ultimately destroying—the great maritime empire of Carthage.

Gaius Duilius's victory at Mylae would shatter the perception of Carthage's naval invincibility, eventually helping lead Rome to ultimate victory. The chained prisoners forced to trudge up the Palatine Hill before the general were material evidence of Rome's successful capitalization of stolen intellectual property—proof of the lethal effectiveness of reverse engineering. Rome had gained a critical capability in maritime warfare, not through years of development, but through a sudden, single stroke of technological acquisition. The balance of power had forever shifted as a result. More than two thousand years later, the echoes of Rome's industrial cunning resonate vividly in a different global rivalry.

At the turn of the twenty-first century, China, like ancient Rome before it, found itself technologically outmatched, enviously observing the sophisticated military machinery of its distant rival across the Pacific, the United States. Against those odds, China's rulers had recognized that the quickest path to power lay not necessarily in innovation but in imitation, theft, and rapid mastery.

Today, China's pursuit of cutting-edge military technologies echoes the ancient story of Rome. The People's Republic has systematically employed an unprecedented whole-of-society campaign fusing the entirety of its civil and military might. From cyber-espionage to corporate infiltrations, financial acquisitions, joint ventures, lawfare, talent recruitment programs, academic exchanges, and classic human source recruitments, it has acquired the critical blueprints necessary to take on the United States. Beijing's rapid ascent to the heights of global economic and military power, without such a campaign, would have been impossible.

Nations today, just like those in the past, must fiercely protect their secrets if they are to ensure their core interests. History reveals to us quite clearly the dangers if they fail to do so. The openness of Western societies, the free exchange of ideas, and the porous nature of modern digital infrastructures have all provided countless proverbial shipwrecks for Chinese engineers to exploit and turn against its geopolitical rivals.

Perhaps most ominously China appears to be more actively escalating the stakes of the Great Heist. The PRC is shifting from mere surveillance, theft, and innovation from illicit acquisitions to a more immediate and threatening playbook of wielding the global economy to covertly deliver kinetic effects, whether that be through malware installed in critical infrastructure, booby-trapped solar panel inverters, or potential agro-terrorism weapons smuggled into our ecosystem in the form of dangerous funguses.

Despite such ominous escalations, Washington appears to still lack the political will or policy tool kit necessary to combat the full scale and persistence of the Chinese espionage threat. In early 2022, for instance, even as Beijing's campaign of economic theft accelerated, the Biden administration quietly dismantled the Department of Justice's China Initiative, the program launched in 2018 to prioritize and combat PRC-linked technology and intellectual property theft. The reason? Like similar efforts to shut down investigations into the origins of the Covid-19 pandemic, Democrats claimed that it supposedly led to a "harmful perception" in fueling bias against Chinese Americans.

According to a DOJ insider, however, an internal review at the department found no such evidence for discrimination in the cases it pursued. Pulling the plug on the initiative signaled to field offices across the country that pursuing China theft cases was no longer a priority and the number of prosecutions dwindled as a result. Political optics trumped American national security interests against our greatest geopolitical foe—one that has stolen everything from hypersonic missile technology to cutting-edge AI. As of July 2025, Republicans in Congress are now trying to revive the effort in order to "counter China's malign ambitions to steal American research."

The consequences of Washington's naivety toward this threat continue to surface. A July 2025 ProPublica investigation revealed that Microsoft had employed engineers based in China to help maintain the Department of Defense's cloud infrastructure, in effect laying out a red carpet for Beijing's cyberoperatives to potentially exploit a back door into the Pentagon's digital mainframe. Secretary of Defense Pete Hegseth responded swiftly, ordering the removal of all China-based personnel and launching a broader audit of contractor exposure. But as Hegseth noted, this potential breach wasn't new but rather the result of a "legacy system created over a decade ago during the Obama administration." That legacy, built on complacency and false assumptions, remains embedded in many of our institutions. Unless it is rooted out entirely, the United States will continue to suffer silent defeats that will be fully realized only long after the damage is done.

Just as Carthage's complacency led to its ultimate destruction—burned and razed to the ground—the emerging power dynamics of the twenty-first century suggest humility and great caution is needed by today's superpower: the United States. Technological supremacy can prove fleeting when rivals are able to capture, dismantle, and replicate state-of-the-art advancements with exponentially more speed and less cost. In the game of great power competition, mastery over critical technologies can shift the tectonic plates of power swiftly and devastatingly.

The story of the Great Heist is a testament that stolen knowledge is not a trivial matter: It can rewrite the rules of global dominance. Having gained entry to the World Trade Organization, China used that achievement as a launching pad to penetrate and steal intellectual property across the global trading ecosystem. Later, in 2015, President Xi would set forth a highly ambitious plan, Made in China 2025, to seize the commanding heights of the twenty-first-century global economy. To execute his plan, Xi would turn to his primary henchmen, the MSS. And now, as we write in 2025, the end stage of this plan, the Great Heist, can be described as nothing less than an overwhelming success.

For instance, having laid out the strategic goal of conquering the electric vehicle industry in 2015, less than ten years later China's flagship EV giant BYD would surge past Elon Musk's Tesla to seize the mantle of the world's largest market share—an achievement that would once have seemed impossible. In other industrial sectors, from stealth technology to drones to AI to hypersonics, China has likewise rapidly become a world leader. According to the critical technology tracker of the ASPI, a prominent Australian think tank, China has now seized the global lead in thirty-seven out of the forty-four of the world's most important future technologies it tracks. At the same time, China's GDP growth has skyrocketed from around $1 trillion in 2000, when it first entered the WTO, to nearly $20 trillion in 2025, going from the sixth largest economy in the world to the second. By almost every available economic metric, China's rise has been undeniable.

While undoubtedly benefiting from other advantages such as its massive population size, state-command economy, and lavish government subsidies, China's rapid ascent to the heights of global economic and military power would have been impossible without its unprecedented campaign of state-sponsored espionage. Indeed, Made in China 2025, Xi's ambitious road map seeking to rejuvenate Chinese power, was more successful than any CCP leader could have ever envisioned. In fact, it's arguably the most impactful government-driven industrial strategy ever designed or executed. The leviathan of both official and non-traditional Chinese intelligence collectors spanning the globe across government halls, office parks, agricultural fields, courthouses, and university classrooms, along with China's other use of non-traditional intelligence collection methods such as VC investments and lawfare, no doubt bears much of the credit.

There is an old adage in a Chinese guide on espionage that states, "There are no walls which completely block the wind." While leaders in America's security apparatus have started to wake up to the threat before us, and take relevant countermeasures accordingly, Washington must also be prepared to adapt and counter how China will inevitably evolve its own intelligence capabilities and tactics. New technologies such as AI and quantum computing will inevitably reshape—and indeed already are fundamentally reshaping—the world of intelligence and counterintelligence. And no one has proven savvier, and more effective, at identifying, creating, and mastering new tools of espionage than Beijing. Fighting back against the Great Heist will therefore require an ongoing heightened state of alert and an enduring commitment from political leadership in Washington, DOJ prosecutors, intelligence collectors, FBI field agents, and corporate leaders. Perhaps most critically the gap between the public and private sectors must be bridged, with government and industry executives more willing to work hand in hand to counter this ominous and ever evolving threat.

History, echoing across millennia, reminds us that to ignore the lesson of Carthage is to risk becoming its reflection—dominant today, yet tomorrow nothing more than ruins in the dust. Now, more than ever before, knowledge *is* power. And it must be protected accordingly. Nothing less than the fate of the free world is at stake.

For too long, the Chinese have been on the offensive. It's time for America to finally put an end to the Great Heist—before it's too late.

Epilogue

THE PRECEDING chapters have laid bare a hard truth: China has waged an industrial espionage campaign of unprecedented scale and ambition, one that has hollowed out America's technological edge in a zero-sum contest for power. The time has come for the United States to reconceptualize national security as economic security. In the twenty-first century, the decisive battles are no longer fought on distant front lines but within industrial ecosystems, where knowledge (code, data, algorithms, AI model weights) is the arsenal and rapid innovation the high ground.

Indeed, this is not merely a story of espionage as we traditionally know it but that of an existential struggle over the *DNA* of military and economic might. And it will not be won with bureaucratic half measures. Safeguarding America's future requires full-spectrum mobilization across government, industry, and academia. It demands an urgent mindset shift: to see today's front lines as running through corporate boardrooms, academic labs, courtrooms, energy grids, start-up accelerators, and cloud infrastructure. Ensuring American preeminence in the decades to come will require abandoning a posture of *passive* defense and mounting an *active* counteroffensive. The seven-pillar *Counter* Heist strategy outlined by the authors below is a blueprint for doing exactly that: to defend, disrupt, and outcompete the Chinese espionage apparatus and to reassert America's place as the world's innovation superpower.

Pillar One: Protect the Crown Jewels of Twenty-First-Century Power

A recently published report called "AI 2027," authored by some of the leading global experts in the sector, paints a dystopian picture of the decade ahead: China's rise in superhuman AI will be seismic, exceeding even the impact of the Industrial Revolution. But unlike past revolutions, the report predicts this breakthrough will not be led solely by innovation. It will be driven by theft. Recent incidents at Google and xAI underscore that China's path to AI dominance is already being paved by industrial espionage. Beyond just AI, Beijing is also targeting the technologies that form the bedrock of American strategic advantage: semiconductors, quantum computing, biotechnology, hypersonics, and advanced energy platforms. These are not just commercial products. They are national security assets and must be treated as such.

To do so, the United States must adopt a Crown Jewels Doctrine: a living, government-maintained list of priority technologies that receive national security–grade protection at every stage of their life cycle, from R&D to export, acquisition, and investment. Nowhere is this more urgent than in AI. The trained model weights of frontier systems, the proprietary methods for scaling and optimizing them, and the advanced semiconductor designs and tools that enable their training should be treated no differently than classified military systems. In the Cold War, nuclear weapons shaped global power. In this era, whoever controls AI will dominate the commanding heights of economic and military innovation. As former Deputy National Security Advisor Matt Pottinger has argued, the defensive concept of "small yards with high fences" is insufficient. These technologies demand entire compounds with "walls guarded by .50-caliber machine guns." That means applying national security–grade protection to crown jewel technologies in the form of physical security, export controls, trade secret enforcement, and robust cyber defenses, not just for government labs, but for cloud servers, venture portfolios, and start-up clean rooms.

Pillar Two: Modernize Legal Deterrents

America's legal frameworks and architecture have failed to keep pace with the scope and sophistication of China's industrial espionage. Laws built for Cold War–style spying are no match for the gray-zone tactics of today's Great Heist, where proprietary knowledge is siphoned through academic partnerships, forced IP transfers, insider threats, and lawfare. To restore real deterrence, Congress must modernize the legal definition of economic espionage to account for this "knowledge laundering," crowdsourced espionage, and other indirect transfer mechanisms. Penalties must be more commensurate with the damage to national security, prosecution pathways streamlined, and thresholds for federal action more clearly defined. The Defend Trade Secrets Act should be expanded to include enhanced sentencing, fast-track DOJ referral mechanisms, and priority handling for cases involving critical technologies or links to foreign states. Companies found complicit in enabling China's espionage machine, whether knowingly or through gross negligence, should be placed on the US Department of Commerce's Entity List, cutting them off from US markets, capital, and technical talent. Just as financial sanctions are intended to deter money laundering and terrorism, economic espionage must carry material consequences for those involved.

Central to this legal modernization must be the revival of the China Initiative: a prosecutorial framework originally launched in 2018 to prioritize and coordinate espionage-related cases targeting the PRC. Its quiet dismantling in 2022 sent a dangerous message: that political optics can override national security. Reinstating the initiative will help align law enforcement priorities, empower US attorneys, and make it unmistakably clear that the theft of American innovation by a strategic adversary is not just criminal but a national security threat. Deterrence depends not only on capability but on clarity of will and credibility of punishment.

Pillar Three: Secure the Physical and Digital Perimeter

Beijing's Great Heist is evolving, from the covert theft of secrets to the ability to deliver real-world, kinetic effects. The front lines are no longer defined by military bases alone, but by ports, power grids, cloud servers, and industrial control systems. China isn't just stealing IP; it's positioning itself to sabotage America's physical and digital nervous systems.

The recent exposure of Microsoft's "digital escorts" program—where China-based engineers provided remote support for Pentagon cloud systems—was an embarrassing wake-up call. Even with "escorts," these engineers maintained dangerous access to sensitive infrastructure, potentially rolling out the red carpet to MSS hackers. This was not an isolated failure. Incidents involving Volt Typhoon, Salt Typhoon, Chinese-made solar inverters, and remote-access vulnerabilities in ZPMC port cranes reveal just how deeply Chinese state–linked actors have penetrated the soft underbelly of US infrastructure. America urgently needs a nationwide strategic security audit of its critical infrastructure—spanning both digital and physical domains—to expose hidden vulnerabilities and prioritize hardening efforts. That audit must be followed by a transition from today's patchwork defenses to a cohesive, forward-leaning national perimeter capable of withstanding twenty-first-century threats.

In a world of software-defined systems and globally integrated supply chains, adversaries are targeting both "bits and bolts." Cybersecurity and supply chain security must be treated as one. Procurement standards must emphasize not just cost and performance, but vendor trustworthiness, cyber resilience, and provenance. Programs like the DOD's Cybersecurity Maturity Model Certification (CMMC) should be strengthened and expanded across all sectors touching dual-use or sensitive technologies, not just the traditional defense industrial base. Mandatory breach disclosure laws must be enacted for all critical technology operators, with real consequences for concealment. Every federal agency, subcontractor, and private sector partner must be seen as part of securing America's physical and digital perimeter. Every day of inaction allows Beijing to burrow deeper into our most vital systems.

Pillar Four: Shield the Innovation Pipeline

China's civil-military fusion strategy has transformed American universities and laboratories into key targets for intellectual property theft and talent recruitment. According to the FBI, in 2019 alone, more than one thousand military-affiliated Chinese researchers were quietly withdrawn from US institutions following FBI scrutiny, many tied to state-backed talent programs like the Thousand Talents Program and elite PLA-linked universities known as the Seven Sons of National Defense. The scale of the risk is staggering: In any one year up to 290,000 Chinese students enroll at US universities, many in STEM fields with sensitive, dual-use applications. Under China's 2017 National Intelligence Law, all citizens must cooperate with state intelligence efforts if requested, including students abroad. No domain is off limits: From vaccine research to cancer treatments, next-gen semiconductors to quantum computing, the full spectrum of American scientific achievement is now in Beijing's crosshairs.

To reclaim America's intellectual edge, comprehensive reforms in both academia and national laboratories are essential. That includes mandatory disclosure of all foreign affiliations, funding sources, and research commitments; enhanced visa scrutiny for high-risk doctoral candidates in STEM fields; a ban on academic partnerships with PLA-linked institutions; and more active coordination with the FBI. Universities must no longer treat these risks as bureaucratic issues but as part of the national defense ecosystem. Like private corporations, academic institutions must bear fiduciary responsibility for safeguarding strategic knowledge, and face consequences when they fail. As former DOJ official John Demers observed, when prosecutors reframed the espionage threat as "conflicts of interest" or "conflicts of commitment," terms familiar to university compliance officers, institutions finally began to respond. That cultural shift must now be codified. America must harden the shield protecting its innovation base before more breakthroughs are quietly siphoned into the arsenals of our greatest rival. Dr. Charles Lieber, the former chair of Harvard's Department of Chemistry and Chemical Biology and a pioneer in nanotechnology—the science of manipulating matter at the atomic and molecular scale with potential applications in EV batteries and advanced materials—was convicted for concealing ties to China's Thousand Talents Program, was given a light sentence by a federal court, and is now continuing his research seven thousand miles from Cambridge: in Shenzhen, China.

Pillar Five: Cut the Capital Lifeline

Lenin is reported to have once warned, "The capitalists will sell us the rope with which we will hang them." In the age of the Great Heist, that warning has become prophecy. America's own capital markets—venture and private equity firms and institutional investors—have, wittingly or not, helped finance the rise of China's techno-authoritarian state. From private equity funding for Chinese AI, semiconductor, and drone firms to the purchase of farmland near Grand Forks Air Force Base in North Dakota, described as "the backbone of all U.S. military communications across the globe," by a CCP-tied agribusiness, our financial system has become a strategic vulnerability exploited by Beijing's civil-military fusion strategy.

To counter this novel threat, the United States must adopt a robust national security doctrine toward investments and capital flows, one rooted in strategic long-term clarity and national resilience. First, *outbound* capital must be screened with the same rigor as *inbound* flows. Legislation like the Foreign Investment Guardrails to Help Thwart (FIGHT) China Act and the Comprehensive Outbound Investment National Security (COINS) Act must be passed to prevent US dollars from funding Beijing's next-generation military and surveillance technologies. Second, land acquisitions and greenfield investments by foreign adversaries, especially near critical infrastructure and military sites, must be banned or brought under expanded oversight by the Committee on Foreign Investment in the United States (CFIUS). These loopholes represent not just commercial risks, but national security vulnerabilities. Third, Wall Street must be held to a national security standard, not just a fiduciary one. Finance is no longer neutral; it is a domain of strategic geopolitical competition. We need a new ethic of patriotic capital. The United States should adopt what the authors coin a "Soviet Test" for investment decisions: If the deal would've been unthinkable with the USSR during the Cold War, it should be unthinkable with the CCP today. America must stop underwriting its own decline and finally cut the rope it's hanging itself with.

Pillar Six: Harden the Corporate Front Lines

In an era of systemic competition, America's most innovative companies are no longer just engines of economic progress; they are now primary targets in a new form of hybrid warfare. From Silicon Valley to the Research Triangle, corporate campuses have become central battlefields in the Great Heist. China's civil-military fusion strategy has weaponized the global innovation ecosystem, turning research partnerships, talent flows, and joint ventures into vectors of infiltration and exfiltration. But its most insidious and distinctive tactic is "crowdsourced espionage": luring students, researchers, and foreign employees with implicit promises of funding, prestige, or future market access without explicit state control or involvement. These "nontraditional collectors" act without formal tasking or tradecraft but their cumulative impact is devastating, pilfering American innovation in plain sight.

Countering this threat begins with a cultural shift. Companies must adopt an operational security (OPSEC) mindset like that of a military unit or intelligence agency and treat their most sensitive assets as national security infrastructure. Boards must prioritize this risk with real accountability, designating leadership roles like chief risk officers and embedding counterintelligence responsibilities at the C-suite level. Every company must start by mapping its own "crown jewels": What code, models, data, or designs—and accessible by whom—would be most catastrophic if stolen? Once these are identified, companies should invest in insider threat programs, implement strict role-based access, ensure regular trainings, develop foreign travel risk protocols, and run regular Red Team exercises. Private sector firms like Strider Technologies that specialize in economic threat intelligence and supply chain risk can also help supercharge corporate defenses. Too often, businesses issue loaner laptops for China travel while keeping the same users connected to core systems—locking the front door while leaving the back door wide open. China-facing infrastructure must be fully isolated.

Above all, companies need to forge stronger ties with law enforcement. But that trust must be mutual. The FBI and Department of Homeland Security must offer clear assurances of confidentiality, legal protection, and relevant intelligence to reassure companies to come forward in confidence. And the government needs to resist the ingrained reflex to overclassify sharing threat data in timely, *actionable* formats. National resilience depends not just on government agencies but on the thousands of private firms that house America's most sensitive innovation. Patriotism alone won't necessarily drive action, but market survival will. Intellectual property theft isn't just a security risk; it's an existential threat to any company's survival in the free market. Just ask Elon Musk.

Pillar Seven: Make Economic Security a National Imperative

As underscored above, the defining contest of the twenty-first century is for *knowledge*: for the intellectual property, data, code, and critical technologies that underpin material economic and military power. Yet the United States remains institutionally unprepared to defend this new high ground. Just as the Cold War demanded the creation of the National Security Council (NSC) to coordinate defense and diplomacy, the nature of today's great power competition requires a new structure of equal weight and priority: an Economic Security Council (ESC) housed in the White House and chaired by the vice president. The ESC would elevate economic security to a core function of national strategy. It would unify fragmented authorities across export controls, investment screening, research protection, and cybersecurity. Crucially, it would bring together senior representatives from key federal departments—Commerce, Treasury, Energy, Defense, Homeland Security, State, Justice, and the Intelligence Community—with leaders from the private sector and academia. For unlike in the Cold War, today's most strategic assets do not reside in classified vaults, but in cloud servers, start-up incubators, university labs, and advanced manufacturing clean rooms.

The ESC's mandate would be clear: actively identify and ensure adequate protection for technological crown jewels, coordinate interagency disruption of state-backed industrial espionage, align outbound capital flows with national interest, harmonize export regimes with allies, and publish regular threat assessments to elevate risk awareness across the private sector. By embedding this body within the White House and giving it a direct line to the Oval Office, the United States would send a powerful message: that defending America's innovation base is not a bureaucratic afterthought but rather a top-tier national imperative. Only with this level of sustained whole-of-nation commitment can the United States move beyond fragmented and passive defense, mount a strategic counteroffensive, and reclaim the initiative in the defining economic and technological contests of our time.

Strategy, as ever, is the disciplined use of limited means toward prioritized ends. Confronting the Great Heist will require hard choices amid competing national security demands, sustained focus, and national commitment to invest in the defense of our economic future. America must ensure that no foreign adversary, especially one bent on authoritarian dominance like Beijing, can exploit the openness of our free-market system to build their strength at our expense. With clear priorities, strong public-private partnerships, and unified resolve across government, industry, and academia, America can prevail—if it has the will to do so.

ACKNOWLEDGMENTS

WRITING THE *Great Heist* has been both an intellectual journey and a counterintelligence exercise. This book could not have been written without the insights, candor, and trust of an extraordinary set of voices—individuals who have spent their careers tracking, confronting, and exposing the scale of what we call the Great Heist: the systematic theft of Western innovation, industry, and advantage by the Chinese Communist Party.

First and foremost, we are deeply grateful to Seth Kaufman and Luke Argue, whose disciplined editorial instincts ensured that quality consistently triumphed over quantity. Their fingerprints are on every chapter, and their commitment to sound research and intellectual clarity sharpened the story we sought to tell.

We would also like to thank Sean Desmond and the rest of the HarperCollins team for their hard work, partnership, and dedication to this project. Their support has been invaluable. We would also like to thank our agents David Vigliano and Tom Flannery for their early commitment to this project and steadfast guidance to making it happen.

A special thanks goes to William "Bill" Evanina, former director of the National Counterintelligence and Security Center, whose unflinching perspective on the PRC as an omnipresent counterintelligence threat was instrumental in shaping the urgency and tone of this narrative. Now leading the Evanina Group, Bill remains one of the nation's clearest voices on the intersection of espionage and national security.

We are indebted to Greg Levesque of Strider Technologies for his pioneering work mapping China's strategic talent programs and commercial targeting. His research, and the strategic lens he brings to it, provided a crucial foundation for analysis.

Thanks as well to Frank Miller, former US defense attaché in Beijing, whose behind-the-scenes insights into PLA operations and diplomatic deception helped us see the chessboard more clearly. Now at Exovera, Frank remains an invaluable mentor to many navigating the complexities of the PRC threat.

We are grateful to Duncan Jepson—filmmaker, writer, human rights activist, and one of the most compelling voices on CCP behavior—for never being fooled by the WTO's lofty expectations or the rhetoric of America's political class and for laying bare the ideology behind Beijing's actions.

Craig Singleton, of the Foundation for Defense of Democracies, provided a clear-eyed, deeply researched perspective on how China weaponizes finance and lawfare in ways few in the West are prepared for.

We also benefited immensely from the insights of Michael Brown, former director of the Department of Defense's Defense Innovation Unit. He reminded us just how early in the innovation pipeline China begins its targeting—and what's truly at stake if we fail to protect it.

Several interviews brought the story to life. We thank former National Security Advisor Robert O'Brien, former Deputy National Security Advisor Matt Pottinger, former DOJ National Security Division head John Demers, and John O'Connor, whose reflections on capital markets and the CCP's strategic investments helped connect powerful dots. From Australia, Adam Leslie of ASPI guided us through the Milo case and PRC academic networks. L. J. Eads and Bill LaPlante, the former under secretary of defense for acquisition and sustainment, offered deep albeit always unclassified insights into hypersonic technologies and more generally the defense innovation ecosystem.

We're also grateful to Dennis Wilder, the former CIA deputy assistant director for East Asia and the Pacific, whose stories—like the

Coca-Cola can-lining theft—anchored complex ideas into a compelling narrative. James Mulvenon, David Goldman, Anna Puglisi, Rudy Guerin, and Ray Mislock shared vital insights on cyber, chemicals, and the critical legacy of past cases like DuPont and Cisco.

Thank you as well to fellow authors and strategists: Robert Spalding, Elbridge Colby, Elliott Abrams, and Nick Butterfield, whose encouragement and examples helped us navigate the chaos of first-time book authorship. Other expert contributors whose work, ideas, or time influenced this book include Lee Branstetter, Tai Ming Cheung, Patrick Jenevein, Jonathan Ward, Matt Brazil, Andrew May, and Margaret Harker (whose continued work on the Hill we deeply respect).

David gives thanks to God for His enablement in bringing this project to fruition. To Him be all the glory and honor.

Andrew would like to thank his colleagues and mentors, including Ron Wahid, Charles Eberly, and Larry Henderson. He would also like to thank his former teacher Rosalie Mackay.

We have not included some names at their own request. To them, and others who remain anonymous, we extend our sincere thanks.

Finally, to our families and those closest to us—thank you for putting up with late-night calls, disrupted weekends, and the intensity that researching and writing this book demanded. Your patience was the quiet force behind every page. And for that we owe you a debt of gratitude not easily repaid.

NOTES

A NOTE FROM THE AUTHORS

1. PRC State Council, "Made in China 2025," Center for Security and Emerging Technology, Georgetown University, May 8, 2015, translation date March 8, 2022, https://cset.georgetown.edu/wp-content/uploads/t0432_made_in_china_2025_EN.pdf.
2. Gordon Corera, "MI5 Head Warns of 'Epic Scale' of Chinese Espionage," BBC, October 17, 2023, https://www.bbc.com/news/uk-67142161.

PROLOGUE | The Billion-Dollar Thumb Drive

1. "The 2018 Complete List of World's Billionaires," Areppim, accessed January 14, 2025, https://stats.areppim.com/listes/list_billionairesx18xwor.htm.
2. Mara Hvistendahl, "How Elon Musk Became 'Kind of Pro-China,'" *New York Times*, March 27, 2024, https://www.nytimes.com/2024/03/27/world/asia/musk-china-tesla-explained.html.
3. "Tesla, Inc.(TSLA), Historical Prices," Yahoo! Finance, https://finance.yahoo.com/quote/TSLA/history/?period1=1277784000&period2=1532736000&interval=1d&filter=history&frequency=1d.
4. Authors' interview with source who requested anonymity, April 24, 2024.
5. Authors' interview with source who requested anonymity, May 20, 2024.
6. "Kevin J. Webb," Purdue University, accessed March 15, 2025, https://engineering.purdue.edu/Kevin-Webb/research/group.
7. Tesla, Inc., v. Guangzhi Cao, United States District Court, Northern District of California, March 21, 2019, https://storage.courtlistener.com/recap/gov.uscourts.cand.339740/gov.uscourts.cand.339740.1.0_1.pdf.

CHAPTER 1 | Foreshadowings

1. Patrick Hunt, "Late Roman Silk: Smuggling and Espionage in the 6th Century CE," Stanford University, August 2, 2011, https://archive.ph/20130626180730/http://traumwerk.stanford.edu/philolog/2011/08/byzantine_silk_smuggling_and_e.html#selection-553.581-553.639.
2. *Procopii Caesariensis Historiarum Temporis sui Tetras Altera. De Bello Gothico*, trans. Claudius Maltretus (Venice, 1729), Lib. IV, cap. XVII, 212;

reprinted in Roy C. Cave and Herbert H. Coulson, eds., *A Source Book for Medieval Economic History* (Biblo and Tannen, 1965), 244–45.

3. Authors' interview with Rudy Guerin, April 15, 2024.

4. Deng Xiaoping, *Selected Works of Deng Xiaoping*, vol. 3 (Foreign Languages Press, 1994), 73, https://ebook.theorychina.org.cn/ebook/upload/storage /files/2022/07/28/f77a1a130ad7a1b14c88b839e0671e7073068/mobile/index .html#p=74.

5. Yudhijit Bhattacharjee, "A New Kind of Spy," *New Yorker*, April 28, 2014, https://www.newyorker.com/magazine/2014/05/05/a-new-kind-of-spy.

6. Deng, *Selected Works of Deng Xiaoping*, 73, https://ebook.theorychina.org.cn/ebook /upload/storage/files/2022/07/28/f77a1a130ad7a1b14c88b839e0671e7073068 /mobile/index.html#p=74.

7. "National High-Tech R&D Program (863 Program)," Ministry of Science and Technology of the People's Republic of China, https://en.most.gov.cn /programmes1.

8. "The Other Tiananmen Papers," ChinaFile, July 8, 2019, https://www.chinafile .com/conversation/other-tiananmen-papers.

9. While Scowcroft reported that his conversations with Deng had been benign, David Shambaugh, writing in ChinaFile, reported that Deng Xiaoping told Scowcroft at the July 2 meeting in the Great Hall of the People that the American side had been a principal source of the "counter-revolutionary rebellion" and it would be up to the United States to "untie the knot." Shambaugh, "The Other Tiananmen Papers," ChinaFile, July 8, 2019, https://www.chinafile.com /conversation/other-tiananmen-papers.

10. Authors' interview with source who requested anonymity, April 20, 2024.

11. "Full Text of Clinton's Speech on China Trade Bill," *New York Times*, March 9, 2000, https://archive.nytimes.com/www.nytimes.com/library/world/asia /030900clinton-china-text.html.

12. David H. Autor, David Dorn, and Gordon H. Hanson, "The China Shock: Learning from Labor Market Adjustment to Large Changes in Trade," National Bureau of Economic Research, January 2016, https://www.nber.org/papers /w21906.

13. "Gallagher, Williams Seek Answers from DOJ on Chinese IP Theft," The Select Committee on the CCP, June 15, 2023, https://selectcommitteeontheccp.house .gov/media/press-releases/gallagher-williams-seek-answers-doj-chinese-ip-theft.

14. "Survey of Chinese Espionage in the United States Since 2000," CSIS, March 2023, https://www.csis.org/programs/strategic-technologies-program/survey -chinese-espionage-united-states-2000.

CHAPTER 2 | The Great Leap Everywhere

1. "Background Information on China's Accession to the World Trade Organization," Office of the United States Trade Representative, December 11, 2001,

https://ustr.gov/archive/Document_Library/Fact_Sheets/2001/Background _Information_on_China%27s_Accession_to_the_World_Trade_Organization .html.

2. "China Joins W.T.O. Ranks," *New York Times*, December 12, 2001, https://www .nytimes.com/2001/12/12/world/china-joins-wto-ranks.html.

3. "In Bush's Words: 'Join Together in Making China a Normal Trading Partner,'" *New York Times*, May 18, 2000, https://www.nytimes.com/2000/05/18/world /in-bush-s-words-join-together-in-making-china-a-normal-trading-partner .html.

4. Scott Lindlaw, "U.S. Normalizes China's Trade Status," *Washington Post*, December 28, 2001, https://www.washingtonpost.com/archive/business/2001/12/28 /us-normalizes-chinas-trade-status/7f97942b-3fe4-46c1-bd1b-72c7ee4f4e57.

5. "Background Information on China's Accession to the World Trade Organization."

6. Jim Mann, *Beijing Jeep: A Case Study of Western Business in China* (Simon & Schuster, 1989).

7. Authors' interview with A. J. Khubani, May 31, 2024.

8. Authors' interview with Duncan Jepson, October 31, 2024.

9. Seymour Martin Lipset, "Some Social Requisites of Democracy: Economic Development and Political Legitimacy," *American Political Science Review* 53, no. 1 (1959): 75, https://eppam.weebly.com/uploads/5/5/6/2/5562069/lipset1959 _apsr.pdf.

10. National Bureau of Statistics of China, "National Data, Annual Query," accessed January 14, 2025, https://data.stats.gov.cn/english/easyquery.htm?cn=C01.

11. PRC State Council, "Made in China 2025."

12. PRC State Council, "Made in China 2025."

13. Jennifer Wong Leung, Jamie Gaida, Stephan Robin, and Danielle Cave, "ASPI's Critical Technology Tracker," Australian Strategic Policy Institute, March 1, 2023, https://www.aspi.org.au/report/critical-technology-tracker.

CHAPTER 3 | Inside China's Intelligence Labyrinth

1. Authors' interview with William Evanina, July 25, 2024.

2. "PRC National Intelligence Law (as Amended in 2018)," China Law Translate, June 6, 2017, https://www.chinalawtranslate.com/en/national-intelligence-law -of-the-p-r-c-2017.

3. Nicholas Eftimiades, *Chinese Espionage Operations and Tactics*, 2nd ed. (Vitruvian Press, 2025), 28.

4. Peter Mattis and Matthew Brazil, *Chinese Communist Espionage: An Intelligence Primer* (Naval Institute Press, 2019), 55–56.

5. "PRC National Intelligence Law (as Amended in 2018)," China Law Translate.

6. "PRC National Intelligence Law (as Amended in 2018)."

7. "2016 Cybersecurity Law," China Law Translate, November 7, 2016, https:// www.chinalawtranslate.com/en/2016-cybersecurity-law/.

8. Koh Ewe and Laura Bicker, "United Front: China's 'Magic Weapon' Caught in a Spy Controversy," BBC, December 18, 2024, https://www.bbc.co.uk/news/articles/c878evdp758o.

9. Mao Zedong, "The Communist," October 4, 1939.

10. Marcel Angliviel de la Beaumelle, "The United Front Work Department: 'Magic Weapon' at Home and Abroad," China Brief, July 6, 2017, https://jamestown.org/program/united-front-work-department-magic-weapon-home-abroad.

11. Sun Tzu, *The Art of War* (Canterbury Classics, 2014), https://classics.mit.edu/Tzu/artwar.html.

12. Sun Tzu, *The Art of War*.

13. Mike Giglio, "China's Spies Are on the Offensive," *Atlantic*, August 26, 2019, https://www.theatlantic.com/politics/archive/2019/08/inside-us-china-espionage-war/595747/.

14. Paul Moore, quoted in David Wise, *Tiger Trap: America's Secret Spy War with China* (Houghton Mifflin Harcourt, 2011), 16.

15. Moore, in Wise, *Tiger Trap*.

16. George J. Tenet and Louis J. Freeh, "Report to Congress on Chinese Espionage Activities Against the United States," Federation of American Scientists, December 12, 1999, https://irp.fas.org/threat/fis/prc_1999.html.

17. Latika Bourke, "British Parliamentary Aide Denies Being a Chinese Spy," The Sydney Morning Herald, September 13, 2023, https://www.smh.com.au/world/europe/british-parliamentary-aide-denies-being-a-chinese-spy-20230913-p5e470.html; Harrison Jones, "Two Men Deny Spying for China," BBC News, October 4, 2024, https://www.bbc.co.uk/news/articles/c9qve471ydqo.

18. William Evanina, quoted in Giglio, "China's Spies Are on the Offensive."

19. Authors' interview with Greg Levesque, May 8, 2024.

20. Giglio, "China's Spies Are on the Offensive."

21. Sun Tzu, *The Art of War*.

CHAPTER 4 | The Playbook Exposed

1. "Professor Helena Hamerow," School of Archaeology, Oxford, accessed March 12, 2025, https://www.arch.ox.ac.uk/people/hamerow-helena#tab-4542436.

2. Jordan Robertson and Drake Bennett, "A Chinese Spy Wanted GE's Secrets, But the US Got China's Instead," Bloomberg, September 15, 2022, https://www.bloomberg.com/news/features/2022-09-15/china-wanted-ge-s-secrets-but-then-their-spy-got-caught.

3. William Evanina, "Statement of William R. Evanina, CEO, The Evanina Group, Before the House Select Committee on the Chinese Communist Party," July 26, 2023, https://www.congress.gov/118/meeting/house/116281/witnesses/HHRG-118-ZS00-Wstate-EvaninaW-20230726.pdf.

4. Robertson and Bennett, "A Chinese Spy Wanted GE's Secrets."

5. Yudhijit Bhattacharjee, "The Daring Ruse That Exposed China's Campaign to Steal

American Secrets," *New York Times Magazine*, March 7, 2023, https://www
.nytimes.com/2023/03/07/magazine/china-spying-intellectual-property.html.

6. Robertson and Bennett, "A Chinese Spy Wanted GE's Secrets."

7. Bhattacharjee, "The Daring Ruse."

8. Paula Christian, "'People in Intelligence Like Us—We Focus [on] Aviation,' FBI
Testifies About Xu's Texts, Emails," WCPO, October 25, 2021, https://www
.wcpo.com/news/local-news/i-team/people-in-intelligence-like-us-we-focus
-on-aviation-fbi-testifies-about-xus-texts-emails.

9. Paula Christian, "GE Aviation Leaders Testify Against Accused Chinese Spy
Charged with Stealing Their Trade Secrets," WCPO, October 29, 2021, https://
www.wcpo.com/news/local-news/i-team/ge-aviation-leaders-testify-against
-accused-chinese-spy-charged-with-stealing-their-trade-secrets.

10. Bhattacharjee, "The Daring Ruse."

11. "Federal False Statement Charges—18 U.S.C. §1001," Eisner Gorin LLP, accessed January 5, 2025, https://www.keglawyers.com/false-statements.

12. Bhattacharjee, "The Daring Ruse."

13. "Constitution," Jiangsu Association for International Science and Technology
Cooperation, http://www.jaistc.com/en/a/about/charter.

14. Bhattacharjee, "The Daring Ruse."

15. Robertson and Bennett, "A Chinese Spy Wanted GE's Secrets."

16. "Chinese National Sentenced to Eight Years for Acting Within the United States as
an Unregistered Agent of the People's Republic of China," US Department of Justice, January 25, 2023, https://www.justice.gov/archives/opa/pr/chinese-national
-sentenced-eight-years-acting-within-united-states-unregistered-agent-people.

17. United States v. Xu, Unsealed Opinion, US Court of Appeals, Sixth Circuit, July 24,
2024, https://law.justia.com/cases/federal/appellate-courts/ca6/22-4020/22
-4020-2024-08-07.html.

18. Christian, "GE Aviation Leaders Testify Against Accused Chinese Spy."

19. Intelligence Report: "Huge Fan of Your Work: How Turbine Panda and China's Top Spies Enabled Beijing to Cut Corners on the C919 Passenger Jet,"
Crowdstrike, October 2019, https://passle-net.s3.amazonaws.com/Passle
/5c752afb989b6e0f5cda12f4/MediaLibrary/Document/2019-10-18-10-42-26
-646-huge-fan-of-your-work-intelligence-report.pdf.

20. Bradley Hull, witness, Criminal Complaint: United States of America v. Xu
Yanjun (a/k/a Qu Hui), United States District Court for the Southern District of
Ohio, March 21, 2018, https://www.justice.gov/d9/press-releases/attachments
/2018/10/10/xu_complaint.pdf.

21. Robertson and Bennett, "A Chinese Spy Wanted GE's Secrets."

22. Jeff Sedlin, "Chinese Intelligence Official Sentenced to 20 Years in US Prison,"
VOA News, November 16, 2022, https://www.voanews.com/a/chinese
-intelligence-official-sentenced-to-20-years-in-us-prison-/6837568.html.

23. Christian, "'People in Intelligence Like Us.'"

24. "Chinese Government Intelligence Officer Sentenced to 20 Years in Prison for

Espionage Crimes, Attempting to Steal Trade Secrets From Cincinnati Company," US Department of Justice, November 16, 2022, https://www.justice.gov /opa/pr/chinese-government-intelligence-officer-sentenced-20-years-prison -espionage-crimes-attempting.

25. United States v. Xu, Unsealed Opinion.

26. "Chinese Government Intelligence Officer Sentenced."

CHAPTER 5 | The Attack of the Clones

1. "Intellectual Property Rights Seizure Statistics, Fiscal Year 2024," U.S. Customs and Border Protection, January 2025, https://www.cbp.gov/sites/default /files/2025-01/intellectualpropertyrightsseizurestatisticsfiscalyear2024 _pbrb_approved_with_publication_number_508.pdf.

2. Dharmesh Mehta, "Amazon Makes It Easier for Brands to Join Amazon Transparency Through New Interoperability Features," AboutAmazon.com, October 16, 2023, https://www.aboutamazon.com/news/policy-news-views/amazon -makes-it-easier-for-brands-to-join-amazon-transparency-through-new -interoperability-features.

3. Julia Faria, "Largest Advertisers in the United States in 2022," Statistica, September 10, 2024, https://www.statista.com/statistics/275446/ad-spending-of -leading-advertisers-in-the-us.

4. Lauren Feiner, "Apple Ramped Up Lobbying Spending in 2022, Outpacing Tech Peers," CNBC, January 23, 2023, https://www.cnbc.com/2023/01/23/apple -ramped-up-lobbying-spending-in-2022-outpacing-tech-peers.html.

5. "2002 Report to Congress on China's WTO Compliance," Office of the United States Trade Representative, https://china.usc.edu/sites/default/files/article /attachments/2002-report-chinas-wto-compliance.pdf.

6. Lee G. Branstetter, "China's Forced Technology Transfer Problem—and What to Do About It," Peterson Institute for International Economics, June 2018, https://www.piie.com/sites/default/files/documents/pb18-13.pdf.

7. The State Council, The People's Republic of China, "The National Medium- and Long-Term Program for Science and Technology Development (2006–2020)," 2006, https://www.itu.int/en/ITU-D/Cybersecurity/Documents/National _Strategies_Repository/China_2006.pdf.

8. Office of the United States Trade Representative, "Findings of the Investigation into China's Acts, Policies, and Practices Related to Technology Transfer, Intellectual Property, and Innovation Under Section 301 of the Trade Act of 1974," March 22, 2018, https://ustr.gov/sites/default/files/Section%20301%20FINAL.PDF, 4.

9. Office of the United States Trade Representative, "Findings of the Investigation into China's Acts, Policies, and Practices," 54.

10. Office of the United States Trade Representative, "Findings of the Investigation into China's Acts, Policies, and Practices," 7.

11. Sebastien Roblin, "Is China's J-11 Fighter Copied from Russia's Su-27 'Flanker'?,"

The National Interest, April 6, 2021, https://nationalinterest.org/blog/reboot
/chinas-j-11-fighter-copied-russias-su-27-flanker-182096.

12. Authors' interview with Tai Ming Cheung, December 30, 2024.

13. "Nathan Cluett, "Is the Shenyang J-11 just a Copy/Paste Su-27?," Plane Historia,
February 17, 2024, https://planehistoria.com/is-the-shenyang-j-11-just-a-copy
-paste-su-27.

14. The State Council, The People's Republic of China, "The National Medium- and
Long-Term Program for Science and Technology Development (2006–2020)."

15. Tai Ming Cheung, *Innovate to Dominate: The Rise of the Chinese Techno-
Security State* (Cornell University Press, 2022), 16.

16. Branstetter, "China's Forced Technology Transfer Problem."

17. Office of the United States Trade Representative, "2022 Review of Notorious
Markets for Counterfeiting and Piracy," accessed March 12, 2025, https://ustr
.gov/sites/default/files/2023-01/2022%20Notorious%20Markets%20List%20
(final).pdf.

CHAPTER 6 | Crossed Circuits: The Electric Vehicle Wars

1. Walter Isaacson, *Elon Musk* (Simon & Schuster, 2023), 284–85.

2. Criminal Complaint: United States of America v. Xiaolang Zhang, US District
Court for the Northern District of California, July 9, 2018, https://regmedia
.co.uk/2022/08/23/readable_complaint.pdf.

3. Criminal Complaint: United States of America v. Xiaolang Zhang.

4. Joint Stipulation of Dismissal with Prejudice, Fed R. Civ. P. 41(A)(1)(A)(ii).
Tesla, Inc., A Delaware Corporation, Plaintiff, v. Guangzhi Cao, An Individual,
Defendant, United States District Court Northern District of California, April
15, 2021, https://storage.courtlistener.com/recap/gov.uscourts.cand.339740
/gov.uscourts.cand.339740.127.0.pdf.

5. Authors' interview with Charles Finrock, May 20, 2024.

6. "Party Secretary Li Visits Tesla Gigafactory, Meets Musk," Shanghai Lignang
Development Group, January 11, 2020, https://www.shlingang.com/en
/lingangjituan/xwzx/jtdt/202001/t20200111_19272.shtml.

7. Emma Jarratt, "Tesla Acquires Canadian Battery Specialist, Hibar Systems,"
Electric Autonomy, October 4, 2019, https://electricautonomy.ca/news/2019
-10-04/tesla-acquires-canadian-battery-specialist-hibar-systems.

8. "Klaus Pflugbeil," LinkedIn, accessed March 14, 2025, https://www.linkedin
.com/in/klauspflugbeil.

9. "Resident of China Pleads Guilty to Conspiracy to Send Leading Electric Vehicle Company's Trade Secrets to Undercover U.S. Agent," US Department of
Justice, June 13, 2024, https://www.justice.gov/opa/pr/resident-china
-pleads-guilty-conspiracy-send-leading-electric-vehicle-companys-trade
-secrets.

10. Scott Kennedy, "The Chinese EV Dilemma: Subsidized Yet Striking," Center for

Strategic and International Studies, June 20, 2024, https://www.csis.org
/blogs/trustee-china-hand/chinese-ev-dilemma-subsidized-yet-striking.

11. Park Jae-hyuk, "Chinese Battery Maker Probed for Alleged Technology Theft
from Samsung SDI, SK On," *Korea Times*, January 17, 2024, https://www
.koreatimes.co.kr/www/tech/2024/11/129_367098.html.

12. Tycho de Feijter, "A Deep-Dive into the History of China's Bizarre Jeep Cherokee XJ Clones," The Autopian, March 29, 2022, https://www.theautopian.com
/wip-a-deep-dive-into-how-china-started-building-bizarre-jeep-cherokee-xj
-clones.

13. Jay Nagley and Emma Smith, "Invasion of the Chinese Clones," *Sunday Times*,
January 29, 2006, https://www.thetimes.com/travel/destinations/asia-travel
/china/invasion-of-the-chinese-clones-qdqmnd3mtbf.

14. Associated Press, "GM Settles Case with Chery," *Los Angeles Daily News*, updated August 29, 2017, https://www.dailynews.com/2005/11/19/gm-settles
-case-with-chery.

15. Associated Press, "China Assailed on Capitol Hill for Pirated Goods," NBC
News, June 7, 2006, https://www.nbcnews.com/id/wbna13183395.

16. Kevin Bullis, "Tesla Roadster," MIT Technology Review, August 19, 2008,
https://www.technologyreview.com/2008/08/19/219217/tesla-roadster-2.

17. We will discuss this issue later in the book, but Buffett's stock purchase underscores the problematic nature of free trade investment clashing against national
interests. US investors' pumping up Chinese companies to the detriment of US
companies may be good for the bottom line, but at what cost to our nation?
Berkshire Hathaway's leaders and many of its shareholders live in America, not
China. Bolstering a Chinese firm at the detriment of American car manufacturers, such as Tesla, which, at the time of Berkshire's stock purchase, was committed to building its cars in America, poses a conflict of national interests. To be
fair, Tesla was not yet a publicly traded company. And Buffett and Berkshire
Hathaway have the right to spend their money any way they please. But again,
at what cost?

18. Nicholas Gordon, "Charlie Munger Says BYD Was His Best Investment at Berkshire Hathaway—It's 'Almost Ridiculous' How Much It's Beating Elon Musk's
Tesla," *Fortune*, February 16, 2023, https://fortune.com/2023/02/16/charlie
-munger-byd-stake-warren-buffett-berkshire-hathaway-china-tesla.

19. Bloomberg TV, "Tesla's Musk Laughs at BYD," YouTube, November 15, 2011,
https://www.youtube.com/watch?v=_9ftbRWqkj0.

20. Keith Bradsher, "What Elon Musk Needs from China," *New York Times*, November 22, 2024, https://www.nytimes.com/2024/11/22/business/elon-musk
-tesla-china.html.

21. "Tesla's China-Made EV Sales Fall 18% in April; Shares Slip," Reuters, May 7, 2024,
https://www.reuters.com/business/autos-transportation/teslas-china-made-ev
-sales-fall-18-yy-april-2024-05-07.

22. Phate Zheng, "Tesla Offers 0-Interest Loans for Up to 5 Years in China to Boost

Sales," CnEVPost, April 3, 2024, https://cnevpost.com/2024/04/03/tesla
-offers-0-interest-loans-in-china-boost-sales.

23. Edward White and Gloria Li, "The Relentless Innovation Fuelling China's 'Brutal' Car Wars," *Financial Times*, April 6, 2025, https://www.ft.com/content/70e602c7-768c-4b1c-846f-eaf64d38984b.

24. "Fact Sheet: President Biden Takes Action to Protect American Workers and Businesses from China's Unfair Trade Practices," The White House, May 14, 2024, https://bidenwhitehouse.archives.gov/briefing-room/speeches-remarks/2024/05/14/remarks-by-president-biden-remarks-by-president-biden-on-his-actions-to-protect-american-workers-and-businesses-from-chinas-unfair-trade-practices.

25. Dan Milmo, "Tesla Boss Elon Musk Criticises US Tariffs on Chinese Electric Vehicles," *Guardian*, May 24, 2024, https://www.theguardian.com/technology/article/2024/may/24/tesla-boss-elon-musk-criticises-us-tariffs-chinese-electric-vehicles-distort-market.

26. "Elon Musk Visits China as Tesla Seeks Self-Driving Technology Rollout," Reuters, April 28, 2024, https://www.reuters.com/business/autos-transportation/elon-musk-heading-china-visit-teslas-second-biggest-market-sources-say-2024-04-28.

27. "Notice on the Testing of Four Safety Requirements for Automotive Data Processing" [in Chinese], China Association of Automobile Manufacturers, April 28, 2024, http://www.caam.org.cn/chn/1/cate_2/con_5236385.html.

28. Mara Hvistendahl, "How Elon Musk Became 'Kind of Pro-China,'" *New York Times*, March 27, 2024, https://www.nytimes.com/2024/03/27/world/asia/musk-china-tesla-explained.html.

29. Tara Patel, "Jeep Pulls Out of China over Government Meddling in Business," Bloomberg, July 28, 2022, https://www.bloomberg.com/news/articles/2022-07-28/jeep-pulls-out-of-china-over-government-meddling-in-business.

30. Marco Quiroz-Gutierrez, "Tesla Is Getting Pummeled in the Stock Market, but Elon Musk's Other Companies Are Having a Field Day in the Secondary Market—Especially xAI," *Fortune*, March 14, 2025, https://fortune.com/2025/03/14/elon-musk-private-company-valuations-soar-tesla-stock-falls.

31. Phate Zhang, "Tesla Passes Data Security Requirements in China amid Elon Musk Visit," CnEVPost, April 28, 2024, https://cnevpost.com/2024/04/29/tesla-passes-data-security-requirements-china-musk-visit/.

32. Authors' interview with Mike Caudill, December 3, 2024.

33. Edward White and Gloria Li, "The Relentless Innovation Fuelling China's 'Brutal' Car Wars," *Financial Times*, April 6, 2025, https://www.ft.com/content/70e602c7-768c-4b1c-846f-eaf64d38984b.

CHAPTER 7 | Chip Spy Wars

1. "The Basics of Microchips," ASML, accessed January 21, 2025, https://www.asml.com/en/technology/all-about-microchips/microchip-basics.

2. Authors' interview with Shoshana Raphael, January 8, 2024.

3. FemtoMetrix Inc. v. Chongji Huang et al., Case No. 8:22-cv-01624, Complaint for Misappropriation of Trade Secrets and Breach of Contract, filed August 31, 2022, https://pdfserver.amlaw.com/legalradar/45849544_complaint.pdf.

4. John Shiffman and Joshua Schneyer, "US Wants to Contain China's Chip Industry. This Startup Shows It Won't Be Easy," Reuters, December 29, 2023, https://www.reuters.com/technology/us-wants-contain-chinas-chip-industry-this-startup-shows-it-wont-be-easy-2023-12-29.

5. Femtometrix Inc. v. Chongji Huang et al., https://pdfserver.amlaw.com/legalradar/45849544_complaint.pdf.

6. "About Aspiring" [in Chinese], Aspiring, accessed January 15, 2025, http://www.aspiring.com.cn/#page2.

7. Alon Raphael, witness, "Standing United Against the People's Republic of China's Economic Aggression and Predatory Practices," Testimony Before the House Foreign Affairs Committee, Indo-Pacific Subcommittee, May 18, 2023, https://docs.house.gov/meetings/FA/FA05/20230518/115921/HHRG-118-FA05-Wstate-RaphaelA-20230518.pdf.

8. Authors' interview with a retired tech CEO familiar with Femtometrix who requested anonymity.

9. "ASPIRING and FemtoMetrix reach settlement on dispute," Aspiring.com, September 22, 2024, http://www.aspiring.com.cn/news/22.html.

10. Jordan Robertson and Michael Riley, "Engineer Who Fled Charges of Stealing Chip Secrets Now Thrives in China," Bloomberg, June 6, 2022, https://www.bloomberg.com/news/articles/2022-06-06/engineer-who-fled-us-charges-of-stealing-chip-technology-now-thrives-in-china.

11. Robertson and Riley, "Engineer Who Fled Charges of Stealing Chip Secrets Now Thrives in China."

12. "Board of Directors," China Oriental Group, accessed March 14, 2025, http://www.chinaorientalgroup.com/e/about_bod.php#1.

13. "China Semiconductor Market: Industry Analysis and Forecast (2024–2030)," Maximize Market Research, accessed March 14, 2024, https://www.maximizemarketresearch.com/market-report/china-semiconductor-market/85973.

14. Dong Cao, "China Chip Firm Seeking to Rival ASML Weighs IPO Filing, Sources Say," Bloomberg, May 16, 2023, https://www.bloomberg.com/news/articles/2023-05-16/china-chip-firm-seeking-to-rival-asml-is-said-to-mull-ipo-filing.

15. Thomas Claburn, "Dutch Chip Equipment Maker Denies Trade Secrets Theft Was Chinese Espionage," The Register, April 12, 2019, https://www.theregister.com/2019/04/12/dutch_china_theft_claim.

16. "Statement by ASML's Board of Management in light of the XTAL Court Case," ASML, April 17, 2019, https://www.asml.com/en/news/press-releases/2019/statement-by-asmls-board-of-management-in-light-of-the-xtal-court-case.

17. Authors' interview with Matt Brazil, April 9, 2024.

CHAPTER 8 | Telecommunications

1. Ray Le Maistre, "Huawei Is Still the World's Biggest Telecom Equipment Vendor," TelecomTV, March 22, 2023, https://www.telecomtv.com/content/access-evolution/huawei-is-still-the-world-s-biggest-telecom-equipment-vendor-47048.

2. PR Newswire, "Huawei Cloud Launches New Brand Motto 'Grow with Intelligence' to the Hong Kong Market," Business Insider, March 14, 2019, https://markets.businessinsider.com/news/stocks/huawei-cloud-launches-new-brand-motto-grow-with-intelligence-to-the-hong-kong-market-1028029192.

3. "Copper Tower—Head Office for Plesner (Law Firm)," EUmies Awards, 2005, https://eumiesawards.com/heritageobject/copper-tower---head-office-for-plesner-law-firm.

4. Jordan Robertson and Drake Bennett, "When a Huawei Bid Turned into a Hunt for a Corporate Mole," June 15, 2023, https://www.bloomberg.com/news/features/2023-06-15/how-huawei-got-caught-spying-and-lost-a-200-million-5g-contract.

5. Frederik Kulager and Fie Dandanell, "Operation Pellegrino," Zetland, June 2, 2024, https://www.zetland.dk/historie/s8D34NZJ-aOZj67pz-be97a.

6. Drake Bennett and Jordan Robertson, "Huawei, TDC Holding and a 5G Network Corporate Spying Tale," Bloomberg, June 16, 2023, https://www.bloomberg.com/news/newsletters/2023-06-16/huawei-tdc-holding-and-a-5g-network-corporate-spying-tale.

7. Kulager and Dandanell, "Operation Pellegrino."

8. Frederik Kulager and Fie Dandanell, "Operation Pellegrino: #3," June 16, 2024, https://www.zetland.dk/historie/sO0VZpna-aOZj67pz-159e4.

9. Kulager and Dandanell, "Operation Pellegrino: #3."

10. Kulager and Dandanell, "Operation Pellegrino: #3."

11. Kulager and Dandanell, "Operation Pellegrino: #5," June 30, 2024, https://www.zetland.dk/historie/sO0VZXx7-aOZj67pz-3998d.

12. Kulager and Dandanell, "Operation Pellegrino: #5."

13. Dov Goldstein, "Posts," LinkedIn, 2020, https://www.linkedin.com/posts/dov-goldstein-12689b_jeg-er-klar-til-nye-udfordringer-min-activity-6665867318867951618-AU1Q.

14. Malte Oxvig, "TDC har udskiftet sin sikkerhedschef: 'Med Ray fungerede det ikke godt nok'" ["TDC Has Replaced Its Security Manager: 'With Ray, Things Didn't Work Well Enough'"], ITWatch, January 9, 2020, https://itwatch.dk/ITNyt/Brancher/tele/article11863011.ece.

15. Simon Kruse and Lene Winther, "Banned Recording Reveals China Ambassador Threatened Faroese Leader at Secret Meeting," *Berlingske*, December 10, 2019, https://www.berlingske.dk/internationalt/banned-recording-reveals-china-ambassador-threatened-faroese-leader.

16. Laurens Cerulus, "Huawei Put Pressure on Denmark in Wake of Diplomatic Row," Politico, May 13, 2020, https://www.politico.eu/article/huawei-put-pressure-on-denmark-in-wake-of-diplomatic-scandal.

17. Thomas Brienstrup, "Huawei bliver droppet på Færøerne til 5G-mobilet" ["Huawei Is Dropped in the Faroe Islands for 5G Mobile Networks"], Berlingske Tidende, August 20, 2021, https://www.berlingske.dk/virksomheder/huawei-bliver-droppet-paa-faeroeerne-til-5g-mobilnet.

18. Qiao Liang and Wang Xiangsui, Unrestricted Warfare (Beijing: PLA Literature and Arts Publishing House, February 1999), 10, https://www.c4i.org/unrestricted.pdf.

19. Sun Tzu, The Art of War (Canterbury Classics, 2014), https://classics.mit.edu/Tzu/artwar.html.

20. "Who Is Ren Zhengfei?," U.S.-China Perception Monitor, August 16, 2021, https://uscnpm.org/2021/08/16/value-6.

21. Superseding Indictment, United States Against Huawei Technologies Co., Ltd., Huawei Device. Usa Inc., Skycom Tech Co. Ltd., Wanzhou Meng, United States District Court, Eastern District of New York, January 23, 2019, https://www.justice.gov/opa/press-release/file/1125021/dl?mod=article_inline.

22. Authors' interview with an academic leader with knowledge of Ren meetings, November 2024.

23. Laura Wamsley, "A Robot Named 'Tappy': Huawei Conspired to Steal T-Mobile's Trade Secrets, Says DOJ," NPR, January 29, 2019, https://www.npr.org/2019/01/29/689663720/a-robot-named-tappy-huawei-conspired-to-steal-t-mobile-s-trade-secrets-says-doj.

24. Indictment, United States of America v. Huawei Device Co., Ltd., and Huawei Device Usa, Inc., United States District Court for the Western District of Washington at Seattle, January 16, 2019, https://www.justice.gov/opa/press-release/file/1124996/dl.

25. Indictment, United States of America v. Huawei Device Co., Ltd., and Huawei Device Usa, Inc.

26. Indictment, United States of America, v. Huawei Device Co., Ltd., and Huawei Device Usa, Inc.

27. Rachel Lerman, "Jury Awards T-Mobile $4.8M in Trade-Secrets Case Against Huawei," Seattle Times, May 18, 2017, https://www.seattletimes.com/business/technology/july-awards-t-mobile-48m-in-trade-secrets-case-against-huawei.

28. Chuck Goudie and Barb Markoff, "Decade After China Secrets Case, Suburban Woman Off the Hook," abc7chicago.com, March 7, 2018, https://abc7chicago.com/hanjuan-jin-motorola-trade-secrets-chinese-spy-craft/3183288/.

29. Third Amended Complaint, Motorola, Inc., v. Lemko Corporation, Xiaohong Sheng, Shaowei Pan, Hanjuan Jin, Xiaohua Wu, Xuefeng Bai, Nicholas Labun, Bohdan Pyskir, Hechun Cai, Jinzhong Zhang, Angel Favila, Ankur Saxena, Raymond Howell, Faye Vorick, Nicholas Desai, and Huawei Technologies Co., Ltd., Case No. 08 Cv 5427E, United States District Court for the Northern Dis-

trict of Illinois, Eastern Division, July 16, 2010, https://dig.abclocal.go.com
/wls/documents/2019/060719-wls-motorola-huawei-doc.pdf.

30. "Motorola Solutions and Huawei Issue Joint Statement," Motorola, April 13, 2011,
https://www.motorolasolutions.com/newsroom/press-releases/motorola
-solutions-and-huawei-issue-joint-statement.html.

31. Jeff Ferry, "Top Five Cases of Huawei IP Theft and Patent Infringement," Coalition for a Prosperous America, December 13, 2018, https://prosperousamerica
.org/top-five-cases-of-huawei-ip-theft-and-patent-infringement.

32. Mark Chandler, "Huawei and Cisco's Source Code: Correcting the Record,"
Cisco, October 11, 2012, https://blogs.cisco.com/news/huawei-and-ciscos
-source-code-correcting-the-record.

33. Phil Hochmuth, "Cisco Drops Suit Against Huawei," IT World Canada, July 27,
2004, archived at https://web.archive.org/web/20210127233518/; https://www
.itworldcanada.com/article/cisco-drops-suit-against-huawei/16764.

34. Kate O'Keeffe, "Huawei Secretly Backs US Research, Awarding Millions in
Prizes," Bloomberg, May 2, 2024, https://www.bloomberg.com/news/articles
/2024-05-02/huawei-secretly-backs-us-based-research-with-millions-in
-prizes-through-dc-group.

35. Authors' interview with source who requested anonymity, November 15, 2024.

36. O'Keeffe, "Huawei Secretly Backs US Research."

37. Frank Lucas and Zoe Lofgren, letter to Optica CEO Elizabeth Rogan, July 29,
2024, https://democrats-science.house.gov/imo/media/doc/2024.07.29%20FL
%20and%20ZL%20to%20Optica%20pt2%20(fd).pdf.

38. Christopher Balding and Donald C. Clarke, "Who Owns Huawei?," SSRN, April
17, 2019, https://ssrn.com/abstract=3372669.

39. Craig Chambers, "Out of Sight but Not Invisible: Defeating Fileless Malware
with Behavior Monitoring, AMSI, and Next-Gen AV," Microsoft Security, September 27, 2018, https://www.microsoft.com/en-us/security/blog/2018/09/27
/out-of-sight-but-not-invisible-defeating-fileless-malware-with-behavior
-monitoring-amsi-and-next-gen-av.

40. "Volt Typhoon Targets US Critical Infrastructure with Living-off-the-Land
Techniques," Microsoft Security, May 24, 2024, https://www.microsoft.com
/en-us/security/blog/2023/05/24/volt-typhoon-targets-us-critical
-infrastructure-with-living-off-the-land-techniques.

41. "PRC State-Sponsored Actors Compromise and Maintain Persistent Access to
U.S. Critical Infrastructure," Cybersecurity & Infrastructure Security Agency,
February 7, 2024, https://www.cisa.gov/news-events/cybersecurity-advisories
/aa24-038a.

42. Dustin Volz, "Dozens of Countries Hit in Chinese Telecom Hacking Campaign,
Top U.S. Official Says," Wall Street Journal, December 4, 2024, https://www
.wsj.com/politics/national-security/dozens-of-countries-hit-in-chinese
-telecom-hacking-campaign-top-u-s-official-says-2a3a5cca.

43. Ellen Nakashima, "Top Senator Calls Salt Typhoon 'Worst Telecom Hack in

Our Nation's History,'" *Washington Post*, November 21, 2024, https://www
.washingtonpost.com/national-security/2024/11/21/salt-typhoon-china-hack
-telecom.

44. David Shepardson, "US House to Vote to Provide $3 Billion to Remove Chinese
Telecoms Equipment," Reuters, December 7, 2024, https://www.reuters.com
/world/us/us-house-vote-provide-3-billion-remove-chinese-telecoms
-equipment-2024-12-08.

CHAPTER 9 | Artificially Subsidized Intelligence

1. Superseding Indictment, United States of America v. Linwei Ding, a.k.a. Leon
Ding, Case No. 24-cr-00141 VC. United States District Court, Northern District of California, San Francisco Division, February 4, 2025, https://www
.justice.gov/opa/media/1388341/dl?inline.

2. "Our Approach to Search," Google, accessed April 16, 2025, https://www
.google.com/intl/en_us/search/howsearchworks/our-approach.

3. Superseding Indictment, USA v. Ding.

4. Superseding Indictment, USA v. Ding.

5. Superseding Indictment, USA v. Ding.

6. PRC State Council, "Made in China 2025."

7. "Director Wray Discusses Potential Misuses of AI During the FBI's Emerging
Technology and Securing Innovation Security Summit," FBI, October 17,
2023, https://www.fbi.gov/video-repository/101723_fireside_chat_02.mp4
/view.

8. Robert McMillan, Dustin Volz, and Aruna Viswanatha, "China Is Stealing AI
Secrets to Turbocharge Spying, U.S. Says," *Wall Street Journal*, December 25,
2023, https://www.wsj.com/tech/ai/china-is-stealing-ai-secrets-to-turbocharge
-spying-u-s-says-00413594.

9. Superseding Indictment, USA v. Ding.

10. Superseding Indictment, USA v. Ding.

11. Superseding Indictment, USA v. Ding.

12. USAO Northern District of California, "USA Ramsey Announces Ding Indictment," YouTube, March 6, 2024, https://www.youtube.com/watch?v=l64VlrA
-GUA.

13. Didi Kirsten Tatlow, "Exclusive: U.S. Gave $30 Million to Top Chinese Scientist
Leading China's AI 'Race,'" *Newsweek*, November 1, 2023, https://www.newsweek
.com/us-gave-30-million-top-chinese-scientist-leading-chinas-airace-1837772.

14. Irene Zhang, "AI Proposals at 'Two Sessions': AGI as 'Two Bombs, One Satellite'?," China Talk, March 8, 2023, https://www.chinatalk.media/p/ai
-proposals-at-two-sessions-agi.

15. Yuan Yuan, "Song-Chun Zhu: The Race to General Purpose Artificial Intelligence Is Not Merely About Technological Competition; Even More So, It Is a
Struggle to Control the Narrative," Center for Security and Emerging Technology,

January 29, 2025, https://cset.georgetown.edu/wp-content/uploads/t0618_ai_narrative_battle_EN.pdf.

16. Tatlow, "Exclusive: U.S. Gave $30 Million."

17. Samantha Subin, "Nvidia Sheds Almost $600 Billion in Market Cap, Biggest One-Day Loss in U.S. History," CNBC, January 27, 2025, https://www.cnbc.com/2025/01/27/nvidia-sheds-almost-600-billion-in-market-cap-biggest-drop-ever.html.

18. Marc Andreessen (@pmarca), "Deepseek R1 is one of the most amazing and impressive breakthroughs I've ever seen – and as open source, a profound gift to the world," X, January 24, 2025, https://x.com/pmarca/status/1882719769851474108.

19. Jess Weatherbed, "OpenAI Has Evidence That Its Models Helped Train China's DeepSeek," The Verge, March 13, 2025, https://www.theverge.com/news/601195/openai-evidence-deepseek-distillation-ai-data.

20. Jaime Hampton, "Ai2 Launches Tülu3-405B Model, Scales Reinforcement Learning for Open Source AI," AIwire, January 31, 2025, https://www.aiwire.net/2025/01/31/ai2-launches-tulu3-405b-model-scales-reinforcement-learning-for-open-source-ai.

21. Zak Doffman, "DeepSeek Warning—New Chinese Security Threat Puts You at Risk," *Forbes*, January 28, 2025, https://www.forbes.com/sites/zakdoffman/2025/01/27/warning-deepseek-is-a-chinese-security-nightmare-come-true.

22. Authors' interview with Charles Finrock, October 18, 2024.

CHAPTER 10 | Sneak Attacks on the Department of Defense

1. *Military and Security Developments Involving the People's Republic of China 2024: Annual Report to Congress*, U.S. Department of Defense, December 18, 2024, 30, https://media.defense.gov/2024/Dec/18/2003615520/-1/-1/0/MILITARY-AND-SECURITY-DEVELOPMENTS-INVOLVING-THE-PEOPLES-REPUBLIC-OF-CHINA-2024.PDF.

2. Colin Freeze and Alexandra Posadzki, "Canadian Resident Charged in U.S. for Directing Chinese Spy Ring," *Globe and Mail*, July 22, 2014, https://www.theglobeandmail.com/news/national/canadian-charged-in-us-for-directing-chinese-spy-ring/article19703820.

3. Jim Sciutto, "'The Shadow War': How a Chinese Spy Stole Some of the Pentagon's Most Sensitive Secrets," CNN, May 14, 2019, https://www.cnn.com/2019/05/14/politics/shadow-war-chinese-spy/index.html.

4. Jeremy Page, "Plan B for China's Wealthy: Moving to U.S., Europe," *Wall Street Journal*, February 21, 2012, https://www.wsj.com/articles/SB10001424052970203806504577181461401318988.

5. Criminal Complaint, United States of America v. Su Bin, aka Stephen Su, aka Stephen Subin, United States District Court, Central District of California, June 27, 2014, https://exportlawblog.com/docs/us_v_su_complaint.pdf.

6.   Criminal Complaint, United States of America v. Su Bin.

7.   Criminal Complaint, United States of America v. Su Bin.

8.   Criminal Complaint, United States of America v. Su Bin.

9.   Garrett M. Graff, "How the US Forced China to Quit Stealing—Using a Chinese Spy," Wired, October 11, 2018, https://www.wired.com/story/us-china -cybertheft-su-bin.

10. Wendell Barnhouse, "The Y-20: A (Big) Chinese Knockoff," avgeekery.com, February 3, 2016, https://avgeekery.com/y-20-big-chinese-knockoff.

11. Authors' interview with source who requested anonymity, April 20, 2024.

12. Rachanee Srisavasdi, "Wife of Engineer Gets 3 Years for Acting as Chinese Agent," *The Orange County Register*, October 2, 2008, https://www.ocregister .com/2008/10/02/wife-of-engineer-gets-3-years-for-acting-as-chinese-agent./

13. "Chinese Agent Sentenced to over 24 Years in Prison for Exporting United States Defense Articles to China," US Department of Justice, March 8, 2008, https://www.justice.gov/archive/opa/pr/2008/March/08_nsd_229.html.

14. "Former Boeing Engineer Convicted of Economic Espionage in Theft of Space Shuttle Secrets for China," US Department of Justice, July 16, 2009, https:// www.justice.gov/archives/opa/pr/former-boeing-engineer-convicted -economic-espionage-theft-space-shuttle-secrets-china.

CHAPTER 11 | Hard Lessons in Hypersonics and National Security

1.   "Philippines Arrests Chinese National on Suspicion of Espionage," Reuters, January 20, 2025, https://www.reuters.com/world/asia-pacific/philippines -arrests-chinese-national-suspicion-espionage-2025-01-20.

2.   "Video: Kendall on the State of the Forces at AFA's Air, Space & Cyber '21," *Air & Space Forces Magazine*, September 23, 2021, https://www.airandspaceforces .com/video-kendall-on-the-state-of-the-forces-at-afas-air-space-cyber-21.

3.   Demetri Sevastopulo and Kathrin Hille, "China Tests New Space Capability with Hypersonic Missile," *Financial Times*, October 16, 2021, https://www.ft .com/content/ba0a3cde-719b-4040-93cb-a486e1f843fb.

4.   "China's 2021 Orbital-Weapon Tests," *Strategic Comments* 28, no. 1 (2022): vii–ix.

5.   Sevastopulo and Hille, "China Tests New Space Capability with Hypersonic Missile."

6.   "HRL Laboratories LLC," Military Aerospace Electronics, accessed December 29, 2024, https://www.militaryaerospace.com/directory/rf-and-microwave /mmics/company/14183636/hrl-laboratories-llc.

7.   Igor Neyman, Special Agent, affidavit, United States of America v. Chenguang Gong, Defendant, United States District Court for the Central District of California, February 5, 2024, https://www.justice.gov/archives/opa/media/1337756 /dl?inline.

8. Igor Neyman, Special Agent, affidavit, United States of America v. Chenguang Gong, Defendant.

9. "LTN4323 Product Brief," Fairchild Imaging, accessed December 29, 2024, https://fairchildimaging.com/ltn4323-product-brief.

10. "Justice Department Announces Charges and Arrest in Two Separate Illicit Technology Transfer Schemes to Benefit Governments of China and Iran," US Department of Justice, February 7, 2024, https://www.justice.gov/opa/pr /justice-department-announces-charges-and-arrest-two-separate-illicit -technology-transfer.

11. "System Technology Modernization," Los Alamos National Laboratory, accessed March 1, 2025, https://www.lanl.gov/about/lab-agenda/technology -modernization.

12. "The Los Alamos Club," Strider Technologies, September 2022, https://content .striderintel.com/wp-content/uploads/2022/09/Strider-Los-Alamos-Report .pdf.

13. "The Los Alamos Club."

14. Emily Weinstein, "Chinese Talent Program Tracker," Center for Security and Emerging Techology, accessed December 30, 2024, https://chinatalenttracker .cset.tech.

15. "Harvard University Professor and Two Chinese Nationals Charged in Three Separate China Related Cases," US Department of Justice, January 28, 2020 https://www.justice.gov/opa/pr/harvard-university-professor-and-two -chinese-nationals-charged-three-separate-china-related.

16. "Harvard University Professor and Two Chinese Nationals Charged in Three Separate China Related Cases."

17. "Former West Virginia University Professor Pleads Guilty to Fraud That Enabled Him to Participate in the People's Republic of China's 'Thousand Talents Plan,'" US Department of Justice, March 10, 2020, https://www.justice.gov /opa/pr/former-west-virginia-university-professor-pleads-guilty-fraud -enabled-him-participate-people.

18. U.S. Department of Defense, "Military and Security Developments Involving the People's Republic of China, 2024," December 18, 2024, 155, https://media .defense.gov/2024/Dec/18/2003615520/-1/-1/0/MILITARY-AND -SECURITY-DEVELOPMENTS-INVOLVING-THE-PEOPLES-REPUBLIC -OF-CHINA-2024.PDF.

19. SpaceRef, "Wolf Letter to NASA's Bolden Correcting Record on Restrictions Involving Chinese Nationals," SpaceNews, October 8, 2013, https://spacenews .com/wolf-letter-to-nasas-bolden-correcting-record-on-restrictions-involving -chinese-nationals.

20. China DOI [in Chinese], accessed April 16, 2025, http://www.chinadoi.cn.

21. Authors' interview with L. J. Eads, October 18, 2024.

22. "FY 2025 Budget Request Agency Summary," NASA, March 2024, https://

www.nasa.gov/wp-content/uploads/2024/03/fy-2025-budget-agency-fact
-sheet.pdf?emrc=65ef896cd78d9.

23. L. J. Eads, email to author, October 18, 2024, listing NASA-tied Wichita research.

24. Ali Asgari et al., "Multivariable Degradation Modeling and Life Prediction
    Using Multivariate Fractional Brownian Motion," *Reliability Engineering &
    System Safety* 248 (2024): 110146, https://doi.org/10.1016/j.ress.2024.110146.

25. Yutong Xue et al., "Designing Hybrid Aerogel-3D Printed Absorbers for Simul-
    taneous Low Frequency and Broadband Noise Control," *Materials & Design*
    242 (2024): 113026, https://doi.org/10.1016/j.matdes.2024.113026.

26. "Presidential Memorandum on United States Government–Supported Research
    and Development National Security Policy," The White House, January 14, 2021,
    https://trumpwhitehouse.archives.gov/presidential-actions/presidential
    -memorandum-united-states-government-supported-research-development
    -national-security-policy.

27. Authors' interview with L. J. Eads, October 18, 2024.

28. Authors' interview with L. J. Eads, October 18, 2024.

29. *Military and Security Developments Involving the People's Republic of China
    2024*, U.S. Department of Defense.

30. Lesley Kennedy, "Why Reagan's 'Star Wars' Defense Plan Remained Science
    Fiction," History, February 17, 2025, https://www.history.com/news/reagan
    -star-wars-sdi-missile-defense.

31. Robert Spalding and Seth Kaufman, *Stealth War: How China Took Over While
    America's Elite Slept* (Portfolio, 2019), 183–86.

32. Donald Trump, "The Iron Dome for America," Executive Order, White House,
    January 27, 2025, https://www.whitehouse.gov/presidential-actions/2025/01
    /the-iron-dome-for-america.

CHAPTER 12 | Financial Instruments of Destruction: Venture Capital and Private Equity

1. "We Are Milo," Milo, accessed May 10, 2024, https://www.okmilo.com/en-us
   /our-story/.

2. "Milo—The Action Communicator," Kickstarter, accessed March 20, 2025,
   https://www.kickstarter.com/projects/okmilo/milo-the-action-communicator.

3. "China Internet Report 2020," SCMP Research, July 2020, https://web
   .archive.org/web/20230209141150/http://www.invest-data.com/eWebEditor
   /uploadfile/202007300944091123 6297.pdf.

4. Gill and James Reilly, "The Tenuous Hold of China Inc. in Africa," *Washington
   Quarterly* 30, no. 3 (2007): 37–52, https://doi.org/10.1162/wash.2007.30.3.37;
   Rahul Karan Reddy, "China's Going Global Policy: A Prelude to the BRI," Organization for Research on China and Asia, January 16, 2023, https://orcasia.org
   /chinas-going-global-policy-a-prelude-to-the-bri.

5. Reddy, "China's Going Global Policy."

6. PRC State Council, "Made in China 2025."

7. Cory Bennet and Bryan Bender, "How China Acquires 'the Crown Jewels' of U.S. Technology," Politico, May 22, 2018, https://www.politico.com /story/2018/05/22/china-us-tech-companies-cfius-572413.

8. "A Machine-Learning Approach to Venture Capital," CSC Group, November 3, 2017, https://www.leadvc.com/2017/new_en_1103/855.html.

9. "Overview," CSC Group, accessed March 17, 2025, https://www.leadvc.com /business_en.

10. Krysten Crawford, "Purvi Gandhi, BS 92 Partner and CFO, Hone Capital," BerkeleyHass Magazine, Fall 2019, https://newsroom.haas.berkeley.edu /magazine/winter2019-20/purvi-gandhi.

11. Purvi Gandhi-Kapoor v. Hone Capital LLC, C.A. No. 2022-0881-JTL-1 (Del. Ch. Nov. 22, 2023), https://law.justia.com/cases/delaware/court-of-chancery/2023 /c-a-no-2022-0881-jtl-1.html.

12. Tabby Kinder, "FBI Probes Whether Silicon Valley Venture Firm Passed Secrets to China," *Financial Times*, September 25, 2024, https://www.ft.com/content /d94a5467-ebf9-4992-af13-3e71061707a4.

13. Kinder, "FBI Probes Whether Silicon Valley Venture Firm Passed Secrets to China."

14. "A Machine-Learning Approach to Venture Capital," CSC Group.

15. National Counterintelligence and Security Center, "Safeguarding Our Innovation: Protecting U.S. Emerging Technology Companies from Investment by Foreign Threat Actors," Director of National Intelligence, July 2024, https://www.dni.gov /files/NCSC/documents/products/FINALSafeguardingOurInnovationBulletin .pdf.

16. "Entities Identified as Chinese Military Companies Operating in the United States in Accordance with Section 1260H of the William M. ('Mac') Thornberry National Defense Authorization Act for Fiscal Year 2021 (Public Law 116-283)," U.S. Department of Defense, January 31, 2024, https://media.defense .gov/2024/Jan/31/2003384819/-1/-1/0/1260H-LIST.PDF.

17. Nicholas Borst, "China's Tech Rush," Seafarer Funds, September 2018, https:// www.seafarerfunds.com/commentary/chinas-tech-rush.

18. Yelin Mo, Max A. Cherney, and Stephen Nellis, "Arm's China Relationship Complicates IPO," Reuters, August 22, 2023, https://www.reuters.com/markets /deals/arms-china-relationship-complicates-ipo-2023-08-22.

19. Zhang Erchi, Qu Yunxu, and Guo Yingzhe, "In Depth: How SoftBank Wrested Back Control of Arm China," Nikkei Asia, July 5, 2022, https://asia.nikkei.com /Spotlight/Caixin/In-Depth-How-SoftBank-wrested-back-control-of-Arm-China #selection-2767.218-2767.414.

20. Mo et al., "Arm's China Relationship Complicates IPO."

21. Hanna Dohmen and Jacob Feldgoise, "A Bigger Yard, a Higher Fence: Understanding BIS's Expanded Controls on Advanced Computing Exports," Center for Security and Emerging Technology, December 4, 2023, https://cset.georgetown .edu/article/bis-2023-update-explainer.

22. Ryan McMorrow et al., "China Holds Up Arm's Exit from Troubled Joint Venture," *Financial Times*, March 2, 2023, https://www.ft.com/content/e605a92c-5efc-471c-bd7d-a36c7620420c.

23. David Vergun, "Leaders Say TikTok Is Potential Cybersecurity Risk to U.S.," U.S. Department of Defense, April 6, 2023, https://www.defense.gov/News/News-Stories/Article/Article/3354874/leaders-say-tiktok-is-potential-cybersecurity-risk-to-us.

24. Lauren Hirsch, "The U.S. Investors Caught in the Scrum Over TikTok," *New York Times*, March 26, 2024, https://www.nytimes.com/2024/03/26/technology/tiktok-investors-bytedance.html.

25. Mike Gallagher and Raja Krishnamoorthi, letter to Roelof Botha and Don Vieira, Sequoia Capital, House of Representatives, Select Committee on the Chinese Communist Party, October 17, 2023, https://selectcommitteeontheccp.house.gov/sites/evo-subsites/selectcommitteeontheccp.house.gov/files/evo-media-document/2023.10.17-letter-to-sequoia-capital.pdf.

26. "Investigative Report: How American Financial Institutions Provide Billions of Dollars to PRC Companies Committing Human Rights Abuses and Fueling the PRC's Military," House of Representatives, Select Committee on the Strategic Competition Between the United States and the Chinese Communist Party, April 18, 2024, 6, https://selectcommitteeontheccp.house.gov/sites/evo-subsites/selectcommitteeontheccp.house.gov/files/evo-media-document/4.18.24%20How%20Americsan%20Financial%20Institutions%20Provide%20Billions%20of%20Dollars%20to%20PRC%20Companies%20Committing%20Human%20Rights%20Abuses%20and%20Fueling%20the%20PRC%27s%20Military.pdf.

27. "BlackRock, MSCI Draw Scrutiny from US House Committee on China," Reuters, August 1, 2023, https://www.reuters.com/business/finance/blackrock-msci-face-probe-allegedly-facilitating-china-investments-wsj-2023-08-01/.

28. "2024 Annual Meeting of Shareholders and Proxy Statement," MSCI, Inc., https://www.msci.com/downloads/web/msci-com/discover-msci/corporate-responsbility/sustainability-reports-and-policies/2024%20MSCI%20Proxy.pdf.

29. "Investigative Report: How American Financial Institutions Provide Billions of Dollars to PRC Companies Committing Human Rights Abuses and Fueling the PRC's Military," 7.

CHAPTER 13 | The Health Care Assault

1. "APT 40 Cyber Espionage Activities," FBI, https://www.fbi.gov/wanted/cyber/apt-40-cyber-espionage-activities.

2. United States of America v. Ding Xiaoyang, Cheng Qingmin, Zhu Yunmin, Wu Shurong, United States District Court for Southern California, May 28, 2021, https://www.justice.gov/archives/opa/press-release/file/1412916/dl.

3. Paul Mozur and Chris Buckley, "Spies for Hire: China's New Breed of Hackers Blends Espionage and Entrepreneurship," *New York Times*, August 26, 2021, https://www.nytimes.com/2021/08/26/technology/china-hackers.html.

4. Christopher Bing and Marisa Taylor, "China-Backed Hackers 'Targeted COVID-19 Vaccine Firm Moderna,'" Reuters, July 31, 2025, https://www.reuters.com/article/technology/exclusive-china-backed-hackers-targeted-covid-19-vaccine-firm-moderna-idUSKCN24V38H.

5. United States of America v. Li Xiaoyu (a/k/a "Oro0lxy") and Dong Jiazhi, United States District Court for the Eastern District of Washington, July 7, 2020, https://www.justice.gov/opa/press-release/file/1295981/dl.

6. "China's Collection of Genomic and Other Healthcare Data from America: Risks to Privacy and U.S. Economic and National Security," The National Counterintelligence and Security Center, February 2021, https://www.dni.gov/files/NCSC/documents/SafeguardingOurFuture/NCSC_China_Genomics_Fact_Sheet_2021revision20210203.pdf.

7. Brian Fung, "TikTok Collects a Lot of Data. But That's Not the Main Reason Officials Say It's a Security Risk," CNN, March 24, 2023, https://www.cnn.com/2023/03/24/tech/tiktok-ban-national-security-hearing/index.html.

8. Jack Nicas, Raymond Zhong, and Daisuke Wakabayashi, "Censorship, Surveillance and Profits: A Hard Bargain for Apple in China," *New York Times*, May 17, 2021, https://www.nytimes.com/2021/05/17/technology/apple-china-censorship-data.html.

9. "Apple statement—May 2021," *New York Times*, https://int.nyt.com/data/documenttools/apple-statement/61821a018e163070/full.pdf.

10. Nicas and Wakabayashi, "Censorship, Surveillance and Profits: A Hard Bargain for Apple in China."

11. Jack Nicas, "Apple Removes App That Helps Hong Kong Protesters Track the Police," *New York Times*, October 9, 2019, https://www.nytimes.com/2019/10/09/technology/apple-hong-kong-app.html.

12. "Apple statement—May 2021," *New York Times*.

CHAPTER 14 | The Elements of Infiltration: The American Chemical Sector

1. "Akhan Semiconductor Overview," PitchBook, accessed January 27, 2025, https://pitchbook.com/profiles/company/119466-01#funding; author interview with Adam Khan, February 3, 2025.

2. Erik Schatzker, "Huawei Sting Offers Rare Glimpse of the U.S. Targeting a Chinese Giant," Bloomberg, February 4, 2019, https://www.bloomberg.com/news/features/2019-02-04/huawei-sting-offers-rare-glimpse-of-u-s-targeting-chinese-giant.

3. Schatzker, "Huawei Sting."

4. Erik Schatzker, "Inside the Huawei Sting," Bloomberg, February 4, 2019, https://www.bloomberg.com/news/videos/2019-02-04/inside-the-huawei -sting-video.

5. "Akhan Caught Up in China-US Semiconductor Battle," Intelligence Online, March 6, 2021, https://www.intelligenceonline.com/surveillance--interception/2021 /06/03/akhan-caught-up-in-china-us-semiconductor-battle,109670740-eve.

6. Authors' interview with Adam Khan, February 3, 2025.

7. "Akhan Caught Up in China-US Semiconductor Battle."

8. "CocaCola's Formula Is at the World of CocaCola," The CocaCola Company, accessed April 16, 2025, https://www.coca-colacompany.com/about-us/history /coca-cola-formula-is-at-the-world-of-coca-cola.

9. "Xiaorong You," LinkedIn, accessed February 1, 2025, https://www.linkedin .com/in/xiaorong-you-7581b113.

10. United States of America v. Xiaorong You, aka Shannon You and Liu Xiangchen, United States District Court, Eastern District of Tennessee at Greeneville, February 12, 2019, https://storage.courtlistener.com/recap/gov.uscourts.tned .88983/gov.uscourts.tned.88983.3.0.pdf.

11. Drake Bennett and Jordan Robertson, "The Plot to Steal the Other Secret Inside a Can of Coca-Cola," Bloomberg, May 11, 2023, https://www.bloomberg .com/news/features/2023-05-11/the-plot-to-steal-the-secret-coke-can-liner -formula.

12. United States of America v. Xiaorong You; United States v. Xiaorong You, Case No. 2:19-CR-00014-1-JRG-CRW (E.D. Tenn. 2023), September 11, 2024, https://www.casemine.com/judgement/us/66e3bfe8b14cc9462135d651.

13. United States of America v. Xiaorong You.

14. Caleb Perhne, "Chinese-Born U.S. Citizen Gets 14 Years for Stealing Trade Secrets from Eastman, Coca-Cola," WCYB, September 17, 2024, https://wcyb .com/news/local/chinese-born-us-citizen-gets-14-years-for-stealing-trade -secrets-from-eastman-coca-cola.

15. Del Quentin Wilber, "How a Corporate Spy Swiped Plans for DuPont's Billion-Dollar Color Formula," Bloomberg, February 4, 2016, https://www.bloomberg .com/features/2016-stealing-dupont-white.

16. Wilber, "How a Corporate Spy Swiped Plans for DuPont's Billion-Dollar Color Formula."

17. United States of America v. Walter Lian-Heen Liew, a.k.a. Liu Yuanxuan, Christina Hong Qiao Liew, Robert J. Maegerle, USA Performance Technology, Inc., Tze Chao, Hou Shengdong, Pangang Group Company, Ltd., Pangang Group Steel, Vanadium & Titanium Company, Ltd., Pangang Group Titanium Industry Company, Ltd., and Pangang Group International Economic & Trading Company, Northern District of California, San Francisco Division, March 12, 2013, https:// www.justice.gov/sites/default/files/usao-ndca/legacy/2014/03/05/LIEW %20-%20Second%20Superseding%20Indictment%20-%20Filed%2C %20March%2012%2C%202013.pdf.

18. "Four Chinese State-Owned Industrial Companies Arraigned in Economic Espionage Conspiracy," United States Attorney's Office, Northern District of California, September 7, 2018, https://www.justice.gov/usao-ndca/pr/four-chinese-state-owned-industrial-companies-arraigned-economic-espionage-conspiracy.

19. Wilber, "How a Corporate Spy Swiped Plans for DuPont's Billion-Dollar Color Formula."

20. United States of America v. Walter Liew and Christina Liew, United States District Court, Northern District of California, August 23, 2011, https://storage.courtlistener.com/recap/gov.uscourts.cand.244399.16.0.pdf.

21. U.S. Attorney's Office, Northern District of California, "Former DuPont Scientist Pleads Guilty to Economic Espionage," FBI, March 2, 2012, https://archives.fbi.gov/archives/sanfrancisco/press-releases/2012/former-dupont-scientist-pleads-guilty-to-economic-espionage.

22. Ross Todd, "Wife Gets Probation in DuPont Trade Secrets Case," Law.com, September 29, 2015, https://www.law.com/therecorder/almID/1202738537839.

23. "United States v. Pangang Group Co.," *Harvard Law Review* 135, no. 6 (April 2022), https://harvardlawreview.org/print/vol-135/united-states-v-panganggroup-co.

CHAPTER 15 | Energy: Gale Force Theft

1. Patrick Jenevein, *Dancing with the Dragon: Cautionary Tales of the New China from an Old China Hand* (Christmas Lake Press, 2024), 172.

2. Jenevein, *Dancing with the Dragon*, 180.

3. DeWolf, a veteran pilot who owned two airplanes, died when his SNJ/T-6 Texan caught fire after takeoff on April 25, 2018. Authors' interview with Patrick Jenevein, December 19, 2024.

4. Tang Energy Group et al. v. Catic USA et al., final award, American Arbitration Association–International Centre for Dispute Resolution, December 21, 2015, https://jusmundi.com/en/document/decision/en-tang-energy-group-ltd-soaring-wind-energy-llc-jan-family-interests-ltd-the-nolan-group-inc-keith-p-young-mitchell-w-carter-v-catic-usa-inc-a-k-a-avic-international-usa-inc-avic-international-holding-corp-aviation-industry-of-china-china-aviation-industry-general-aircraft-co-ltd-avic-international-renewable-energy-corp-ascendant-renewable-energy-corp-avic-international-trade-economic-development-paul-e-thompson-final-award-monday-21st-december-2015#decision_10769.

5. "Sinovel Corporation and Three Individuals Charged in Wisconsin with Theft of AMSC Trade Secrets," US Department of Justice, June 27, 2013, https://www.justice.gov/archives/opa/pr/sinovel-corporation-and-three-individuals-charged-wisconsin-theft-amsc-trade-secrets.

6. American Superconductor Corporation, "AMSC and Sinovel Expand Strategic Partnership," AMSC, May 25, 2010, https://ir.amsc.com/news-releases/news-release-details/amsc-and-sinovel-expand-strategic-partnership.

7. "Sinovel Corporation and Three Individuals Charged."

8. "Former AMSC Employee Sentenced," *Windpower Monthly*, September 27, 2011, https://www.windpowermonthly.com/article/1095536/former-amsc-employee -sentenced.

9. "Court Imposes Maximum Fine on Sinovel Wind Group for Theft of Trade Secrets," US Department of Justice, Friday, July 6, 2018, https://www.justice.gov /archives/opa/pr/court-imposes-maximum-fine-sinovel-wind-group-theft -trade-secrets.

10. United States of America v. Wang Dong, Sun Kailiang, Wen Xinyu, Huang Zhenyu, and Gu Chunhui, United States District Court, Western District of Pennsylvania, May 1, 2014, https://www.justice.gov/iso/opa/resources /5122014519132358461949.pdf.

11. "Chinese Energy Company, U.S. Oil & Gas Affiliate and Chinese National Indicted for Theft of Trade Secrets," US Department of Justice, October 29, 2020, https://www.justice.gov/archives/opa/pr/chinese-energy-company-us-oil-gas -affiliate-and-chinese-national-indicted-theft-trade-secrets.

12. "Forum Energy Technologies, Inc," YetterColeman, accessed June 15, 2025, https://www.yettercoleman.com/case-studies/forum-energy-technologies -inc/.

13. The PRC's military strategy to control the South China Sea and other areas in the Pacific involves building islands and reefs. Ultrabouyant materials are of vital importance to such constructions.

14. United States of America v. Shan Shi, et al., Indictment, United States District Court for the District of Columbia, November 3, 2016, https://www.andrewjowett .net/wp-content/uploads/2019/07/Shi-Shan-et-al-superseding-indictment-2018 .pdf.

15. "American Businessman Who Ran Houston-Based Subsidiary of Chinese Company Sentenced to Prison for Theft of Trade Secrets," US Department of Justice, February 11, 2020, https://www.justice.gov/archives/opa/pr/american-businessman -who-ran-houston-based-subsidiary-chinese-company-sentenced-prison-theft.

16. Edward Wong, Lara Jakes, and Steven Lee Myers, "U.S. Orders China to Close Houston Consulate, Citing Efforts to Steal Trade Secrets," *New York Times*, July 22, 2020, https://www.nytimes.com/2020/07/22/world/asia/us-china-houston -consulate.html.

CHAPTER 16 | The Seeds of Agri-Espionage

1. "Read the Complaint Charging Mo Hailong with Stealing Trade Secrets," *Los Angeles Times*, October 6, 2016, https://documents.latimes.com/read -complaint-charging-mo-hailong-stealing-trade-secrets.

2. United States of America v Approximately $111,516.68 From US Bank Account Ending In 2686, in the Name Of Investors Title Company - Escrow Account, Sup-

porting Check 387143, Dated August 22, 2016, Payable To Jiunn-Ren Chen And Irma Khoj, US District Court Eastern District of Missouri, February 17, 2017, https://www.documentcloud.org/documents/23257165-chen-in-rem-complaint /?responsive=1&title=1.

3. United States of America v. Haitao Xiang, No. 22-1801 (8th Cir. 2023), US Court of Appeals, Eighth Circuit, May 5, 2023, https://law.justia.com/cases /federal/appellate-courts/ca8/22-1801/22-1801-2023-05-05.html.

4. Nicholas Phillips, "Haitao Xiang Was a Quiet Scientist at Monsanto. Then the Feds Began to Suspect Him of Economic Espionage," *St. Louis Magazine*, November 3, 2022, https://www.stlmag.com/longform/monsanto-economic -espionage-haitao-xiang-china.

5. Phillips, "Haitao Xiang Was a Quiet Scientist at Monsanto."

6. Phillips, "Haitao Xiang Was a Quiet Scientist at Monsanto."

7. "Chinese National Sentenced for Economic Espionage Conspiracy," US Department of Justice, April 7, 2022, https://www.justice.gov/opa/pr/chinese-national -sentenced-economic-espionage-conspiracy.

8. Vaclav Smil, "China's Great Ramine: 40 Years Later," *British Medical Journal* 319, no. 7225 (1999): 1619–21, https://pmc.ncbi.nlm.nih.gov/articles/PMC1127087.

9. Tania Branigan, "China's Great Famine: The True Story," *Guardian*, January 1, 2013, https://www.theguardian.com/world/2013/jan/01/china-great-famine -book-tombstone.

10. PRC State Council, "Made in China 2025."

11. "China's New Seed Law with IP Protection over Plant Variety," Rouse, January 28, 2022, https://rouse.com/insights/news/2022/china-s-new-seed-law-with -ip-protection-over-plant-variety; "Members of the International Union for the Protection of New Varieties of Plants," International Convention for the Protection of New Varieties of Plants, updated February 27, 2025, https://www.upov .int/edocs/pubdocs/en/upov_pub_423.pdf.

12. "What Is UPOV?," International Union for the Protection of New Varieties of Plants, accessed March 18, 2025, https://www.upov.int/about/en/faq.html.

13. "International Convention for the Protection of New Varieties of Plants," March 19, 1991, https://www.upov.int/edocs/pubdocs/en/upov_pub_221.pdf.

14. Mara Hvistendahl, *The Scientist and the Spy* (Riverhead Books, 2020), 11.

15. "The Spy Who Came in from the Cornfields," ABC News, October 6, 2016, https://abcnews.go.com/International/spy-corn-fields/story?id=42618588.

16. "Read the Complaint Charging Mo Hailong with Stealing Trade Secrets."

17. "Read the Complaint Charging Mo Hailong with Stealing Trade Secrets."

18. Trish Mehaffey, "Charges Dropped Against Wife of Chinese Billionaire in Corn Conspiracy Case," *Gazette* [Cedar Rapids, Iowa], July 30, 2015, https://www .thegazette.com/agriculture/charges-dropped-against-wife-of-chinese -billionaire-in-corn-conspiracy-case.

19. David Pitt, "Man Charged in Seed Corn Theft Must Pay $425,000 Restitution,"

Associated Press, December 22, 2016, https://apnews.com/general-news
-521316f292354197b1d7774489b32341.

20. "China's New Seed Law with IP Protection over Plant Variety."

21. Constitution of the People's Republic of China, State Council, November 20, 2019, https://english.www.gov.cn/archive/lawsregulations/201911/20/content_ WS5ed8856ec6d0b3f0e9499913.html#:~:text=Article%2035%20Citizens%20 of%20the,%2C%20association%2C%20procession%20and%20demonstration.

22. US v. Yunquing Jian and Zunyong Liu, Criminal Complaint, US District Court for the Eastern District of Michigan, June 2, 2025, https://static.foxnews.com /foxnews.com/content/uploads/2025/06/chinese-smuggling-complaint -6.2.25.pdf.

CHAPTER 17 | Inside the Situation Room: Stopping the Great Heist

1. Colleen Long, "White House Situation Room Gets Cutting-Edge Tech in $50M Upgrade," *Federal Times*, September 8, 2023, https://www.federaltimes.com /management/leadership/2023/09/08/white-house-situation-room-gets -cutting-edge-tech-in-50m-upgrade.

2. Derek Scissors, testimony, "Oversight of US Investment into China," House Select Committee on the Chinese Communist Party, July 26, 2023, https://select committeeontheccp.house.gov/sites/evo-subsites/selectcommitteeontheccp .house.gov/files/evo-media-document/scc-expert-written-testimony_20230726 _derek-scissors.pdf.

3. John Hyatt, "Why a Secretive Chinese Billionaire Bought 140,000 Acres of Land in Texas," *Forbes*, August 9, 2021, https://www.forbes.com/sites /johnhyatt/2021/08/09/why-a-secretive-chinese-billionaire-bought-140000 -acres-of-land-in-texas/.

4. Grace Zhu and Karen Wang, "Doing Business in China: How to Repatriate Profits," PNC Financial Services Group, February 4, 2019, https://www.pnc .com/insights/corporate-institutional/go-international/doing-business-in -china-how-to-repatriate-profits.html.

INDEX

ABOUT THE AUTHORS

DAVID R. SHEDD is the former deputy director and acting director of the Defense Intelligence Agency (DIA). He also served as chief of staff for the director of national intelligence and National Security Council senior director and as special assistant to the president for intelligence under George W. Bush. He began his intelligence career in 1982 immediately after his studies at Geneva College and Georgetown University, and served nearly thirty-three years in a wide variety of positions both inside and outside of the CIA during his career.

ANDREW BADGER is a former DIA case officer and graduate of the CIA's elite training program, The Farm. He served on the front lines of human intelligence operations, including a 2014 deployment to Afghanistan in support of US military operations. In the private sector, Badger has advised global firms such as McKinsey & Company and Deutsche Bank on geopolitical risk. He holds a bachelor's degree in government from Harvard and a master's in diplomatic studies from the University of Oxford, where he is a research associate and lectures on state-sponsored espionage.